BOOKS BY KAY CASSILL

Twins: Nature's Amazing Mystery   1982
The Complete Handbook for Freelance Writers   1981

TWINS:
Nature's Amazing Mystery

TWINS:

Nature's Amazing Mystery

KAY CASSILL

New York

ATHENEUM

1984

LIBRARY OF CONGRESS CATALOGING IN PUBLICATION DATA

Cassill, Kay.
Twins : nature's amazing mystery.

Bibliography: p.
Includes index.
1.Twins.   1. Title.
GN63.6.C37   1982   305'.9045   81–69126
ISBN0–689–70663–4 (pbk.).   AACR2

Published simultaneously in Canada by McClelland and Stewart Ltd.
Composition by American–Stratford Graphic Services, Inc.,
Brattleboro, Vermont
Manufactured by Fairfield Graphics, Fairfield, Pennsylvania
Designed by Mary Cregan
First Atheneum Paperback Edition

For my twin Marilyn Adams Holmes especially,
and for all multiples everywhere—
past, present and future.

Acknowledgments

Because the genesis of this volume lies far back in time, the number of people to whom I am indebted for their many kinds of largess has become legion. Since it is impossible to single out all individually, I can only hope that they know who they are and are aware of my deep gratitude. I do wish, however, to name some names.

A special thank you is extended to the many doctors, scientists and researchers with whom I have spoken or corresponded and whose particular work has offered fresh insights into the condition of twinning, the lives of twins and the new and exciting work in twin studies. They include: Gordon Allen, Frank X. Barron, Andrew Blazar, Thomas Bouchard, Rune Cederlof, Joe C. Christian, Piet

Colaert, Luigi Gedda, Jules Glenn, Irving I. Gottesman, George Engel, Judy W. Hagedorn and Janet W. Kizziar, Isaac Halbrecht, Zdenek Hrubec, Joe Jaffe, Lissy F. Jarvik, Louis G. Keith, H. Warner Kloepfer, Frederic Lepage, Salvator Levi, David Lykken, Ian MacGillivray, Jean Milner, Walter E. Nance, Paolo Parisi, Ivo Pitanguy, Jack A. Pritchard, Hugh P. Robinson, Richard Rose, Lucien Schneider, Jeanne Smith, Steven G. Vandenberg, Ronald S. Wilson, Morris A. Wessell and Rene Zazzo.

Thanks go, too, to the many twins and other multiples whom I interviewed and who responded to my question-naire. Because of the bond of twinship we share, I consider you all my special friends.

But behind this book are many others: Some are twins; some are parents of twins; some are singletons with widely varying backgrounds but a common bond. In one way or another, they furthered my exploration of the many facets of twins' lives and twin studies: Roberta Ashley, Maria Blair, Felicia Connors, Ray Diersing, Dorothy Foltz-Gray and Deane Foltz-Koontz, Diana Galligan, Gordon Gibson, Arnold D. and Susi Goldstein, Donald M., Gail and Phyllis Keith, Jim and Jon Hager, Ann Harrell, Bernard Hurwood, Mary Lou Kavanaugh, Helen Kirk Lauve, Tom Mahoney, Joyce E. Maxey, Kathryn McLaughlin Abbe and Frances McLaughlin Gill, Karen Termohlen Meehan, Michelle Minor, Ellen Mulroney, Robert Ostermann, Marvin Breckenridge Patterson, Harriet Rosenberg, Carlo and Angela Ruggeri, Carl H. Scheele, Jose Schorr, Mitchell Shields, Victoria Sprague, Josie Stanmyre, Pat Stewart, Frank and Sodi Swinehart, Christi Tarasevich, Dennis White, Daniel Whitman and Betty Yarmon.

Certainly the arduous research and interviewing could not have been managed without the thoughtfulness, patience and skill of the following: Paul Bannister, Kathleen E. Digan, Anita Singer, Donald Share and, most especially, Janice Mercurio. For typing and clerical help, often under difficult circumstances, I sincerely thank Janet Cardin, Elaine Coccoli and Joyce Randall.

To the many members of the following organizations I am also deeply in debt: American Society of Journalists and Authors; International Twins Association, Inc.; International Society for Twin Studies; National Organization of Mothers of Twins Clubs, Inc.; Overseas Press Club; and Women in Communications, Inc.

I am truly grateful to Barbara Anderman for her superb editorial judgment and to all of the others at Atheneum for their efforts on behalf of this volume, as I am to Elise and Arnold Goodman, my agents, for their continuing kindness and support.

My special thanks, however, are reserved for my mother, Mrs. Arnolda Adams; my sister, Marilyn A. Holmes; her children, Jeffrey, Vivian and Whitney Holmes; my children, Orin, Erica and Jesse Cassill; and my husband, R. V. Cassill, for their patience, sympathy and forbearance throughout a project with so many endings, one of which is this volume.

Author's Preface

Matthew Arnold compared the condition of each mortal to that of an island separated from others by "the unplumbed, salt, estranging sea." His image, however, applies less forcibly to twins than to their singly born fellow beings. If twins appear to the uninitiated observer as islands, they know themselves to be connected, at high tide or low, only a little beneath the surface, by complex strata of shared sympathies, insights, and destinies. Their self-recognition is always complicated by an acknowledgment of the duality which binds and sustains them.

Consciously as well as subconsciously, I have been exploring and explaining this curious world of multiples all my life. I imagine I always will. My identical twin sister Marilyn and I traveled in tandem throughout our early years. Not until others remarked on our parallel development or put an obstacle in our thoroughly shared paths did we truly question where such progress might be leading. We knew we need not worry for, while there was a tug-of-war between our evolving personalities, there was a compensating sense of solidarity and reciprocity between

us that more often than not made up for any flickers of
animosity. Reinforced by what we profoundly shared, we
were able to face oncoming challenges with an extra dose
of confidence that singletons of our acquaintance had to do
without. Heraclitus observed that the hidden harmony is
better than the obvious one; we seemed to know that in
our bones.

From our early years we found delight, too, in discovering the stories of other duos. Tweedle-dee and Tweedle-
dum and the Bobbsey Twins come readily to mind. As we
matured, each newly found pair added validity to our experience. In a sense, we knew in advance what awaited
Alice in Wonderland since we had been from infancy
each other's mirror. Wherever we might ramble individually we knew our secret sharer would be there on our
return.

With all this, we were also aware of an urgency that
all twins feel to be recognized as distinct personalities. So,
as we grew, our comfortable sharing was tested repeatedly
by competitive strains. One instance of this occurred in
childhood when we were equally enamored of the idea of
becoming nurses. (I think we were six then.) When I
actually contracted scarlet fever it was my fate to "get
to go to the hospital," as my sister put it. While I had the
privilege of being with the nurses we revered, she had to
be quarantined at home. While I faced the rigors of disease
and separation from her, she encountered anxiety and
jealousy of my adventure in a distressing way. What balanced our separate traumas may never be entirely clear to
us. What appears more meaningful now is that the jolt
of dislocation turned out to be a blessing in disguise. It
accelerated our initiation into the other—singleton—world
and indicated forcibly the individual resources our adult
lives would demand. Thereafter we could never quite slide
back into the unexamined assumptions that are perilously
easy for very young twins.

Nevertheless, a great deal of that first effortless harmony persisted. Over a period of eight years we spent innumerable hours working side by side in an effort to excel as synchronized swimmers. Apart from the excessive toil required for any stellar athletic achievement, however, we had the natural advantages of easy synchronicity. We challenged the notion of the poet Howard Nemerov that "the universe induces a different tremor in every hand." (Like Matthew Arnold, Nemerov does not seem to grasp the exceptional nature of twins.) That basic harmony between us was profoundly reinforced when we brought home trophies to prove our hands were as well synchronized as our ambitions.

Such satisfactions were sufficient for a while. As a duo we were not presented with the singleton's metaphysical dilemma of the choice between either/or. In a certain way we could have our cake and eat it, too. We prepared for adult responsibilities as individuals without giving up the rich benefits of our twinship. I have found we were by no means unique in our assessment of our good luck.

During the process of gathering information for this book, I questioned hundreds of twins who graciously gave of their time to speak openly of the pleasures and perils of their twin lives. In an overwhelming majority of cases these multiples mentioned their conviction of having been specially blessed. Despite the well-known fact that twinning is far more hazardous in humans than among animals, most twins believe it is better to have a twin than not. They realize they have been given a lifetime partner by the grace of one brief, still unexplainable sequence of events that occurred at their conception.

The perception multiples have of their situation at times contrasts sharply with the way singletons view it. The latter are inclined to believe that twins consider themselves special merely because they are given special treatment as children, or that, by dressing alike and staying together, as a small minority of adult twins do, they call attention to themselves. There is some substance to such a belief, but on fuller examination there appears much, much more that distinguishes the nature and experience of twinship. For one thing, twins are conditioned by the idea that their walking, talking other self is an ever-present second chance, a guarantee of their invulnerability to some of the slings and arrows of fortune. This intuition feeds their wish to touch base with each other when they have been separated by distance or the ordinary distractions of common life. It is surely infused in the complicated parallels Dr. Glenn discovers in the creative works of the Shaffer twins. In his eloquent examination of his dreams, George Engel alludes to it when he describes the death of his twin and its traumatic aftermath in his own life. Many duos sum it up as does the Catholic credo *et nunc manet in te*—and now he lives in thee.

Still to be accomplished is a closing of the gap between what twins have gleaned from their extraordinary experience and what the rest of the world imagines them to be. In this book I have attempted to narrow that gap significantly. As I gathered, sifted, deciphered and evaluated the enormous amount of available material about twins, other multiples and twin studies, I became ever more aware that there is a missionary task to be completed. The best informed scientists, physicians and researchers still have much to unravel about the enigmas surrounding twin gestation and birth, as well as the twin condition in general, but from the wealth of knowledge they have thus far amassed, there is much to be disseminated to the general public. With that in mind I have written this book, and I hope to kindle and reward your interest with my own.

Kay Cassill
Providence, Rhode Island
November 1, 1981

Contents

Introduction

Kay Cassill is an identical twin. As such, she knows only too well the different views people hold about twins. The media focuses on the unusual, always searching for a fresh story. The public also scrutinizes twins intensely, viewing them—especially identicals—as a unit. Differences often are seen as eccentricities, and similarities are singled out for approval. Each twin is compared to the other, and in some instances one comes off as "second best." Although the twins often try to see themselves as unique individuals, they also recognize they are parts of a whole.

Within recent years, scientific studies have answered many questions about twins, but they have also added several others. As a result, behavioral psychologists, sociologists, obstetricians, gynecologists, pediatricians and other health care professionals are taking a new look at twins. Publication of their findings in the scientific and lay press renews the interest twins have always generated among singletons. Twins and their parents are increasingly aware of their special destiny as an assimilated minority.

When we met Kay Cassill at the Third International Congress of Twin Studies in Jerusalem in 1980, we knew instantly she had willingly undertaken a difficult writing task—a labor of love for her fellow twins. This definitive and timely book is the successful culmination of her endeavor. The whole range of past and current "twin lore" has come under the scrutiny of a gifted writer. As a twin, Kay Cassill brings the insights of her own personal experience to bear on this fascinating subject. Through her formal and informal research, she has made the acquaintance of many of the current leaders in this area of scientific interest.

It is not by accident that *Twins: Nature's Amazing Mystery* has a dual purpose. One of them is to sort out selected scientific studies and present their conclusions to an intensely curious public. The other is to attempt to answer the question, "why is the public so interested in twins?" It would be difficult, if not impossible, to hold a reader's interest if the book were merely a recitation of the results of the scientific reports. Cassill had to search for relationships, common threads, and clarifications whether the research came to divergent conclusions or the scientists agreed. She also had to answer the reader's natural question, "how does this relate to me?" As twins first and scientists later, we knew long ago we were among a small group of persons considered by some to be "nature's living laboratory." What this means is that the answers to questions and tests results about our bodies and lives will help scientists better understand all people, including our singleton brothers and sisters. The threads of information Cassill has expertly woven together mingle the rich anecdotes of life as a twin or as multiples of all ages have experienced it with equally fascinating data from twin studies' laboratories around the world. Together these make an exotic tapestry.

Twins frequently are uncertain about the specially complex relationship they have with their "partners in life." The bond between twins may be greater than that between mother and child, although it varies in intensity. It is a link that is present at birth and continues throughout life. Twins who are raised together spend an incredible amount of time in each other's company—far more than other siblings. During this period they learn to communicate with each other in many ways: verbally, with body language, and with other private signals. This communication is often not hampered by societal barriers experienced by other people. Thus, part of the bond of twins can be looked at as an ability to communicate in special ways, in much the same manner that husbands and wives and friends and lovers of long standing share their thoughts and feelings. For many of our close friends who, over the years, have expressed a "secret" desire to be a twin, we can only wish that everyone were fortunate enough to experience the special bonds that many twins share.

This book will be a welcome addition to many libraries—those of obstetricians, gynecologists, pediatricians, general practitioners, students and the general public. This volume is also directed to parents, who are blessed and baffled by twin children and often dismayed by the contradictions found in legends and hearsay about them. The rewards as well as the problems of parenting twins are spelled out with insight and good humor, against a backdrop of solid research.

Twins, Nature's Amazing Mystery could not have been written without Kay Cassill's tenaciousness. The research she conducted and the resulting book attest to her skill in ferreting out obscure data and her ability in making the information understandable to all.

Twins themselves—there may be over four million of them in our country alone—will welcome the mirror Cassill holds up to them. In it they will see much that is familiar, and no doubt learn even more about the fascinating world of multiples.

Louis G. Keith, M.D.
President, The Center for Study of Multiple Birth
Fellow, International Society for Twin Studies
Past Co-Vice President, International Twins Association

Lt. Col. Donald M. Keith, U.S.A. (Ret.), M.B.A.
Chairman of the Board,
The Center for Study of Multiple Birth
Fellow, International Society for Twin Studies
Past Co-Vice President,
International Twins Association

From the Other Side

When I first heard that my twin sister (alias sin twister) had received a contract for writing a book on twins, I was angry, hurt and jealous. After all, I, too, am a writer. I felt the public might be far better served by a book on this subject written by identical twins.

After repeating the motions of the old competitive ritual, however, I examined my true feelings and realized that this was *her* particular interest and *her* book.

In a typical twinlike way, of course, I did ask for the opportunity to add a few comments, get into the act and say, "me, too." Because of her lengthy research on twins, Kay knew what I was doing and was very patient with me.

She brought me a copy of the manuscript to read while

we were at the International Twins Convention. She had attended a previous such meeting while researching the book. I, on the other hand, had not and wasn't too sure that I wanted to "go through all that dressing alike and twinning again after I had found my own individuality." We attended the convention together, and I discovered it was a lovely and most rewarding experience: accepting what is. That weekend, with 300 twins from all over the world, and this book have given us a renewed and comfortable level of communication.

Even at the convention, however, I felt that we were—different. People would read our name tags and say: "*You* live in Denver and *she* lives so far away—in Providence?" Or vice versa. It's that vice versa that is so endemic to twinship.

I am very pleased and proud of Kay for the work she has done to produce this book, which I hope and trust will give many others a real insight into themselves as well as the world of multiples and especially of twins.

A parting thought: As usual, there is always so much more we have to say. When God makes twins, he should also give them stock in the telephone company.

Much love and best success for *Twins: Nature's Amazing Mystery*.

Marilyn Adams Holmes
Denver, Colorado
November 1, 1981

TWINS:
Nature's Amazing Mystery

1. The Fascination Factor

The cocks have not yet begun to crow when Leelannee begins her journey to the birthing hut. The simple building—a small, peaked enclosure of tree branches covered with animal skins—is open to the sky and stands 380 paces from the edge of the village. At regular intervals along the way upright poles five feet high emerge from the cracked earth. They stand like sentinels, and Leelannee thinks of them both as guards and guides now that her time has come. Most of all, however, they are stark reminders of her duty to the forefathers and to the gods. The hut is far enough away so that any cries escaping her lips during labor will not be heard by the men in the village. Giving birth to the next generation is a woman's duty and eventual glory, but it is surrounded by strong taboos. As pains wrack her pelvis and back, Leelannee grasps each pole in succession, dropping to her knees and panting like a dog. Behind her the midwife wraps strong arms around her. She places her gnarled hands on Leelannee's overly full belly and pushes hard. Despite daily applications of tightly rolled leaves between her legs and other painful preparations the midwife swore by, Leelannee's baby has failed to appear. It is this omen Leelannee ponders in her slow and painful journey. Then she reaches the hut and eyes the tallest, strongest pole in its center. She begs the midwife to tie her to it. Hanging thus suspended and covered with perspiration, Leelannee is finally delivered. Her ordeal is over.

The midwife's incantations halt. For one long moment there is silence. Then she grins. She begins her ritual thanks to the gods. The midwife's words are music to Leelannee's ears. "Tonight the drums will pound your sign double, oh noble mother. There are two children instead of one!"

Leelannee's twins were unexpected, but even before they arrived and lay beside their exhausted mother, legend and myth had begun to assert themselves. There was and is, after all, a need to explain this divergence from the common order of things.

Multiple births have always fascinated people, although cultures have varied widely in dealing with the arrival of more than one infant at a time. In American Indian Leelannee's case, the midwife repeats certain prescribed prayers, since the two babies represent a reincarnation of cosmic myths that have been understood since the dawn of the tribe's memory. The elder twin, the first born, has been fathered by the Sun. He sips the water of the great hero. He is the earthly representative of Good and will accomplish many great deeds. The younger baby, the secondborn, is the offspring of the waters welling up from below the earth and represents Evil. If he is unlucky, he may be dragged down to the underworld by monsters reclaiming their own. But if the gods are good to him, he will drink the water of the magician. He will become wise and powerful as a medicine man.

Halfway around the globe in Africa, in a mud and straw lean-to built by her grandfather, Mobutee lies on smooth, hard stones. The men of the village left early to hunt and are a half-day upriver, which is fortunate since Mobutee, too, has just been delivered of twins. What an evil omen for the harvest! She is so ashamed that she weeps uncontrollably as the midwife turns her back in disgust. The words the woman flings at her as she leaves the hut are even more painful. They imply that Mobutee is a slut, or at the very least nothing more than an animal. As quickly as she is able, the shamed mother gathers up the second, most sickly child, binds him to her now shrunken belly, covers herself and rushes into the bush. She knows what she must do. Without another thought, she digs a shallow grave and thrusts him headfirst into it. With luck, she may be able to return to her village and raise the firstborn without the taint of twinship.

December 9, 1981, in the obstetrical wing of a modern American hospital: Twenty-nine-year-old Martha Peeples goes into labor at 5:03 A.M. She has been attended by labor-room nurses monitoring the fetal heartbeat and checking the condition of her cervix. There have been minor complications throughout her pregnancy, but the doctor has assured her that all is proceeding normally. He scrubs in preparation for the delivery. An anesthetist waits in the wings. Martha is wheeled into the sterile atmosphere, already groggy from muscle-relaxing drugs. The next thing she knows, the doctor is speaking: "Congratulations. You've just become a mother—twice. You have two fine, healthy boys. Everything is going to be all right. But, I have to admit, you've surprised us all." Behind the encouraging words, Martha thinks she detects a shade of consternation in her doctor's voice. There seems to be a look of outright dismay on the face of the attending nurse. For one brief instant, Martha herself has misgivings. Most women have one child at a time. What on earth has she done to deserve twins? How will she nurse or care for them both? Then she sees her two handsome boys. They are tiny, but the doctor has assured her they are healthy. She's overwhelmed with pride. A sense of exhilaration and joy that will carry her through the next few weeks replaces her momentary feeling of anxiety.

It's easy enough to understand why the American Indian and African twins have arrived unexpectedly. Primitive childbirth methods have always been surrounded by ignorance, superstition, religious and cultural taboos. It's more of a jolt when a multiple birth takes a twentieth-century physician so much by surprise. Yet the scene in the sophisticated atmosphere of the hospital is far from uncommon. In spite of all that modern medicine has accomplished, a large percentage of multiples born daily are not expected. Several mothers of twins, married to obstetricians, tell with relish how their husbands refused to believe them when they insisted they were carrying more than one child. When it turned out that they were right, occasionally even they had to endure the wisecracks and old wives' tales all too familiar to mothers of multiples.

Such stories fascinate and trouble us—simply because they push us beyond the comfortable platitudes of ordinary life. Even in a civilized society, in which meticulous research has illuminated many of the real hazards as well as the opportunities awaiting them, twins still come into the world surrounded by myths and superstitions not much less murky than those that followed their primitive counterparts born in the desert, on the high plateaus of mountainous countries or near the ice floes that hug the stark regions of the Arctic.

There are reasons for the persistence of the fables. As twin expert Frederic Lepage puts it, "The weight of the binary logic [twins] incarnate is . . . stronger in primitive societies, where they are eagerly mythified." In other words, the myths spring from the recognition of a duality in human relations and in the elementary processes of human nature. Searching for images to represent such doubleness, the human imagination fastens on twins.

Mythological Roots

The fascination and grave concern with twins is older than civilization; it predates the oldest known religions. If people have been eager to convert the birth of twins into legends and myths, it is, then, surely because twins bring to the surface of our consciousness profound intuitions and fears.

At one time, many people believed twins had magic control over the wind and rain. Peruvian Indians living in the area between Quito and Cuzco, for example, revered twins Apocatequil and Piquerao as those who produced the thunder and lightning. Apocatequil was known as "Prince of Evil" and was by far the most respected of the Gods. American Indian tribes in the Northwest believed that twins were salmon in human guise; further north, their primitive brothers believed they were related to grizzly bears. African primitives believed that crocodiles were born as twins of single human children. Twins and their double afterbirth were thought by some to be four identical infants. Ugandans, for instance, believed that each person's placental afterbirth was an incomplete twin possessing a soul. The afterbirth was therefore considered dangerous and treated, particularly in the birth of royal children, according to a special ritual. The ancient Egyptians had similar beliefs. Some Egyptian stories tell of two tombs—one built for a dead king, the other for the king's placenta, which had been carefully preserved during his lifetime. To date this is the only reason that has been found to account for a second pyramid having been erected for some Egyptian kings. While a number of primitive notions about twins and twinning link the present to the past, this one shared by Ugandans and ancient Egyptians hits with uncanny accuracy upon something that modern science, centuries later, has learned to be true. Recognition of the importance of the placenta has led to the newly uncovered mystery of the "vanishing twin," discussed in a later chapter.

Among the Iroquois, one twin was supposedly good, the other evil. The evil one was banished to the underworld. For the Sioux, the Algonquins and other tribes of the Plains, the younger twin was "attacked by monsters and carried away," never to be seen again. (Some human help speeded the poor things on their way, no doubt.)

If the appearance of two humans at one birth is a reminder of the doubleness of nature, it is often also seen as a manifestation of the supernatural—that which "the gods" may know from direct perception but which man can only comprehend obscurely by means of his symbols. In art and literature, there are many twin images relating to divinities. The sun and moon, for instance, seem more readily accessible to our imagination through the myths of Apollo and Diana, who, as deities with human attributes, were supposed to be the twin offspring of Latona, fathered by Zeus.

In an attempt to sort out a number of the myths, it is useful to see how anthropologists have separated and compared twin fables and anthropological fact. Myths displaying hostility to or fear of twins could probably be attributed, according to anthropologists, to such factors as: inadequate food supplies; the need to deny that humans bear

the kind of litters that many animals do; the mother's presumed adultery; a concern for the overburdening of a
mother whose work was needed to ensure tribal survival;
a nomadic or other such precarious existence; and birth-
order quandaries in tribes which revered their elders.
Myths that held twins in high esteem, even deifying them,
appeared to grow out of a more stable society in which
the arrival of more than one infant at a time threatened
neither survival nor long-established tribal customs and in
which there was a less stringent treatment of the females,
especially in regard to sexual matters. There are tracks in
anthropological records that show instances where the
second, more humane views sometimes evolved from the
earlier, more cruel practices.

All twin myths appear to satisfy certain general psychic
needs of a tribe or culture. Some anthropologists believe
that most cultural myths may have their roots in semi-
historical reminiscences of communal experiences. Others
suggest they portray more remote tribal histories con-
densed as legend. If, as author Mark Schorer says, "Myths
are the instruments by which we continually struggle to
make our experience intelligible to ourselves," then twin
myths have a continuing value and can never be entirely
superseded by factual data. Psychologist Carl Jung is another who thought myths were indispensable as organizers
of human action. At least it may be said that everyone is
aware that the shortcomings of literal, factual language
can be remedied to a degree by the truths incorporated in
the images of myths. That is one of the reasons a well-told
story still manages to capture our credulity sooner than
other forms of communication.

Speaking as a twin who has been enchanted throughout
my life by the hodgepodge of twin stories from all sources
—and amused, insulted, threatened, supported or sometimes
truly edified by the persistence of twin myths in the atti-

tudes of my contemporaries—I heartily welcome whatever flickering light they can shed on my nature and the circumstances in which I live.

Some writers (frequently singletons with medical training) have set out to debunk primitive stories and attitudes toward twins. Twins and their parents should be grateful for that, of course, since it is time that unreasonable customs and damaging misconceptions about multiples disappeared.

If, however, we throw out all of the earlier explanations for twins, forgetting in the process some of the subtleties encoded in the myths, more distortions arise. We are made up, after all, of bits and pieces of our past—our personal and immediate past as well as the greater combined past of the human race. So twins may well look at the roots of those curious stories for some answers to their very special condition.

Looking Back to See Ourselves

The story in the Old Testament of Jacob and Esau is the archetype for the notion that the bond of twins may be the linking of opposites. It also suggests that twins are wellsprings of fertility. This pair was born to a mother who had been sterile until God answered their father's prayer and intervened. While she was pregnant, Rebekah heard the Lord say: "Two nations are in thy womb, and two manner of people shall be separated from thy bowels." The boys she bore were indeed different, from infancy on. "Esau was a cunning hunter, a man of the field; and Jacob was a plain man, dwelling in tents." Esau, as the elder, sold his birthright to Jacob for a mess of pottage. Rebekah's trickery, however, obtained the father's blessing for her favorite. Angered at being cheated of the blessing due him as elder son, Esau threatened to kill Jacob, so Jacob was sent to live with his uncle. There, serving as overseer of his uncle's flocks, Jacob did very well. The flocks flourished and multiplied "unto a multitude." Later, when his uncle had agreed to give Jacob, as his share, the spotted and speckled cattle from the flocks, it was the spotted and speckled which multiplied, while the uncle's share of the animals dwindled miserably. Such is the power of the twin favored by God.

Fraternal hostility, as in the Jacob and Esau story, is also the dark side of the story of Romulus and Remus. These twins collaborated in the founding of Rome. Then Romulus killed Remus in a climactic power struggle. (Fratricide between twins has occurred—rarely—in modern times as well, as we'll see later.)

Twins have been associated with ideas of fertility in many other primitive cultures and antique civilizations. They were preferred as herdsmen so their influence would encourage the animals to multiply. They were also required to live near rivers or lakes so the fish would be plentiful.

In ancient Greece, the enigma of twin births gave us the myth of Leda. Since no one could account for her twins in any other way, it was said that Leda was raped by Zeus in the guise of a powerful and beautiful swan. She had four children born from two huge eggs: Pollux and Helen were fathered by Zeus and came from one egg; Castor and Clytemnestra, fathered by Leda's husband, came from the second egg. Interestingly, Castor and Pollux, actually half-brothers, were called the Dioscuri and were seen as twins. Helen and Clytemnestra were regarded simply as sisters. Leonardo da Vinci and his followers painted Leda as a symbol of fecundity with indistinguishable twin boys frolicking beside her against a background of broken eggshells. The boys have become symbols of brotherly love: the girls have not.

Sometimes twins were cast as military heroes. Leda's sons Castor and Pollux played this role in the folklore of the Romans and Greeks. In addition, their story enshrines the well-documented observation that a twin is linked to his double by extraordinary devotion. Pollux begged for death so that he would not be separated from his mortal twin, who was killed in battle. As a reward for such loyalty, Castor was permitted by the father of the gods to return to life. Doubles appear as gods or goddesses of such peoples as the Aztecs, Babylonians, Zunis, Ashantis and many others. The most prevalent legends about mortal twins show them as warriors, builders, healers, fertility symbols, symbols of light, offspring of air and water or of thunder. According to Christian legend, twin saints Cosmas and Damian are patrons of potency and fecundity—an association echoed by figures in the stories of other religions.

In Roman and Babylonian times, twins were regarded as portents to be consulted by the guardians of the state. Food shortage was predicted by the birth of quadruplets. (Many parents in our difficult times might have the impulse to agree with that one!) Here it is easy to see how hostility toward twins may have grown directly from the economic need to control population. Abandonment of twins was evidently commonplace in early Greece and Rome. Romulus and Remus turned to a she-wolf for nourishment after being left in the wilderness as unwanted children.

In Greek and Roman as well as in primitive American legend, the fact that twins were sometimes thought to be born from the union of air and water produced a quaint set of associations. The noise of thunder accompanying rainfall became an omen linked to the advent of twins, and since the sound of galloping horses is thunderous, an imaginary connection between twins and horses came about. Warrior twins are often shown on horseback or riding in horse-drawn chariots.

In Africa, twins occur more frequently than elsewhere, and so, too, do fables of twin gods and twin demons. In certain black cultures, twins are considered heroes and receive special favors and adulation. Among tribes in Upper Guinea, for instance, they are set apart from the rest of the tribe, given their own special houses—built for them by other twins—special clothing and special tasks permitted only to twins. Scholar Daniel Whitman reports that currently in Mouyandi, a village in the Bouenza region of the Congo, women who are barren are put through a ritual of fasting, during which time they are isolated from society and their husbands. Once reunited with the husbands, they very often produce twins, and the tribe rejoices in this evidence of fertility. Sometimes, Whitman says, there is grumbling about the cost of raising twins, but there is no murmur of regret at having them.

In contrast, the Hottentots used to express their dread of twins with a law which required each male to cut off one of his testicles as a prophylactic measure to prevent the conception of twins. Newly married women were not supposed to couple with their mates until they verified that the requirement had been met. Elsewhere, infanticide has been not uncommon. For this the tribal justifications were expressed as fears that the twins, being "abnormal," would kill any sick people they came near, that they were inherently evil or that they were born of adultery—all these probably rationalizations of a response to the hardships brought on by multiple births. In desperately poor cultures, twins were simply too much for a hardworking, undernourished mother to cope with. To meet her other responsibilities, the mother had to sacrifice her twins, consoling herself as best she could with the superstitions.

Albert Schweitzer's *African Notebook* tells us more about this kind of problem, noting that where twins are not threatened with death, they are sometimes subject to strict rituals intended to limit their supposed capacity for mischief. Among the Galoas, for example, all twins are given the same names. With no distinction as to sex, the firstborn is always called Wora, the second Yeno. It is primarily the mother's responsibility to see that the twins are always treated exactly alike—dressed the same, fed the same, put to sleep on either side of her each night without any variation permitted. They have to marry at the same time, or the one left single will never be allowed to marry. When one dies, the survivor is also presumed dead until complex ceremonies reinstate him in life. The Pahoins take it for granted that twins have bad characters, so bad behavior on their part is tolerated, since they can't help it. "If somebody is very irascible, it is usual to inquire whether he happens to be a twin. If he answers that he is, no resentment is felt against him," writes Schweitzer.

Among those primitives who see twins as bad omens, the response to a multiple birth may be not only to reject one or both of the infants, but the mother as well. She may be isolated and forbidden to take part in the planting or harvesting, as Mobutee dreaded, on grounds that her touch might ruin the crops. In extreme instances, she may be put to death in an effort to halt the evil signaled by the ominous multiple delivery. Such extreme forms of rejection probably stem from the notion that a male is capable of fathering no more than a single child in any given birth. Therefore (according to primitive logic), multiple births are powerful evidence of adultery or even of extramarital intercourse with an evil spirit.

Again and again anthropologists have encountered the notion among primitives that multiple births are a throwback to the animal level of life. Since many animals give birth to litters and most human births are single, benighted tribes imagined that the mother of twins must somehow be an animal who had taken a human guise, or that she had copulated with an animal to become pregnant. Thus, the antipathy toward twins when it appears in primitive societies seems to stem from an impulse to preserve at all cost the human distinction from animals. As one researcher said, "It is even believed in Dahomey that unless proper ceremonies are performed over twin babies they will become monkeys again."

It is easier to interpret these preposterous ideas if we see how they grew out of the conditions in which primitives lived. They represent a stage of evolution at which sexual patterns had developed to a point where men and women no longer automatically mated at intervals dictated purely by their genes and hormonal secretions. Instead, in the perilous, hard-won ascent toward full humanity, there came to be individual selection between men and women, the stirrings of love and the accompanying feelings of marital loyalty and jealousy. Taboos against incest are said to have formed during this phase of the human journey, and the appearance of twins suggested a range of unacceptable sexual activity that could include incest. Today, before we judge too harshly the barbarism of primitive misconceptions, at least we should note that their vestiges linger in the minds of our supposedly civilized contemporaries. I know of many twins who have been shocked and dismayed by innuendos about their origin and their presumed sexual preferences and habits.

As they have through history, cultural attitudes around the world still swing wildly—and often blindly—between extremes of rejoicing and horror toward twins and whatever processes led to their birth. Although shadows of the incest taboo have intermittently blighted the acceptance of twins, it is also true that among the ruling dynasties of Egypt, where the desire to create an exclusive family unit was strong, incest between brother and sister was permitted, encouraged and even enforced. A union between fraternal twins was considered even more propitious.

Symmetrically opposed responses to twins are a puzzle

not easily solved. Perhaps the best clue lies simply in the symmetry of the opposites. They seem to be reversed as in mirror images. Together they have the powerful balance that is suggested by twinship itself. As cultures change, the attitude of one era will revert to its opposite at a later time. This, in fact, is the conclusion of anthropologists—that a custom of killing twins may be motivated by precisely the forces that earlier dictated their joyful acceptance. Among the Yoruba tribe in Africa, for example, it was once the custom to kill twins. At a crisis period when many of the tribe died mysteriously, the Yorubas consulted their oracle. The word from it was clear to them: Stop killing twins. Honor them instead, and they will stop killing other tribesmen. The mothers of twins began to worship their offspring; they created special ceremonial dances, for which they were paid. Suddenly, the families for whom twins had been an affliction were relatively rich. Now the arrival of twins is considered a sign that the family's fortune will take a turn for the better. There is happiness and general rejoicing. When one of a pair of twins dies, the Yorubas build a household shrine and have a statuette made as a memorial. The surviving twin then keeps the replica of the dead one with him always. Thus, he never needs to be separated from his sibling.

In our time and place, when we think of the nightmarish customs and superstitions that have plagued twins, our minds also strain toward the happier opposite of what we have read and been told.

Twins naturally and instinctively cheer for other twins and rejoice in tales of the individuals or pairs who somehow survived. Even in the worst circumstances, there have always been some. One "former" twin, from a tribe where the custom was to put both twins in a jar and let them die, lived to tell how his brother died first and how he was saved in the nick of time by rebels against the gruesome practice. "The Twin Who Survived," by Iris Andreski, tells of a woman in Ibibioland who, as an infant, was placed atop her mother's grave with her twin after the mother had been killed for producing a pair. She did not know what happened to her sibling. However, a Good Samaritan—a childless woman—heard her cries and spirited her away to another town, where she was raised as the woman's own.

In 1932, Olivia Phelps Stokes, a traveler going from Capetown to Cairo, noted in her diary: "The whole mission is delightfully simple and suited to the Natives. They have a small hospital. . . . They also have a special place for twins where the mother can bring them as soon as they are born to prevent them from being killed according to tribal custom."

Twins in Literature

The word twin comes from the Anglo-Saxon *getwinn*, meaning that which is divided. As H. H. Newman put it, "Strictly speaking, twinning is twaining or two-ing—the division of an individual into two equivalent and more or less completely separate individuals." The modern English verb *to twin* has two definitions: *to match* and *to link together* one thing with its identical replica and *to divide into two equal parts* something that was originally single. This combining of opposites prevails in social attitudes toward twins and the legends they have inspired.

Plato conceived of sexual love as an attempt to reconstitute a broken twinship. According to him, humans, as first created by Zeus, had two identical faces as well as four arms and four legs. They were hermaphroditic, with male genitals on one side and female on the other. This complete form, however, equipped them so well for life that they were more proud and powerful than Zeus had intended. Aware that he had only two options—either to destroy them or to handicap them—he chose the latter. He directed Apollo to cut them down the middle. Ever after, these divided beings sought to return to their former state of completeness by uniting their two bodies in sexual love.

Plato's version of the quest for the perfect mate is particularly applicable to those twins who were separated at birth or in early infancy. Many twins reared together but later separated, often at their own choosing, still sense unaccountable yearnings for the "lost" twin, even though they are fully cognizant of themselves as individuals and of the necessity of going their separate ways.

References to twins in literature illustrate as many contradictory attitudes as we have seen in primitive societies. From the time of Plautus (200 B.C.) to the present, however, they have fallen into broadly four thematic approaches: (1) Twins who are so much alike that no one can tell them apart. The outcome is usually a series of mistaken-identity crises and/or the substitution of one twin for another; (2) The "astro-twins," actually two unrelated people with enough similarities to pass for twins who use the substitution ploy for fun or profit; (3) Twins' births coming as "the big surprise" that upsets everyone's applecart, especially that of the unsuspecting father, boyfriend or lover; and (4) the "good" twin versus the "evil" twin. The last idea is the most upsetting and potentially most harmful to twins as they attempt to adjust to the single world. Over and over they refer to it as the one idea they wish would be expunged from literature, marital arguments, and wherever and whenever else it appears.

Some of the instinctive dread twins occasionally still seem to inspire in people is exploited by Aldous Huxley in his novel, *Brave New World*. It is a satire concerned with the cultural threats of conformity and standardization. In the society Huxley depicts, breeding techniques deliberately mass-produce twins by exaggerating the natural process so that "the original [single] egg was in a fair way to becoming anything from eight to ninety-six embryos—a prodigious improvement, you will agree, on nature. Identical twins—but not in piddling twos and threes as in the old viviparous days, when an egg would sometimes accidentally divide; actually by dozens, by scores at a time. Standard men and women in uniform batches. The whole of a small factory staffed with the products of a single Bokanovskified egg. 'Ninety-six identical twins working ninety-six identical machines!' The voice was almost tremulous with enthusiasm. 'You really know where you are for the first time in history.' The principle of mass production at last applied to biology."

Which of us hasn't heard that satirical note as it is echoed in jokes about "mass production" whenever the surprise of twin births is announced? But "knowing where you are" with twins is rather another matter. The point of many family anecdotes, as well as of Shakespeare's *Twelfth Night*, is that since one twin can easily pass for another, the possibilities for deception multiply fantastically. As children, twins often escape blame by laying the deed on a look-alike. Eyewitnesses are notoriously confounded by twins who are in fact at two places at once—on the scene of the crime and far from it, establishing an alibi. Shakespeare's twins, Viola and Sebastian, drive a whole dukedom to distraction, get themselves more entangled in troubles than any singleton could and provide entertaining complications of plot before their actual identities are at last straightened out.

The dangers of mistaken identity, of one twin passing for another, are also exploited in Dumas' novel *The Man in the Iron Mask*. The plot of that story hangs on the supposition that King Louis XIV of France was born with a twin brother. To make sure there is no competition for the throne, the twin is not only imprisoned for life but is forced to wear an iron mask so that not even his jailers will ever see his face and think him to be the rightful heir to the throne. Dumas' *The Corsican Brothers*, too, has a theme built around identical twins. In this one, the phenomenon of shared pain adds another significant piece of twin lore to the story. George Sand's novel, *La Petite Fadette*, has hard-to-tell-apart twins, too. These resemble each other so much that one is marked for identification. In this case, a small cross is tattooed on the elder. (This idea of marking one or both of the pair for identification is also found in some stories of primitive African tribes who put daubs of paint on twins so that the singletons around them would never be confused.)

"The Blood of the Walsungs," a short story by Thomas Mann, deals with two decadent, rich twins, Siegmund and Sieglinde. After being subjected to the emotional pull of a Wagnerian concert, they have an incestuous fling which, brother Siegmund finally declares, "will make the life of his sister's fiancé 'less trivial.'"

The idea of "the double"—who may or may not be an actual flesh-and-blood twin—appears in a vast number of literary works. The concept is usually of an imaginary twin, a doppelgänger. This is someone who can take the heat for us when we've done wrong, a scapegoat to be sacrificed to threatening powers. The double is also someone to keep us company when we're lonely or ignored.

In Henry James's "The Jolly Corner," a ghost story with metaphysical implications, an American who has spent thirty years in Europe returns to New York to seek out and confront the self he might have been if he had not gone to live abroad. In a spooky house with as many dark stairs, passages and vacated rooms as the past itself, Spencer Brydon prowls in the late hours of the night, terrified and fascinated by his pursuit of the ghostly twin. When at last he confronts the other self, Brydon has a sensation that he is "dying." This appears to mean that he is abandoning the limits of his personal ego to be joined with something larger. Waking from this transitional "death," Brydon feels himself healed of an incompleteness that has crippled him. He is now ready to love.

Oscar Wilde's *The Picture of Dorian Gray* gives us an unhappier version of the use of the double. In this novel, a painted portrait of the main character grows old, showing all the deterioration of age and dissipation, while Gray himself appears unchanged, as youthful as he was when the portrait was painted. It is a story of vain deception by a man who used his double as a scapegoat.

Then there is *Dr. Jekyll and Mr. Hyde*, another popular exploitation of the idea of twinship. The good Jekyll and the wicked Hyde are "twins" when we look at them under the light of the author's moral code.

More recently, science-fiction writers have played their variations on the enduring idea of the double, often supplying robots as twins or secondary embodiments of the humans with whom they interact. As in *Star Wars*, the robots can run risks that humans can't. Made of metal, the robots don't bleed. They can't be killed by bullets or ray guns. They are invincible and immortal, as everyone would wish his fantasy twin to be. Sometimes the robots rebel against their human prototypes. When they do, their rebellion serves as a projection of the fears which psychologists find at the root of the concept of twinning.

A Chinese tale from the Ming dynasty (1368–1644) describes how one man was allowed to marry both twins in a pair. Twin expert Dr. Luigi Gedda records the story in *Twins in History and Science*. The twins were much sought after for their intelligence and beauty. In an attempt to find suitable mates for them, their mother and father disagreed. So, as was customary, the decision was taken to a mandarin. The wise man announced a literary contest—the twins were the prizes. Two men, Tsin-tsin and Tchi-wen, won the first award, but during an investigation that followed, some subterfuge was discovered. Tsin-tsin had written both poems. Apparently he'd done so to help his friend Tchi-wen, who had been widowed twice and been warned by an astrologer never again to marry only one wife at a time. The mandarin took Tchi-wen's plight to heart and allowed him to marry both women.

"Sticks and stones may break my bones" is the beginning of a popular childish chant. Unfortunately, it holds a key to another aspect of twins' lives—the folklore and jokes that perpetuate the fears and fascination about twins. Primarily, that's because many of these popular giggles are far from free of malice. These guffaws seldom help twins as they attempt to decipher their special relationship to each other. Nevertheless, since they—at least indirectly—help us see how twins haunt our collective subconscious and the way we comprehend our human condition, they may be useful.

Folklore recognizes twins as good omens or bad. In some places there are rituals and charms which are thought effective in procuring the blessing of twins: A stone taken from a deer and carried in the pocket or worn around the neck gives the power to produce twins at will, as does the eating of twin apples or any kind of twin fruit or double-yolked eggs. According to North Carolina folklore, two knots near each other in a first baby's umbilical cord indicates that twins will be next. Then there is the superstition that says that if a newly married couple sees a twin boll of cotton open in the field where other bolls have not yet opened, twins will be born to them in the first year of their marriage.

In a joke that must be at least as old as the idea of democracy, it is said that "All men are created equal—especially twins." For our age of television, the joke is: "Show me a twin birth and I'll show you an infant replay." It's very probable that the clowns who tell these and other twin jokes may not be entirely at ease when confronted by duos.

Happily, though, there are those who can't get enough of us. It is said, for example, that Bolivian women who want large families wear bowler hats; an ambitious salesman once convinced them that if they did so, they would have twins.

Living the Twin Role

For twins, the significance of mythical and scientific stories and family reminiscences is heightened by the awareness that we are both subject and observer of that mystery play enacted by twins everywhere. We can be as confused, shocked and fascinated by twin lore as any singleton, but we know that at the heart of the matter is the fascination of being spectator and actor at the same time. We experience the condition as a blessing and burden. Watching with an insider's eyes, we have another fully human self alongside who shares the field of vision. It is as if we have had a hand in the creation of even the strangest myths—and we know that as our lives unfold, we will inevitably weave new variations into the spectacle that attracts attention to us.

The sense of being special—set apart by nature—is one that all twins share, however their lives may vary from one another's or from that of other pairs. In a time of acute minority consciousness, we know ourselves to be a minority distinguished from others not by race, religion, color or creed, but by a peculiar relationship not fully comprehensible to singletons.

Given the advantages and risks of such a role, is it really any wonder that we twins develop special modes of communication with each other? Such a link may be unspoken or it may be a private code. The possibility that twins—and

particularly identical twins—may possess a high degree of
ESP (extrasensory perception) is perhaps evidence for our
intuition that we actually exist in a psychological union of
a type unique in human experience. Twin children tend
naturally to rely on means of communication indecipherable
by those around them; in later years it is something they
have when and if they need it. Between twins, a few words
are enough to convey elaborate and nuanced meanings.
Often one twin will leave sentences unfinished in the confidence that the other twin will complete them. Unspoken
agreements between twins lead them to meet on the play-
ground, on a certain street corner or in a foreign city.
Subconsciously, they coordinate their choices of careers,
clothing, life-styles and spouses.

In many cases, the uncanny harmonies linking twins will
be baffling to outsiders. Often enough, this bafflement will
stir up envy. Recently, the psychotherapist Bradford Wilson confirmed what most twins learn from their encounters
with singletons: "Yes, people do envy twins . . . [they]
tend to see twins as the embodiment of their own yearning
for an ideal soulmate." While twins may think that envy
not misplaced, it can have a darker side, as when the awe
with which they are welcomed into a family encourages
them to feel superior to their siblings. Along with special
risks of precarious health—particularly in early months—
twins may also run a high risk of being spoiled.

Whether we look into the dark mirror of the mythic
past, into the attitudes of our families and contemporaries
or into our own hearts, we twins have the exhilarating
sense that ours is an extraordinary adventure. In the world's
eyes and in our own, our lives are a splendid show. When
all the twin myths are eventually unraveled or debunked
and when science deciphers all of the biological mysteries
presented by the birth of multiples, people, as they always
have, will still be watching twins.

2. Science Takes a Look

Definitions and Classifications

For all of us, twin or singleton, the great journey into life begins in darkness. Just how it begins is something the wise in every culture have attempted, since the origin of time, to explain. So far we have only a patchwork of answers and must rely on conjecture for the rest. As Nathaniel Hawthorne said of nature: "Our great creative Mother, while she amuses us with apparently working in the broadest sunshine, is yet cleverly careful to keep her own secrets, and, in spite of pretended openness, shows us nothing but results."

Although the efforts of science have cast considerable

sunshine on one of the most fascinating processes in nature, secrets still remain. Researchers would appear to be wrestling a many-tentacled scientific octopus on their way to discovering what causes—or at least influences—twinning in humans. Why or under what conditions will some women bear twins and others not? Why should a particular fertilized egg cell divide to produce twins when others do not? Why, on some occasions, at the time of a given ovulation, is more than one egg cell present and fertilized in the womb? It has long been accepted that all these things happen. The reasons for their occurrence, however, remain in the shadows.

The genes combined by the joining of male and female cells might be thought of as the "blueprint" or "wiring diagram" that determines the characteristics of an individual. Genes are subdivisions of chromosomes. The genes themselves are so tiny as to be invisible. They are subdivisions of the DNA molecules which make up chromosomes, the latter being discernible only through special, high-powered microscopes. These complex molecules are made up of simple sugars, phosphates and proteins linked together in a very precise way. The pattern of their linkage seems to determine the "genetic message" or "blueprint" they will relay to all generations of cells as the organism grows. How many genes does each cell have? Estimates range from 100,000 to 2,500,000 per cell. Although the exact figure is not available, it is known that each new individual gets exactly half his chromosomes from his mother and half from his father.

No two separate egg cells the mother produces contain precisely the same genetic pattern, just as no two sperm cells from the father are exactly alike. Both, however, are enough alike to produce what is called a "family likeness." With identical twins, of course, this likeness is usually much closer.

Most twins fall into two distinct types: the one-egg, identical or monozygotic (MZ) twin; and the two-egg, fraternal or dizygotic (DZ) twin. The identicals, or monozygotics, occur in this way: An egg cell is penetrated and fertilized by a sperm. Then, shortly after it begins the delicate process of cell multiplication, it divides into two replicas of itself. Each of the embryos that grows from this original division has exactly the same type of genes. The twins born from this process usually have identical physical characteristics—hair, skin and eye coloring; shape of head and body weight; height; sex; and so forth—and often possess amazingly similar personalities, ambitions and tastes. These similarities are, of course, what make such twins especially fascinating to their families and to scientists as well.

Fraternal or dizygotic twins result from the fertilization of two separate eggs by two sperms. Since both sperms have been produced by the same father, the gene pattern in the resulting embryos will be similar, as in the case with siblings of different ages but not identical. The combinations of genes available to each tiny cell that will eventually become a human infant are almost beyond comprehension. Thus, genetically speaking, the chances that two dizygotic twins could be identical down to their very last gene is estimated at about one in 200,000 trillion conceptions. These fraternal or dizygotic twins are not, in a strict scientific sense, "true" twins, since there was no "splitting" of the ovum, but are siblings who happen to be born at the same time. The degree to which they resemble one another varies widely. They may be less alike in temperament and physique than are other brothers and sisters of the same family. Occasionally, however, dizygotic twins are very difficult to tell from identical or monozygotic pairs. Identical twins Donald and Louis Keith report that they always thought they were dizygotic twins until, as adults, they took a series of blood tests that revealed they were identical. Many mothers of twins I have interviewed tell how their obstetricians said their two were dizygotic, only to be proved wrong later. And vice versa. This happens for several reasons, but more often than not because the birth of multiples is still an incompletely solved riddle.

A Third Type of Twin?

As if the existence of two quite different types of twins was not puzzling enough, scientists have speculated over the years about yet a third type, one that does not fall neatly into either category.

In the process of meiosis (the division of egg cells prior to fertilization), a large cell (called an oocyte as its transformation begins) divides twice to develop into an ovum or "egg" ready for fertilization. These divisions rearrange and reduce by half the number of chromosomes in the original maternal cell. Each splitting is usually uneven, separating a smaller new cell (called a polar body) from the oocyte as it evolves into an egg. Some scientists believe that in rare cases the oocyte in one of its divisions may split evenly into two oocytes with many of the same chromosomes. Two highly similar eggs will then move into the womb, where they can be fertilized by two separate sperms. When this happens, the genetic mix will show some characteristics special to identical twins and some expected of fraternal twins. In other words, the resulting embryos will have relatively identical genes from the mother (as identical twins do) but different sets from the father (as fraternal twins do). Twins born of this rare variation can conceivably even be of opposite sexes while still appearing more "identical" than dizygotics. These twins are sometimes described as "half-identical."

Meiosis: Steps in Ovarian Production

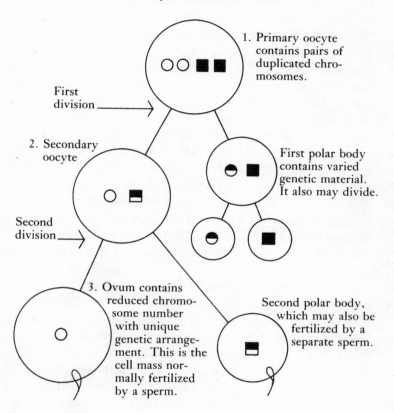

1. Primary oocyte contains pairs of duplicated chromosomes.

First division →

2. Secondary oocyte

First polar body contains varied genetic material. It also may divide.

Second division →

3. Ovum contains reduced chromosome number with unique genetic arrangement. This is the cell mass normally fertilized by a sperm.

Second polar body, which may also be fertilized by a separate sperm.

It is normal for the egg to divide twice before fertilization, each division producing an oocyte and a smaller unit called a polar body. In the process the number of chromosomes is reduced and the genetic pattern is rearranged. There is a hypothesis that, in rare cases, the polar bodies may also be fertilized. This would account for those unusual twins who are sometimes described as "half-identical."

The attempt at classification of twins may not end here. Dr. M. G. Bulmer, author of *The Biology of Twinning in Man*, theorized *five* possible types of twins, which he ranked in increasing order of genetic likeness: primary oocytary, dizygotic, secondary oocytary, uniovular dispermatic and monozygotic. In other words, the twins *least* genetically alike will be those formed when the normal egg divides into two more or less *equal* sections at an extremely early moment (before fertilization). Next in genetic dissimilarity are the dizygotic twins (formed from two eggs and two sperms). The third pair in this hierarchy is formed during the second division of the egg cell (still prior to fertilization). Fourth—and more nearly genetically identical—are those twins formed from one egg that is fertilized by two different sperms. Genetically most alike is the monozygotic pair formed from one egg which is fertilized by one sperm which then splits to form two separate fetuses.

In 1919, one scientific investigator theorized that all twins fell into the third category of twins. Since there seemed to be certain similarities that could not genetically be accounted for, the assumption was made that all twins were identical on the mother's side but not on the father's. According to another theory, the third type of twin, if there really was one, demonstrated that the tendency to twins was passed on through the father's side of the family. It was also suggested by another scientist that the third type of twins might come about if, under certain conditions, the sperm was more forceful during the fertilization process, causing the occasional egg to split into two or more parts.

Generally, because monozygotic twins are genetically very nearly identical, researchers expect them to share the vast majority of traits. When, as sometimes happens, monozygotic twins are not identical regarding mongolism or another such abnormality, the third type of twin comes back into scientific discussion in an attempt to explain this unusual difference.

Nature's Patterns of Multiple Births

One hundred years ago, a ewe normally had a single lamb at each birth. Then Alexander Graham Bell came along. The inventor of the telephone summered in Nova Scotia. That starkly beautiful country is subject to long, cold winters, so the cost of raising sheep—a major part of the economy—was quite high there. With a view to improving productivity, the ingenious Bell became interested in those ewes which had more than two nipples. In 1889, he undertook the job of developing a type of sheep that would consistently bear twins and also have enough functional nipples to nourish them. After Bell's death, the research was continued by Dr. Ernest G. Ritzman at the University of New Hampshire. By 1939, when the Bell flock was broken up, Dr. Ritzman had increased the twinning rate so much that the lambing of 100 ewes produced 184 young. Records of genetic lines developing in the flock have become part of the data banks drawn on by those interested in human multiples.

In the Bell flock, it was observed that a number of factors markedly increased the number of lambs delivered as multiples: (1) Four-, five- and six-year-old mothers bore more twins than did the younger and older ewes; (2) twins were more often produced from October matings; and (3) overfeeding the ewes at the time of mating increased the number of twins born. Comparable animal studies have determined that climate affects the rate of multiple births in some species. For instance, cold, rainy summers increase the number of twin births among goats, while hot, dry summers decrease that number. The Soviet Union has experimented heavily with hormonal methods for increasing twinning among domestic animals and has achieved marked success.

If, so far, none of these results has illuminated the darker mysteries of human twin births, they have provided analogies and clues. Twin studies, for instance, by Dr. Ralph W. Morris at the University of Illinois may be tied in with Russian animal experiments. Dr. Morris finds evidence not only that hormones and enzymes may have their part in human twinning, but that those favorable to twinning are most active when the moon is full. As for weather influences, Dr. Luigi Gedda notes that twinning rates in Japan are generally higher in the colder regions than in the warmer, and Dr. Stephen Rosen finds that ratios of conception and twinning "echo atmospheric changes."

As long ago as 1909 a report told how the nine-banded Texas armadillo, an amazing-looking creature known to zoologists as *Dasypus novemcincintus*, always has four identical offspring from a single egg. Even more interesting is the observation that the usual division process does not happen immediately after fertilization. There is a three-week period of dormancy before the egg splits into four equal parts. Research on this animal offers a slow-motion picture of processes harder to study in other species.

The genetic structure and distribution in bees, ants, wasps, and male tortoiseshell cats may offer promising information about those rare situations in which partial identicalness and related anomalies occur in human twins. Theoretical biologist William Hamilton's fascination with the honeybee demonstrates how the worker bees may share up to three-quarters of their genetic heritage with their sisters. This is unusual indeed since "in most of the animal kingdom the highest degree of relatedness except for identical twins is one-half—as between parent and offspring and between siblings."

How does this supersharing come about? Hamilton points out that the workers inherit a "random assortment of half the mother's genes"—which is the normal case among animals. "Because of this randomness each worker is only one-fourth related to each sister through the mother's contribution." However, the drones, which serve as fathers in the bee society, have the unusual characteristic of possessing only one set of genes instead of the ordinary pairs of genes and chromosomes. Therefore, the entire set of what the drone has is duplicated without division in each sperm cell. All the sperm cells are identical. Each drone's contribution to his offspring is—as in all mating—one-half of the latter's genetic makeup. "The total of one-half and one-fourth renders workers as much as three-fourths genetically identical." Perhaps, Hamilton conjectures, this is why they work in such harmonized cooperation.

In the case of the tortoiseshell cats researchers have discovered that these began as two opposite-sexed twins who, at a very early stage of gestation, fused into one animal. They actually have the genetic makeup of such a pair in one body.

A similar sort of cooperation as among the super-related honeybees exists, as we shall see later, between almost all twins. But when twins marry twins, there is a heightening of genetic similarity of particular interest to scientists. A case in point is the Sproul-Vargo marriages. Keith Sproul married Debbie Vargo, and Mark Sproul married Carol Vargo in a double ceremony in mid-1981. All four were twenty-two years old when they were married. Since the husbands were born on January 7, 1959, and the wives one day later, astrologists as well as other special investigators may well be fascinated with their family futures. The same might be true of the twin sisters in Tulsa, Oklahoma, who gave birth to twins, a son and daughter in each case, on the same day. The mothers shared, incidentally, the same doctor and the same hospital room.

Glancing from bees to botany may also help decipher the riddles of twinning. It was with a study of plants that the Austrian monk Gregor Mendel first established a systematic description of the way dominant and recessive traits are distributed by heredity through successive generations. The patterns he traced hold true for animal species, including humans. The sweet peas Mendel used in his experiments were, in effect, fraternal twins as far as their genes were concerned.

Botanists following Mendel's lead believe that in certain species of plants there may be within a single seed more than one egg cell (macrospore). When the multiple macrospores are fertilized by separate male cells, fraternal twin plants will grow from the single seed. Alternatively, however, one macrospore may be fertilized by a male cell and may then trigger a virgin birth (parthenogenesis) in its partner. "Siamese" twins occur in the plant kingdom, particularly among irises. Only by their flowering is it possible to decide whether such joined twins are identical or fraternal. Fraternals may produce blossoms of different shape and color, according to genetic variations. Identicals cannot.

What Are Your Chances of Having Twins?

For the human mother, an attempt to assess the chances of producing twins during her lifetime or from a particular pregnancy can quickly lead to confusion. Data show that much depends upon race and geographical location. The percentage of probabilities will also vary according to the date of any statistics consulted.

It has long been a popular notion that the appearance of twins in any one family tends to follow some sort of consistent pattern, with probabilities high in every other generation. Whether this is true or not, though, it seems to apply only to fraternal twins. According to Dr. Gordon Allen of the National Institute of Mental Health, there is a reliable probability that in each and every pregnancy there is one chance in 270 for the appearance of identicals. Beyond that bare statistic, there is little known for certain.

Nevertheless, the continuing speculation in medical literature about the causes of twinning can be as fascinating as the twin myths of old. According to Dr. Luigi Gedda, the belief that twins occur in alternate generations in certain families is so firmly held among Italians that their insurance companies take note of it. Dr. Gedda himself takes it seriously enough to conjecture that the explanation of the twinning mechanism may be found in the interaction of dominant and recessive characteristics following a Mendelian configuration among successive generations. In a word, the reasons for dizygotic twin births might be related to a particular family's hereditary makeup.

Case reports continue to reinforce the popular notion that twins tend to run in the family. For example, two pairs of twins were born in 1947 to Mrs. Willard E. Heaps of Cedar City, Utah. Six sets of twins and a lone daughter were born in eleven years to Mrs. Harry Fifield of Putnam, Connecticut. Mrs. Charlotte Ridenour of Glenford, Ohio, has twin sons, twin grandchildren and two sets of twin great-grandchildren. I've spoken with many others with similar evidence of a possible twinning streak in their families. The majority of these twins are fraternals.

Records of 4,000 Mormon mothers have shown that the women who were themselves fraternal twins gave birth to twins at the rate of one set for each 58 pregnancies. When the father was a fraternal twin and the mother was not, the rate was only one set for every 126 pregnancies. The likelihood that a predisposition to dizygotic twinning is passed on only through the female's side of the family has been firmly asserted in some literature, but even on this point controversy persists. The twinning gene—if there truly is such a thing—may also come from the male side.

Scientists do know that the rate of fraternal twinning varies according to race. This conclusion is buttressed by massive amounts of statistics available at The Hague. Among whites, twins occur in about 1 percent of all live births; among blacks and American Indians, the percentage is close to 1.7; while among Orientals, the data point to a much lower rate—about .5 percent. Put another way, among whites about one of every 100 births produces fraternal twins, while among blacks twins occur once in every 79 births. In Nigeria, however, fraternal twins occur once in every 22 births!

Even this preponderance of evidence suggesting a correlation between twinning and race sometimes needs further examination. For instance, although Japanese researchers tabulated some 100 million pregnancies, they found that twins occurred only once in every 155 births. Speculation that swirled around this low twinning rate focused on Japanese traditions. In Japan, it is still considered bad luck to have twins, so some twin births may simply never be reported to the bureaus gathering statistics. The same may well be true in some provinces of China, where, according to Dr. Gedda, twins seem to be almost unheard of. And in Africa, economic, social and cultural conditions probably blur the record. Another important consideration is that the present statistics are all drawn from the reported number of live births. Recently, the use of diagnostic sonography (ultrasound scans of the womb and its contents) suggested a dramatic disparity between the number of twin conceptions and twin births. This discovery may

foretell statistical shifts in the future if more twin pregnancies ultimately terminate in the birth of infant twins.

Hellin's Law (named for the researcher who formulated
it about a century ago) still provides a generally accepted
prediction about the frequency of all multiple births. Hellin said that for the human species altogether there would
be one twin birth for every 89 single births; that for every
89 twin births there would be one triplet birth; that for
every 89 triplet births, one quadruplet birth; and so on
up the scale of mathematical chances.

Although fraternal twinning rates are reported declining
in some areas, they seem to be on the rise, if not nationally,
then at least in certain regions. Ronald S. Wilson, head of
the Louisville Twins Study, reports a steady increase in
the number of twins born in his area over a twelve-year
period from 1968 through 1979. The figures jumped from
8.6 to 13 twin births per 1,000 live births. Donald M.
Keith, executive director of the Center for Study of Multiple Birth, accounts for the upsurge this way: "First
there's a slight rise in the birth rate overall; then, too, more
women are having children later in their child-bearing
years, which increases their chances of having twins; third,
there's evidence that as women come off long-term use of
the pill and become pregnant within the first two or three
months, they more often have twins; and the fourth reason
for the rise in twinning is related to uses of fertility drugs."

Twins are born more often to older mothers. Women
between thirty-five and forty are more apt to have twins
than are women in any other age group. Twin pregnancies
are less than one-third as common in women under twenty
with no previous children as in women thirty-five to forty
with four or more previous children. At least two interrelated factors are involved here: the age of the mother
and the number of previous pregnancies. It has been established by some researchers that the likelihood of bearing

twins grows rather remarkably with each successive pregnancy up to the number of seven. One Swedish survey found that the frequency of multiple births was only 1.27 percent in first pregnancies compared with 2.67 percent in fourth pregnancies. The age of the mothers surveyed might also, of course, have affected these figures.

Do the physical characteristics of the mother—her history of menstruation, the size of her pelvis, her history of diseases, her fertility—have a connection with the likelihood of producing twins? There are few reliable answers yet, but the size of the mother's ovaries and of her pelvis have been scrutinized intensely in recent twin research.

As for the use of the contraceptive pill, a higher than normal rate of twin pregnancies occurs when women stop taking oral contraceptives. This is especially true when the women conceive in the first two months after they stop such use. It is thought that going off the pill releases an extraordinary amount of gonadotropin hormone from the pituitary gland into the mother's system. When that drug is intentionally administered by a physician to induce ovulation, the incidence of multiple pregnancies is increased between 20 and 40 percent. The use of Clomiphene treatments produces comparable though less spectacular rises.

A French study in 1976 turned up some interesting results. Doctors were able to pinpoint seven signs in an expectant mother's medical and family history that serve as clues to whether she might be in line to produce twins. The clues were: the mother's age, whether she had had other children previously, the numbers of pairs of twins on the mother's side of the family, her weight, the regularity of her menstrual cycles, her use or non-use of oral contraceptives and her blood group. Women with the proper answers to five or more of these queries were far more likely to have twins.

Certainly there were a number of factors, recently

brought to light from twin studies research, that might
have alerted doctors to the possibility of twins when Ingrid
Bergman and Roberto Rossellini were expecting a child.
Swedes and Italians have relatively high twinning rates, it
was not Bergman's first pregnancy, she is quite tall and
there was about ten years difference in the couple's ages—
all positive clues to twin-prone pregnancies.

Yet, even taking into account all the suspected causes,
no physician can predict with unerring accuracy the birth
of fraternal twins. As for the arrival of identical twins—
seemingly unaffected by race, heredity, age of mother
or known chemical influence—any prediction of that is
sheer guesswork.

Zygosity Determination

But they do show up, these unpredictable identical
twins. When my sister and I appeared unexpectedly, the
story has it that our grandmother fainted in surprise. Other
twins everywhere tell how their arrivals created havoc
among family members. As they lie for the first time in
their mother's arms—one to the left, one to the right—the
twins do look very much alike. But then, surely, all new-
born babies tend to look alike. They're still strangers—
wrinkled, tiny, their eyes closed, their bodies swathed in
blankets. It's easy to see, in those early moments, why it is
difficult to discern whether any given pair is identical or
not.

Discovering if twins come from one or more than one
egg is called zygosity determination. Much genetic research depends on data obtained from the study of twins,
research aimed at learning how the "wiring diagram" of
inherited genes affects or even determines a vast array of
physical and psychological traits. Scientists make infer-

ences about the relative importance of heredity and environment, drawing their information from tests made on
people whose genetic composition is confidently assumed
to be identical. The validity of the tests depends upon the
twins having nearly identical genes. Since identicals have
very similar genes while fraternals do not, the presence of
the latter in a control group will distort the results of the
tests.

In emergency situations, it can be of crucial difference
to know whether twins are fraternal or identical. Should
transplant of some vital organ—heart, kidney or lung—be
required, the system of an identical twin is less likely to
reject the transplant from his partner than from any other
donor. Skin transplants from one person to another so far
can be accomplished successfully *only* between identical
twins. The graft is accepted as if it had been taken from
another part of the same body.

Mutual aid between twins is the norm, not a rarity.
Twins have been shown to be remarkably generous to one
another in this regard. They often share whatever is necessary with their afflicted soulmates. In 1977, a thirty-three-
year-old California twin made medical history by accepting a testicle transplant from his brother and becoming the
father of a baby boy three years later. A seven-year-old
was readily agreeable to giving up a kidney for transplant-
ing to her sister although the parents had to get court approval because of the children's age. The famed plastic
surgeon, Dr. Ivo Pitanguy of Brazil, tells of a burn case
in which one young twin, however, was more hesitant. He
was willing to offer his skin for transplant to his brother,
but when he learned that it wasn't absolutely necessary, he
said in that case he would rather not.

Since zygosity is clearly of more than incidental interest,
then, it ought to be diagnosed whenever possible. But how?

Even with highly sophisticated methods now available, this is occasionally a very difficult task.

The two primary methods of zygosity determination are placental observation and a comparison of the twins after they are born. The key diagnostic factors in the latter method are the observation of (1) sex (identicals do not show up in boy-girl pairs); and (2) inherited characteristics (identicals will be more similar in color of eyes, shape of features, blood groupings and so forth). Once, it was thought that placental examination alone could determine if a set of twins was identical, since it was believed that monozygotic twins always shared the same placenta. Scientists now know this assumption to be false. Identical twins may have separate placentas, and separate amniotic sacs and chorionic sacs as well. (These are the membranes that surround the developing fetus in pregnancy. The inner, amniotic, sac contains the amniotic fluid in which the fetus lives until just before birth.) On the other hand, it has been well established that the placentas of a two-egg twin pair may grow together at some point in the gestational process. This is called a "fused placenta."

According to Dr. Jack Pritchard, the very thorough examination of the placenta still reveals much essential information on zygosity and at far less inconvenience and expense than many other methods. Dr. Pritchard, professor of obstetrics and gynecology at the University of Texas Health Science Center, points out that placental examination allows physicians to take note of the membranes that have linked the twins to each other before birth, thus learning more about the history of their interuterine development—a history of practical concern in predicting physical problems that the infants may be facing after birth.

There are several variations in the development of the placenta and membranes in identical twins. When the division of the single fertilized ovum takes place within seventy-two hours of conception, each fetus will continue growing with its own amniotic sac and outer membrane (chorion). Twin expert Dr. Ian MacGillivray contends that this appears to happen 18 to 36 percent of the time. But if the outer membrane has formed before the division takes place (sometime between the fourth and eighth day), then the twins will share it, though each may still grow within a separate amniotic sac. If the amniotic sac has also formed (at about the eighth day) before the division, the twins will share it as well.

It is believed that postnatal examination of the placenta and membranes can lead to a definite diagnosis of identical twins if certain formations, impossible in the case of fraternals, can be discovered. If twins are found to have shared an amniotic sac, doctors feel fairly certain that the pair is identical. The same is true if they share a single unfused chorion, although each had a separate and distinct amniotic sac. Such formations, however, are not found even in the majority of identical twin births, and where they cannot be discovered, doctors generally turn to modern refinements of observation of the pair after birth.

Generally speaking, twins are declared monozygotic when all signs that would indicate they are dizygotic are excluded. When and if they show major differences in eye color; form, distribution, texture and color of hair; in skin texture or pigmentation; teeth; shape of ears; size of hands and feet; ratio of skull size to limbs; or in the major and minor blood groups, it is almost certain that they are fraternal rather than identical twins. No single disparity is sufficient proof of dizygosity, but all add up to what is called a "table of resemblances" by H. H. Newman, an eminent exponent of the method. He reminds us that the unaided and even untrained human eye has an almost uncanny ability to distinguish between faces even at considerable distances, in crowds or in poor lighting. This ability permits most people to identify identical twins as well as doctors can. Twins particularly seem to have an almost infallible eye for spotting other twins and telling whether they are identical or fraternal, but, faced with the subtle variations nature invariably provides, this can't always be relied upon either. Twins and twin experts Donald and Louis Keith mistakenly believed until they were adults that they were fraternals. It wasn't until other twins convinced them that they took a complete series of blood tests that proved otherwise.

Doctors and laymen alike take for granted that a difference in sexes between members of a pair indicates the twins are dizygotic. Nevertheless, there is occasionally cause for doubt. Doctors have recorded exceptionally rare instances where monozygotic twins were not of the same sex. In 1974, twin adolescents who were known to share twenty-two blood groups and other biochemical markers which testified that they were identical were discovered to be different in one startling aspect of central importance. One had a sex chromosome with the classic features of *a female* with Turner's syndrome, while the other had the sex chromosomes of a male. By all meaningful standards, these twins had to be classed as monozygotic, although the presence of the female chromosome created a paradox for which there is still no explanation.

Currently, conclusive tests in zygosity determination would seem to rest in a scientific matching of hand- and footprints as well as the extensive blood typing to which the Keith twins resorted. The latter is expensive and in most cases not at all necessary. Dermatoglyphics, the careful examination of finger-, hand- and footprints, is far simpler and may guide future doctors to an easy and accurate diagnosis of zygosity. Identical twins show a very high degree of correspondence in the swirls and ridges of their prints, a degree sufficient to distinguish them from fraternals, as we will see later when we examine the work of Dr. H. Warner Kloepfer, a leader in the field.

How Twins Differ

The terms *concordant* and *discordant* are used by researchers to explain likenesses and dissimilarities in all twins. If both members of the twin pair have the same blood type, say, or eye color, or shape of nose or ears, they are said to be concordant for that specific characteristic. When individual twins differ in regard to a certain characteristic, they are said to be discordant for that characteristic. Of course, scientific investigators do not stop there. Depending upon what phenomenon they are examining, they may record concordance and discordance in physical, intellectual, emotional, sociodevelopmental and other traits.

By noting such point-for-point distinctions, doctors can sort out and codify statistics on separate traits, which are of particular use in studies of the causes of myopia, cancer or heart disease, for example.

Identical twins share many—but never quite all—of their characteristics. They have been found to be discordant in as many as 20 percent of the traits most frequently studied. Sometimes even identical twins won't resemble each other at birth. Their size in particular may be quite different. Much will depend upon how equally the pair was nourished during their time in the womb. Complications stemming from such factors as how closely the embryos were attached to the wall of the womb, whether or not the umbilicals became entwined, as well as whether the pair shared inner and outer gestational sacs all may contribute to their difference in size and health. Fraternal twins typically display more discordant traits, but the exceptions to this rule are as interesting a subject for speculation as conformity to it. These questions keep alive the suspicion that currently accepted causes for concordance or discordance may actually distract attention from the more obscure principles behind the twin phenomenon.

On rare occasions identicals have been found to be discordant when extreme medical problems cropped up. Such pairs are called heterokaryotic twins. The different genetic makeup of their cells was not fully evident while they were in health. Where such discordances occur in an identical pair, doctors believe that the differences are linked to the time of the original separation, when the single zygote split in two.

Mirror-Image Twins

When you look in a mirror, you see a reflection of yourself in reverse. A ring on one hand will appear to be on the other; a mole on your left side will look to be on your right side. Nature accomplishes such a reversal in some sets of twins. These are known as reversed asymmetrical, or more commonly mirror-image, twins. This reversed asymmetry generally manifests itself in clockwise and counterclockwise swirls of the hair, in right-handedness and left-handedness and so forth. In extreme cases, there will be a displacement of internal organs in one twin. In such an instance, one twin will have his heart on the right side and the other will have his on the left.

Reversed asymmetrical twins are almost always monozygotic, although there has been speculation that dizygotics occasionally can be mirror images of each other, too. One theory attempting to account for reversed asymmetry in monozygotics suggests that mirror imaging occurs when the embryo splits after it has begun to develop left- and right-sidedness, a process that is thought to occur rather late in the twinning process. In this case, it is assumed that the left-sided half becomes the left-handed twin, the right-sided the right-handed one.

However, much remains hypothetical about how and why reversed asymmetry occurs in twins. In order to examine the phenomenon further, scientists divide the characteristics of mirror-image twins into four categories: anatomical, functional, pathological and psychological. In the anatomical category, they register such data as left-right body characteristics, location and shape of internal organs, teeth, hair whorls and moles or birthmarks. In the functional category, their concern is with voluntary muscular dominance such as preferential use of right or left hand or foot, favoring the use of one eye and the like. Pathological reversed asymmetry refers to conditions such as congenital malformations, which show up on one side of one twin and on the opposite side of the other. Last of all, psychological reversed asymmetry is a reversal of, or complementary difference between, psychological traits. One of the pair may be very active, the other passive; one may be very verbal and the other especially good at physically coordinated tasks. With the original "Siamese" twins, Chang and Eng, one was hot-tempered, the other quite calm and even-tempered. This fact does not surprise such experts as Dr. Luigi Gedda, who says there is evidence to believe that conjoined or "Siamese" twins tend to be less exactly alike than ordinary one-egg twins.

Such psychological mirror imaging is not only difficult to diagnose with assurance, it is often very confusing to twins themselves and to their parents. Twins often reverse their roles as they grow older, or even on what appears to be the whim of the moment. One twin will dominate in a particular area for a while, then the other will.

A study conducted by Gedda and his colleagues using 537 randomly selected twin pairs focused on functional mirror imaging. The questions asked of the duos: With which hand do you write? With which hand do you throw a ball? With which foot do you kick a football? With which eye do you aim at a target? Results confirmed the notion that mirror imaging was "a result of the natural identical twinning process." Also, the pairs demonstrated more mirror imaging in regard to throwing and kicking than in writing and aiming. Most probably this was due to outside pressure for conformity in the latter categories.

Obviously, science has a long way to go before an exhaustive study of reversed asymmetry in twins will yield all its secerts. Most research so far has, of necessity, concentrated on only one or two observations among many variables.

Supertwins

Buttons and bumper stickers proclaim that twins—any twins—are super. TWINS ARE TERRIFIC, says the bold type of a souvenir placard. Wherever twins or their parents congregate, they are apt to wear buttons with comic pronouncements of superiority—or defensiveness. HAVING TWINS IS A BALL. YES, I'VE GOT DOUBLE TROUBLE. HAPPINESS IS HAVING TWO. PATIENCE . . . IS HAVING TWINS. DON'T SAY THIS COULDN'T HAPPEN TO YOU. TWINS ARE TWICE AS NICE.

In spite of all of that, though, the term "supertwin" was coined by Amram Scheinfeld in his classic book, *Twins and Supertwins,* to define triplets, quadruplets and higher multiple births.

Supertwins, like twins, fall into various categories, depending upon whether they originated from one or more

eggs. A wide variety of mathematical combinations is obviously possible as the number of infants in any group rises.
The Dionne quintuplets, born in 1934 in a remote part of
Canada, are assumed to be identicals, still the only known
case on medical record of five infants having originated
from one egg. Much medical attention was directed at the
doctor and midwife involved with their births and the care
(or lack of it) in the examination of the placenta. The
record shows that the five shared the same placenta, but
it was not saved or very thoroughly studied.

The same cannot be said for the quints themselves. After
unprecedented and prolonged attention from the press and
general public and from physicians as well—with much
elaborate testing (blood types, hand- and footprints, table
of correspondences)—these salient facts have emerged:
(1) The first division of the egg cell left two completely
viable halves; (2) one of these split again to produce the
embryos of Annette and Yvonne; (3) the other half divided to produce Cecile and another fraction; and (4) this
remaining fraction divided to produce Marie and Emilie.

So far, the Dionne quints are living proof that the process
of identical twinning need not produce even numbers. The
possibility remains open, though, that in the case of odd-
numbered multiples, one or more of the embryos may have
miscarried. In Mrs. Dionne's case, as in those of some other
mothers of multiples interviewed, an incident early in her
pregnancy might hold the clue. Mrs. Dionne had complained of pains similar to those of labor and eventually
emitted a "black ovoid object about the size of a duck's
egg."

Mathematically, there are many possible ways an egg
could divide and subdivide to form supertwins. Therefore,
there are also numerous ways the fetuses may or may not
share placentas, amniotic sacs and chorions. Scientists use
the same methods to determine the zygosity of supertwins
as they do for twins.

How frequently might we expect supertwins to appear? Again, we can use Hellin's Law for our computer. Triplets occur only once in 7,569 births. Interestingly, however, some mothers have more than one set of triplets. A look at supertwin statistician Helen Kirk Lauve's records turns up these stories: One Texas woman had three sets of them, but that wasn't all. She also had a set of quintuplets, a set of quadruplets, five sets of twins and nine singletons. By the age of thirty-one, a North Carolina mother had delivered quints, quads, two sets of triplets, two sets of twins and a singleton.

Quadruplets occur once in 658,503 births. And, of course, far rarer are quintuplets, born only once in 57,289,761 births. Until the Dionne quintuplets came along and survived childhood, no complete sets had ever lived more than a few days. According to Lauve, in the United States alone today there are 101 complete sets of living quadruplets and eight sets of quintuplets. Her files reflect twenty-nine complete sets of quintuplets now living worldwide and three complete sets of sextuplets. The Dionnes, however, remain the only known set of *identical* quints.

The term "super" as a prefix pops up in numerous bits of scientific jargon relating to multiple births. Superfecundation describes a situation in which two ova released at the same time are fertilized by two sperm released in two different sexual acts. This means that it is possible for fraternal twins to have two different fathers. Medical literature does record such cases, but they are extremely rare.

In 1938, in Chicago, health officer Dr. Herman Bundesen mediated in a dispute between two men who both claimed to be the father of a set of boy-girl twins. Blood tests showed that either—or both—might claim paternity. Stating correctly that the theory of superfecundation supported the possibility that the twins might have had different fathers, Bundesen suggested that they divide the babies between them, one father taking the girl and the other taking the boy. Unmollified, the men continued their quarrel, loudly protesting their love for mother and children. They almost came to blows. The judge decided the case by a commonsense evaluation of the best prospects for the children's future. Other similar cases occasionally appear in the press. When they do, scientific theories obviously play second fiddle to parental emotions. Perhaps Solomon's judgment—to cut in two one child for the two mothers who were disputing the question of maternity— set a precedent for those judges and doctors who today have to help decide such questions in cases of twins.

With the new blood tests currently available, the heat of that 1938 dispute might have been avoided. In June 1981, the *New York Times* reported a new test, known as HLA (human leukocyte antigen), which identifies inherited genetic "markers" in the blood's white cells with 97.3 percent accuracy. This allows a laboratory to identify and match a child's blood with that of its biological father in almost every case.

Superfetation refers to the possibility that after a pregnancy has been started in one ovarian cycle, another cycle in the following month also produces an egg which is then fertilized. When this occurs embryos of different ages are present side by side in the womb. It is also conceivable that two eggs come into the womb simultaneously but the fertilization of one may trigger an inhibiting process which delays the fertilization of the other. When the inhibiting mechanism is no longer in effect the second egg may possibly be fertilized during another sexual act.

Some physicians argue that alleged cases of superfetation can be better explained by conditions of gestation which produce twins far different in size and development at birth; others dispute this notion. In 1961, when a dizygotic male/female pair was born in Cleveland, the female was declared an "eight-month baby," while her brother was said to be a full-term infant. Diagnoses are therefore still pretty much dependent on the individual doctor's preconceptions.

In a far more unusual case, Mrs. Eugene Kupferstein gave birth to two infants who had grown in two separate wombs inside her body. Doctors wouldn't designate her two babies as twins at all. Her attending physician, however, had known she had two wombs and had even told her during her pregnancy she should expect twins. He had discovered the two wombs during minor surgery but believed that after conception the two fetuses would surely be together in only one womb, while the second womb would become an unused appendage to be pushed out of the way. Obviously, nature has tricks that the experts don't expect.

Conjoined or "Siamese" Twins

On May 11, 1811, on a houseboat in the middle of the village of Meklong in Siam, an unusual pair of twins was born. The pair, Chang and Eng, was destined to give a label to all twins born physically attached to each other. Though these "Siamese" twins were not the first twins born so joined, through chance and the auspices of P. T. Barnum they found fame and fortune touring the world.

They came along at the right time to take their place in the public imagination and in medical lore as the representatives of all those twins whose separation into distinct identicals was halted before completion.

Attached at the breast by a thick band of tissue, the brothers spent their entire lives physically linked together. Naturally, their situation drew the interest of physicians around the world. Arguments raged, especially in England and America, as to whether the two might safely be separated by surgery. With today's technological advances, it is probable that their separation could be accomplished. Several such pairs have been separated successfully within just the past few years. At that time, however, the majority of doctors felt that the surgery would jeopardize the twins' lives. As far as the famous showman Barnum was concerned, this controversial attention only increased the attraction of his sideshow stars, who grabbed headlines and free publicity everywhere, since the press played on the public's pity for brothers caught in such "unnatural bondage."

The pity they aroused is understandable. In many ways, however, their bondage was not all that unnatural. Twins of all types talk of something similar when they discuss the subconscious connections with their partners. They call the "bond between them" a cherished part of their psychic makeup. For Chang and Eng, however, the physical problems often must have seemed insurmountable.

Looking back at what they managed to accomplish—how relatively normal, under the circumstances, their lives were—these two seem indeed amazing. Few singletons, or twins, either, no matter how close they may be, can help but be awed by this pair. Changing their names to Bunker when they came to America, they lived long, full lives. They worked hard and were reputed to be kind and generous. Eventually, they became wealthy farmers, and between them they fathered twenty-one children. In later years, two pairs of normal twins were produced by their grandchildren. Their families were close and loving. The story of the Bunkers' deaths, at age sixty-three, has been told often. On a winter evening Chang became ill. The illness worsened, and one night they went to bed early because he was having difficulty breathing. The next thing Eng was aware of was that Chang had died beside him. Eng called to the children, who came running to the bedside. Then Eng died within an hour of his brother. Some think he died not from any physical cause but from sheer fright. The twins left behind them a large group of friends and admirers who spoke often of their moral character. They had managed to rise above their predicament and to pass on an example of warmth and human compassion.

The story of the Biddenden Maids is equally inspiring. One of the earliest recorded sets of conjoined twins, Mary and Eliza Chalkhurst were born in the year 1100 into a moderately wealthy family in Biddenden, England. They lived for thirty-four years connected at the hips or buttocks. When they died, they bequeathed land and money to the church, directing that it be used to benefit the poor. Once each year, cakes were made in their memory, displaying their image. As late as 1875, an observer at the Easter Monday celebration for the Biddenden Maids wrote, "The cakes, which were simple flour and water, are four inches long by two inches wide and are given away, are distributed at the discretion of the church wardens, and are nearly 300 in number."

According to Dr. Alan F. Guttmacher, noted physician and a monozygotic twin, conjoined pairs are rarities which occur only once in 50,000 to 80,000 births. In the past, not many of them survived infancy, and, aside from the Bunkers and the Biddenden Maids, only a few are mentioned with any frequency in medical texts. They are: Radica-Doodica, conjoined Hindu girls; Simplicio and Lucio Godino, from the Philippines; Daisy and Violet Hilton, born in England; Rosalie and Josepha Blazek, from Bohemia; "The Hungarian Sisters," Helena and Judith; and Millie and Chrissie, born to slave parents in South Carolina in 1851. This last pair were mirror-image twins to the degree that the heart was on the left side of one twin and the right side of the other. They, too, entered a sideshow and, because they had excellent singing voices, were billed in America and Europe as the "two-headed nightingale."

The first autopsy in the New World was performed in

1533 on conjoined twin girls in Santo Domingo. It was done at the request of a priest who had baptized both children but had remained uncertain as to whether one or two souls were involved. Since all organs were found in duplicate, the priest's decision to baptize both was thought to be vindicated.

Seeing a pair of "Siamese"—or conjoined—twins, all observers remark on their high degree of similarity. Surely such a pair must be identical to the core of their genetic makeup. Yet time after time, people who knew the Bunkers commented on a few marked differences. They were, like all twins, unmistakably individual people. As already mentioned, Chang had the more explosive temper and was far more argumentative than his brother Eng. Chang became a heavy drinker, while Eng was a teetotaler. Such differences are still a puzzle to twinning specialists. How does one account for the unexpected dissimilarities? The physiologist is lured to answer the question by more and more exacting analysis of the process by which the original egg, from which "Siamese" and other monozygotic twins emerge, splits to produce two human beings.

"Siamese" twins generally demonstrate a high degree of reversed asymmetricality. It is therefore thought that all mirror-image twins may have just narrowly missed—by a few hours or perhaps a single day—being born conjoined. The pioneer researcher H. H. Newman speculated, "The twin derived from the left half of the embryo will develop a little faster than the other twin but will tend to show the same asymmetries as those characteristic of the species, while the twin derived from the right half will tend to develop more slowly and tend to follow the opposite plan of symmetry, which is the mirror image of the twin derived from the left half." Whether true or not, this presents an avenue of investigation still to be explored. A faint but charming echo of such a thought pops up when one hears

the McLaughlin twins, Frances and Kathryn, photographers, authors and mirror-image twins, describe themselves
as "the country twin" and "the city twin."

The daily lives of most twins will be unaffected by rarities and extreme complications of the twinning process.
Yet each new discovery of minute subdivisions brings us
closer to understanding the origin of all twins. With more
enlightenment, we can look forward to a better determination of our genetic heredity and some answers to the environmental hazards both before and after the birth of
twins. Each discovery may help dispel the heresies that
plague twins. We can look forward to freer lives.

3. The Strange Case of the Vanishing Twin

The physician is astounded. He blinks, not quite able to believe his eyes. His patient, a woman in her twelfth week of pregnancy, is still on the examining table. The sonar machine is displaying on its screen in a series of gray images a picture of the woman's womb. This is the second sonar scan the doctor has ordered. The first was taken six weeks ago. Whereas in the earlier scan two tiny gestational sacs were visible, now only one is being recorded. In fact, there is no evidence at all that another has ever been present.

Over decades many an obstetrician has been embarrassed by the unexpected arrival of twins, or even more multiples, but imagine how this doctor must feel. He confidently predicted twins earlier in this woman's pregnancy. Now he discovers that one is missing from the set!

To the practiced eye of the physician and his assistant, the picture on the screen is as distinct as Mount Everest on a clear day. So what could have happened? There has been no misreading of the earlier data indicating the presence of twins. In fact, a Polaroid picture exists to prove it. There has been no malfunctioning of the equipment. Recovering his composure, the doctor explains that in recent years practitioners from around the world have been reporting other cases such as this.

Because there are many possible explanations for the mystery, the doctor can only speculate. Technological advances have, however, been answering many questions about the reproductive process. Sonography, fetoscopy (also called embryoscopy) and amniocentesis, for instance, have brought about remarkable advances in our understanding of what is happening in a pregnant mother's womb. They can help an obstetrician identify and treat complications early—complications that might have been unobserved even a short while ago.

Sonograpy, or ultrasound, produces a picture of the womb and its contents. Sound waves projected through the opaque tissue of the abdomen work rather like radar to produce a moving picture of the processes within. By the use of sonography, doctors can observe the stages of gestation at an earlier date and can do so more frequently than was formerly feasible, since potentially harmful X rays need not be used.

In fetoscopy, an apparatus for making photographs is actually introduced into the womb to take close-ups of the child (or children) in the making. The technique allows physicians to see previously undetectable abnormalities in a developing fetus. However, at present fetoscopy is considered by many physicians to be a far from harmless procedure. Also, it is not possible with this method, as it is with ultrasound, to see inside the fetus. If, in the future, the risks of fetoscopy can be reduced by technical refinements, there will be many proud parents collecting very early baby pictures, since some of the photos thus obtained show very clear images of tiny embryos afloat in the clear amniotic sac within the womb.

Amniocentesis—a particularly important procedure in the early diagnosis of hereditary defects—involves the insertion of a hollow needle through the abdomen, into the amniotic sac, to withdraw some amniotic fluid for analysis.

These three new diagnostic processes complement each other. Sonographic examination, for instance, is now a most important prelude to amniocentesis. In his book *Know Your Genes*, Dr. Aubrey Milunsky says, "If amniocentesis is done without prior ultrasound and therefore without knowing twins are present . . . serious consequences may ensue. The parents run a high risk [25 percent] of having a defective child, and if the twins lie in two different sacs, only one amniotic fluid is obtained with the needle. The result then pertains to only one twin . . ." The sonographic scan may also show the location of the placenta, so it can be avoided when the needle is inserted. The scan is also most useful in those cases in which multiple fertilization has occurred ectopically; that is, outside the womb. There are even cases on record of "combined" pregnancies where one fetus in the womb is accompanied by another, hidden ectopically in the fallopian tube.

While elucidating many of the mysteries of gestation, sonography, fetoscopy, amniocentesis and other new diagnostic approaches are exposing a whole new set of enigmas. They are, however, closing in on a solution to one of the most baffling puzzles of all, that of the "vanished twin."

As far back as 1945, there were tentative allusions in medical literature to the "vanishing process," but it could not be satisfactorily explored until the appearance of ultrasound techniques. Now it is gradually coming to light that one's chances of having started life in the womb with a twin are much higher than was previously imagined. In

1973, Dr. Louis M. Hellman of the State University of New York reported the results of his study of 140 "at-risk" early pregnancies. He observed that twenty-two of the women started out with twin gestational sacs, and that fourteen of these pregnancies were eventually spontaneously aborted. He noted that the frequency of single-ovum twinning in his sample was twenty-five times greater than expected. By 1975, other doctors had mentioned in passing that twin conceptions were probably more numerous than commonly thought. Evidence was piling up that many gestational sacs contained "blighted ova"—ova that would not continue growth to produce an infant. Some of the blighted ova were found in the presence of perfectly healthy embryos.

In 1976, Dr. Salvator Levi of the University Hospital in Brussels delivered some startling news to the medical community. Ultrasound examinations had been made of nearly 7,000 patients prior to the tenth week of their pregnancies. In that group, at least 71 percent had started with twins in their wombs but eventually gave birth only to singletons. Other doctors later reported loss rates as high as 53 percent in pregnancies that began as twin conceptions. And a recent sonography textbook by Roger C. Sanders and A. Everette James states that about "70 percent undoubted twin pregnancies, identified between 5 and 8 weeks, end in the birth of a single fetus."

Where the second twin of the original pair had thus vanished, the tissue of the embryo and amniotic sac had in many cases been resorbed by the mother's body. In other words, it appeared to have been "withdrawn" by the tissues of the womb, in the same manner that a sponge takes up water without visibly changing form. In Dr. Levi's studies, resorption rate was 78 percent in the first ten weeks of pregnancy, 13 percent in the period between ten and fourteen weeks. There was no complete resorption after fourteen weeks; instead, the presence of a tiny, incompletely formed infant (called a fetus papyraceus) was usually found at the time of delivery of the twin which survived through gestation.

If the early forms of the fetus are thus "withdrawn" by the tissues of the womb, the question automatically arises as to why this should happen only in multiple pregnancies. Well, the fact is that it probably doesn't. Probably it happens in other pregnancies when only one human life has been conceived. According to Dr. Levi, it is not only possible but may indeed be what happens in some pregnancies which are just far enough advanced to have delayed menstruation. For instance, in some cases, Levi has detected by ultrasound an indicated presence of a small gestational sac—only to find later that the woman's other pregnancy tests turn out to be negative and that menstruation is soon resumed. If a mother has such a capacity for resorption, the old joke about being "a little bit pregnant" takes on an additional nuance.

The term "vanished twin" means, then, that at an early stage in the cell division and multiplication process, something happens to terminate the growth of one fertilized ovum. So far doctors simply don't know why that something happens. It is too early to say what the whole phenomenon may mean, though it may well prove to be the case that for every one hundred singletons alive today, way over half of them may have begun life with a twin! Thus, singletons may once have had more in common with twins than they ever would have guessed.

His Brother's Keeper

When Cain went to the fields with his brother Abel and returned without him, the Bible records that the Lord God demanded, "Where is your brother?" And Cain, who had killed his brother, answered guiltily, "Am I my brother's keeper?" Of course, one assumes that the look of guilt was written all over his face. Certainly, the sound of guilt was in his answer. In light, however, of what science has discovered so far about the "vanished twin," the answer to Cain's question might, in a certain physiological way, be, "By all means—yes." No one is suggesting that a reenactment of Cain's crime against his brother or anything so dramatic takes place in the tiny cell masses developing together in the mother's womb. We will see later, however, that there *may be* a truly baffling counterpart of Cain's guilt in the psyche of singletons and twins alike. While neither murder nor cannibalism are at all appropriate terms to apply to what is happening between the cell masses, there may be, eerie as it will sound, a sort of parasitism involved, in which one feeds on the nutritive sources necessary for the other's life. And in some cases, one expanding cell mass seems to envelop the other. Perhaps the larger, hungrier and healthier one simply grows around the smaller, less healthy one. When this happens, the survivor may indeed be keeping his brother (or sister) alive *in some transformed state* within his own body. This most peculiar condition may go on for years, or for a lifetime.

In the winter of 1981, a Rhode Island woman consulted her gynecologist about some chronic troubles. Her doctor explained that these were being caused by a teratoma—a cyst growing on one of her ovaries. She was the mother of a teenager, so her first thought was that the cyst had probably developed as a result of her childbearing. Tests confirmed something that seemed to her far more outlandish. The cyst was more likely the remnant of a twin she had carried within her body from the time before her own birth!

Such cysts are relatively rare. They occur, though, in a variety of forms and are found most usually in the ovaries, testicles, face, neck, stomach, liver or brain, the incompleted but living tissues of long-vanished brothers and sisters.

There is an enormous amount of medical literature by now dealing with these extraordinary teratomas, and less than total agreement as to what they are and how they happen to grow. Some doctors think they represent incomplete attempts to form "Siamese" twins. This theory stems from the observation that the cysts generally appear in body areas where "Siamese" twins are likely to be joined. For instance, sharing a liver or a brain is one of the common anomalies tragically associated with conjoined twins. Teratomas often grow on the liver or brain. The term "parasitic twin" is sometimes used in the literature concerned with teratomas and incomplete "Siamese" twinning. In 1949, a Dr. Kimmel of Philadelphia reported a cerebral tumor containing traces of *five* human fetuses. The matter of teratomas remains highly controversial because the interpretation of the findings depends so heavily on the means used to identify tissue as "embryonic." If the cyst appears to contain a vertebral column, appendages such as fingers and toes or similar features that appear early in the development of the embryo, this is taken by some doctors as conclusive evidence, though eminent doubters have yet to be convinced that such a thing is possible.

Most teratomas are understood to be benign cysts, but even the doctors who doubt that teratomas are related to twinning have not explained how the unusual tissues show up in parts of the body where they are totally unrelated to the function of the afflicted organ. Cysts in a mature adult may vary from the size of a tennis ball to a considerably larger growth sometimes containing vestigial teeth, hair, embryonic limbs and other relics of a partially formed twin.

Very rare but not unheard of are cases scientifically labeled *fetus in fetu*, also called "twin inclusion." Here the complete fetus is enclosed by the body of the superficially normal infant. In a most unusual operation in Portland, Oregon, in the late 1940s, the half-developed fetus of a twin was removed from the abdomen of a thirteen-month-old girl. In 1972, another such instance was reported, in which a six-week-old infant was found to be carrying its unborn twin in its abdomen. And once during the autopsy of an elderly man, doctors turned up what they called an almost fully developed *fetus in fetu*. It weighed about six pounds.

Frightening as they may be, these abnormalities may eventually lead scientists to discover some answers to the mysteries of "the vanished twin." There is some faint support for the belief that incorporation is one of nature's methods of causing a twin to disappear before birth.

In another amazing way, the vanished "other" may be literally carried in the bloodstream of the single survivor. Patricia McDonnell, a British housewife of thirty, has two separate blood types—O and A. For most of her life she had no reason to suspect she might be a medical curiosity. Only when she became pregnant and was given routine tests did her extraordinary condition come to light. "They found my blood couldn't be cross-matched with any other blood . . . I had countless tests—on my blood, saliva, hair, skin and so forth. Skin samples were sent all over the world. The tests went on for three years. Then the doctors told me I had two blood groups. They said my mother should have had twins, but that I absorbed the embryo of my twin into my body, where it has been producing its own blood." Among the examiners in her case were Dr. Michael Glowalla, hematologist of the Kaiser Foundation Hospital, and Dr. George Bird. Bird's findings showed that about 93 percent of Patricia McDonnell's blood was type O and 7 percent type A. It was concluded that the type A was hers, while all the rest belonged to her twin brother.

How could the doctors tell that the vanished twin was a boy? The makeup of the chromosomes in the white blood cells established that. Male and female chromosomes can be distinguished positively. The astonishing discovery of male chromosomes led to three years of exhaustive testing, but there was no discovery of any other tissue whatever that could be identified as belonging to the second fetus. What must have happened is that the twinning process had hardly begun before some of the brother's cells were incorporated—without being destroyed—into the cell clusters which would pass through the ordinary processes of cell differentiation to form the woman's body. Even in the bone marrow which produces blood cells, it would be impossible to locate any of the cells remaining from the vanished brother —and yet Mrs. McDonnell feels she has some other evidence to confirm the diagnosis of the twin she carries about with her. "I have two personalities," she told reporters. "Sometimes I am a cheerful extrovert. The next day I will be an introvert. I have no control over it. It just happens."

One further twist: In this case, the twin within was a fraternal one. An identical twin would have had the same blood type as Mrs. McDonnell. If that had been the case, it might well have escaped detection forever! The potential exists that such an undiscoverable twin *might* be hidden away within *any* singleton. And just possibly, his or her unguessed presence may be the basis for the not uncommon intuition, mentioned by numerous singletons, that they have a lost twin somewhere.

Even the Bible hints at the notion of the vanished twin. At the Third International Congress of Twin Studies, Dr. Gedda said, "It is sufficient to recall . . . the Apostle Thomas. Saint John writes of him, 'The one who was called the twin.' We do not know who his twin brother may have been . . . he is 'the twin.' "

Twins Lost from the Census

The idea that one might once have been a twin is, of course, conjectural. Figures on twinning are based on live births and are far from complete. They seldom indicate the numbers of stillborn or spontaneously aborted pairs. There is confusion, too, in the reporting of cases in which one is born of a pair while one is stillborn. In an eleven-year study in British Columbia, Drs. J. E. Livingston and B. J. Poland examined approximately 2,000 spontaneously aborted embryos and fetuses. The percentage of aborted twins was higher than the rate of twins among live births, and many more identical than fraternal pairs were aborted. The earlier the identicals were aborted, the greater the chance that they were girls. Abortions later in pregnancy were predominantly boys.

In France, Drs. Lucien Schneider, Roger Bessis and Therese Simmonnet have even compared the resorption rates in spontaneous twinning and in twinning stimulated by the use of fertility drugs. In their study, almost two-thirds of the spontaneous twin conceptions diagnosed in the first trimester eventually resulted in the birth of a singleton. Resorption was even more frequent when the drug clomifene was used, though it didn't occur at all when the doctors used cyclofenil. The prebirth risks that twins face are hardly a new discovery. Nor is the fact that over the years doctors have often noted the presence of excess protoplasmic material surrounding a normal afterbirth. What is new is that sonographic scanning offers supporting evidence of how often such material may be the remains of a blighted or scarcely formed twin.

A study bearing on the variable forms of spontaneous abortion was conducted at the Queen Mother's Hospital in Glasgow. Spanning three years, the study covered approximately 10,000 deliveries, including 109 pairs of twins—a ratio of 1 in 91. Besides the 109 mothers who bore living twins, 16 more of the pregnant women were diagnosed by sonar in their first trimester as carrying twins. Six of these aborted both twins. Ten gave birth to singletons. Sonar data established three variations among these 16 cases: Either there were twin blighted ovas, or a single blighted ovum plus an incomplete abortion (in which the fetus was extremely wasted before expulsion); or there was a single blighted ovum plus a normally developing fetus. In some of the cases, when the singleton baby was born, a small blighted sac was found attached to its afterbirth, but in some the sac had evidently been completely resorbed.

In all 16 of the cases in which twin conception failed to result in the birth of twins, one of the sacs was detected by sonar to be considerably larger than the other. Most of the smaller sacs appear to have been resorbed, sometime between the sixth and tenth weeks, since there was no evidence of their presence in the later phases of pregnancy. (In cases in which the second sac was still present after the ninth week, it was at its greatest size at that point, although there was no fetus inside; after that time it shrank dramatically.) Nine of the 10 mothers who eventually bore singletons reported some bleeding in the first trimester, although less than a third of the 109 mothers who carried their twins to term had that problem.

The still tentative nature of their findings has led the Glasgow researchers to recommend extreme caution in the diagnosis of twins until two fetuses, each with detectable heartbeats, can be clearly recognized. Yet they stress that without the use of sonar techniques, a twin pregnancy would not even have been suspected in the majority of cases just cited. Because such discoveries were made, the researchers found it "probable" that the rate of twin conceptions is generally 1 in 60, or even higher. Compare this with the rate of 1 in 89 forecast by Hellin's Law.

Modern scientific techniques can, among other things, determine the weight of fetuses, any heartbeat irregularities, estrogen levels and head measurements. Weight is of obvious importance in diagnosing nutritional deficiencies in one or both fetuses. Ultrasound observation is not an infallible means for determining weight, since it can only show fetal size from which weight is estimated, but, happily, the degree of error is lower for the lighter of the twin fetuses—the one for whom error could be most harmful. Size of the head is related to potential delivery problems, among other things. Ultrasound scans which provide information on these matters help take the surprise and consequent risk out of twin gestations.

Obviously, though, not all the complications facing twin fetuses can be detected with any combination of techniques now available. These complications include such features as what doctors call "locked" twins (fetuses whose heads and necks are tightly entwined in a life-threatening way); tangled umbilical cords which may be a high risk during labor; or something called the "placental steal" syndrome, in which one twin receives the mother's nutrients first before passing on what is left over to the other one. (The second twin in this case is essentially in the same boat as a politician who is demanding equal time on TV. Before he gets it, the voters may have already made their decision.) No matter what the needs of the second twin, he will be the loser if the intrauterine distributing system is not functioning normally.

There is another limitation to sonography to be noted. At about two or three months into the pregnancy—the time when mothers report they can feel a stirring or kicking in the womb—the fetuses have begun to stretch and grow at a remarkable rate. They are jostling for position in their crowded quarters as they begin to work out that pecking order with which their lives are vitally concerned. The amount of normal motion during this period has a tendency to blur the sonar image like snow on a television screen. Even when limbs are more or less fully developed, sonar evidence may remain ambiguous and should merely alert the attending physician to the likelihood of a multiple birth. Until the doctor sees two heads and two distinct bodies displayed in the same physical plane on the screen, he can have no assurance that there are two healthy fetuses within.

The possibility still remains that if two fetuses are clearly visible, there may be even more hidden backstage, as it were. Drs. J. E. Livingstone and B. J. Poland, summing up their use of sonar, say: "It is important to void errors of omission. With four, five or more fetuses, the image becomes very complex, and there is a danger of underestimating the number." These researchers also caution that the complexity of an image may indicate that the mother is carrying conjoined ("Siamese") twins or fetuses with serious malformations. (The first case of conjoined twins identified by sonar was recorded at the University of Texas Medical Branch at Galveston, back in 1976. Dr. L. Charles Powell, the obstetrician in charge, confirmed the diagnosis.)

Diagnostic observations which confirm the frequent occurrence of the vanishing twin appear to agree that the surviving twins in such cases show no physical evidence of having begun as part of a pair. (The exceptions, of course, are those with teratomas or *fetus in fetu* cases previously discussed.) In almost all instances, the twin who vanished existed only for a few weeks. Yet even this brief and preconscious sharing may have left psychic imprints of lasting importance. In cases where one twin died at birth, it is reasonable to believe that the psychic effect on the survivor is even more profound.

Subliminal Memories of Vanished Twins

Dr. Louis Keith and his twin Donald admit their amazement at the number of people who have told them that they always wanted to be a twin . . . or sense that in a former life they were a twin . . . or literally believe they *are* a twin whose partner either vanished or was miscarried early in the pregnancy. I've heard myself of a man who believes he is the survivor of a triplet pregnancy, and a mother of twins who believes her twins started in the womb with a third infant. Is this mere daydream, fantasy or wishful thinking? Poets might declare it to be the memory of a time when one was actually part of a living pair. Wordsworth, for instance, says: "Our birth is but a sleep and a forgetting," and "Nature yet remembers what was so fugitive." Be that as it may, the sense of some prenatal separation or bereavement is indeed widespread and, where it appears most acutely, may be intuitive knowledge on the part of one survivor of a pair of twins.

It is not only the surviving twin, however, who may have such intuition. Mothers of singletons may also be left with a sense of incompleteness. These women who "knew they were carrying twins" are often scorned by their doctors for such "feelings," but after assessing the clinical data on vanished twins, one is less easily persuaded that these mothers were wrong. For all we know, a singleton's phobias or dreams of fratricide might have their origins in the actual life-and-death competition within the womb—from which only one survivor emerged. When a singleton who may, in fact, have lost a twin in the prenatal phase of life feels a stab of longing or sympathy for someone whose

existence has never been confirmed, we can't help but
wonder. The experience, uncanny as it may be, is akin to
that of the amputee who feels a twinge in a foot or arm that
no longer exists. Elvis Presley's twin was stillborn. Part of
the lore about Presley touches on his lifelong yearning for
the missing brother; he has been quoted as saying he "felt
incomplete." That melancholy pervaded his songs.

Out of the depth of uncertainty, one woman with a
single daughter wrote to the Center for Study of Multiple Birth: "For months before the delivery, the doctor
said he could hear two heartbeats." By chance, right after
her baby daughter's birth, the mother had heard the attending doctor and nurse mention "two." In addition, her
daughter always felt strongly that there was another person "just like her" somewhere. In her letter to the Center,
the woman asked for help in checking back through old
medical records to see if there could be some basis for her
persistent hunch.

Another letter came to the Center from a singleton with
fraternal-twin siblings. He asked whether, because he is
left-handed, he might once have had a mirror-image twin.

No positive answer could be given to either of these
inquiries, but the questions they raised were not dismissed
lightly. In both instances, the questioners hoped for con-
firmation of something dimly perceived in the shadowland
of prenatal history. Many of the poignant letters flowing
into the Center express a dilemma in medical ethics: "Please
tell me, if you can, whether there is any truth to the rumor
that doctors don't always tell a mother she had delivered
twins, especially if one baby obviously can't live. When
I woke after childbirth, the doctor said I had only one
baby, but I wasn't completely out of it and I remember
hearing the nurses referring to 'the other one.' " In another
letter, this suspicion is amplified: "I've seen birth certifi-
cates with a mark beside multiple births like this $\frac{1}{1}$ and

am wondering if it means there was one live birth and one stillborn child at the same time." Since the mark is not a standard scientific one, it is conceivable that it indicates what the woman suspected.

Donald Keith, chairman of the board of the Center for Study of Multiple Birth (among his other endeavors in behalf of twins), observes: "In the past, doctors sometimes withheld the truth from the mother to spare her pain and sorrow." Those who feel compelled to find out the facts can, under today's laws, get access to available records, although the search will seldom be an easy one. Finding what is wanted may take weeks of sifting through hospital files, and the meaning of the data obtained may be obscure to anyone without a professional medical background. Mr. Keith advises: "If you can't find out, don't brood or become angry. The past is over; we cannot change it."

One should respect that kindly advice—remembering at the same time that, though it be over, the past has invaluable uses for those who press beyond grief in their quest for greater understanding. While no one expects psychological data to have the same exactitude as physiological findings on the subject of the vanished twin, the former may be of equal importance.

Probing the Twin Fantasy

It may well be that single children, disappointed in one way or another by their siblings or their parents, instinctively search for a companion or partner who will provide them with all the attention, support and love they desire. As long as this search is frustrated by reality, it will produce fantasy partners instead. This, basically, is the theory offered by Dorothy Burlingame in her book, *Twins, A Study of Three Pairs of Identical Twins*.

Citing the most commonly recognized categories of childhood fantasy, Burlingame compares the twin fantasy to the so-called "family romance." In the family romance, the dissatisfied child creates an imaginary family for himself, to replace the actual family of his daily experience. In common forms of such fantasy, the father is replaced by someone richer and gentler; the imaginary mother becomes more tolerant and glamorous; the brothers and sisters are braver, handsomer or more loving than the ones who actually sit down to family meals. Surrounded by the imaginary family, the dreamer becomes, he believes, his "real self."

While twin fantasies have something in common with the "family romance," there is, in the case of the latter, the probability that the dreamer follows certain models in re-creating his ideal situation; he knows, from his actual family, the roles of father, mother and siblings. Thus, the question arises: What role models are used by the child who fantasizes about a twin companion? How could he know that a twin would be the ideal substitute for either a disappointing parent or sibling? To be sure, the daydreamer may have observed twins closely enough to envy them, but the fantasy does not appear to be confined to such cases. Where there is no such obvious influence, we can only guess that some substratum of the psyche has been tapped. Perhaps some unconscious memory of a lost twin dictates the form of the fantasy. As one woman says, "Since childhood I've always felt very lonely. I couldn't overcome it and couldn't figure out why I felt that way. Even as an adult, I still felt this longing. It was when I was about to have my first child that my mother finally told me I was a twin and that my twin had died at birth."

The language in which Burlingame describes animal fantasies suggests that these have similarities to the twin fantasy, although she stops short of conjecturing that they spring from the same root. "The child takes an imaginary animal as his intimate and beloved companion; subsequently he is never separated from his animal friend, and in this way he overcomes loneliness." With the animal companion, *there is no need for speech*. This is particularly interesting because twins, especially very young ones, are not necessarily dependent on language for communication between themselves. Even as they grow and acquire normal language skills, twins repeatedly tell how they do not need to rely on language for the exchange of their most important thoughts. The fantasy animal understands the child and loves him unquestioningly, just as twins love each other (in spite of superficial squabbling) and retain the means to express this love without language. Thus, the animal figure of the typical child fantasy conforms very closely to that of the ideal lost twin.

Sometimes the twin conjured up in fantasy embodies traits of beauty, strength, skill or courage that the dreamer doesn't think he possesses. Burlingame says, "The daydream of the twin hero expresses the idea: I am small and weak in the face of dangers, but if I were twice as big, twice as strong, twice as clever, there is nothing I would not be able to do." Quite a few twin pairs have this attitude and display it in their actions, even when their experience indicates no foundation for it. Perhaps they and Burlingame's daydreamer came by this attitude in the same way—in the womb. In other situations, twins may embody two sides of the personality coin—one dominant, one submissive; one active and one quiet; and so on—just as the fantasy twin may embody traits distinctly opposite from those of the dreamer.

Throughout the literature of twinning and in a number of different contexts, there are instances of bizarre and frequently inexplicable coincidences. Since genetics has explained so many correspondences, one is inclined to expect that all may have a genetic base that will someday be understood. Often the coincidences have little to do with the physiology of the twins in question—they are matters involving taste in clothing or ornaments, choice of careers or spouses, decisions about money or marital problems. In a word, they are psychological coincidences. Yet the careful scientist is inclined to assume a linkage between body and mind even here, hypothesizing that the gene patterns which make twins look alike and grow alike also make them think alike to a large degree, and perhaps govern the timetable of particular coincidental thoughts or decisions. The fact is, however, that, as yet, no one can with assurance distinguish meaningful from meaningless coincidences.

If one is skating on thin ice in ascribing any significance to the coincidences in the lives of twins, the ice becomes thinner still when we guess at the significance of reports on the so-called "astro-twins." These are people of the same sex whose birthdays fall on the same day. They aren't blood relatives. There is no question of genetic determination of coincidences in appearance, life histories or temperament, yet these coincidences—this uncanny parallelism—are matters of record.

Science writer Joseph F. Goodavage has researched hundreds of such cases and compiled statistics like those kept on genetic twins. His records, in fact, include a great many examples that would fit neatly into case histories of those born as twins, showing the same sort of parallel life patterns and coincidental events linking people, however totally unrelated or even unacquainted until strange circumstances drew them together. Even their encounters with each other could be labeled as coincidence, awaiting some explanation better than the astrological one. Here is a sampling from Goodavage's records:

Fred S. and Barrett W. were born on the same day. They became classmates in high school, entered college together, *died in similar but separate accidents on the same day*.

Jackie L. and Elizabeth B., born on the same day in the same European town, married the same day, moved to Los Angeles the same month.

Goran L. and Goran L. (same last names, though not blood kin) born in Sweden, won scholarships to study in the United States, attended the same college in the Midwest and met there.

Jean H. and Joyce R. moved next door to each other when they were about six years old. Their schoolteachers and friends were struck by how much they looked alike. Each girl had the same number of brothers and sisters, and their fathers had similar jobs. They learned that they had been born five minutes apart in the same hospital.

The attractiveness of twinning has its affect on some people's psyches when they are blood relatives, too, as is demonstrated by a remark John Lennon made about his young son: "Sean was born on October ninth, as I was. In many ways we're almost like twins. He seems to know how I'm feeling and what I'm thinking and he plays to that."

Leaving the question of astrological determinism to the astrologers, however, it is still possible to infer from the sheer number of instances how strong and widespread is the impulse to be a twin. Perhaps for the time being, it is enough to point out that people seize on coincidences like birthdays and make them the foundation of relationships so close that more coincidences will probably follow. This suggests in turn that the whole process of twinning may not be fully accomplished by a single biological stroke. It is an ongoing process of amalgamation and synthesis, a matter of conscious and unconscious choices lasting for a lifetime. Even those of us who were born identical know very well that the full dimensions of our twinship emerged from the creative and sometimes deliberate choices we made at various points along the way.

Such phenomena as astro-twins are not as yet as useful to science as those reported from clinic or laboratory, but there is still so much to learn about twins and the process of twinning that anything hinting, however obliquely, at information that may eventually lead to new revelations is a welcome addition to the mounting data. In a field in which so much mystery remains, it is inevitable that one should skate sometimes on very thin ice.

While researching this book, I quite accidentally came upon the story of two couples named Cipolla, each of whom had a pair of twins and a singleton daughter. The twins' names were quite unusual—not a "matched" pair, as are so many—Yolanda and Evelyn Cipolla. The singleton daughters were named Anne, and both fathers' first names begin with "A." One pair of twins was born on June 4, and the other pair was born a few years later on June 7— both under the sign of Gemini, the Twins. Both families lived in Cranston, Rhode Island. One pair of twins appeared at City Hall to register to vote and were told that they were already registered. Prior to that time, neither family had any intimation of the other's existence. A newspaper notice about a death in one family brought notes of condolence to the other. The overwhelming strangeness of these circumstance sticks in my mind as I turn over other baffling fragments of twin lore. I would not yet venture to suggest what all this may mean.

In Memoriam

How far the dead have gone
Does not at first appear.
They seem to linger near at hand
For many an ardent year.

EMILY DICKINSON

The prenatal disappearance of twins, as well as any psychological aftereffects that might stem from this early vanishing act, remains an inviting field for researchers.

Perhaps an inescapable emotional pattern is imposed by this early loss. It would seem so when one remembers how vulnerable twins are, later in life, to the pangs of enforced separation. Such separation may be just for hours or days—no matter; its effect is deep. The separation may occur when one twin is hospitalized; it may be brought about by a broken family, forcing twins to grow up in separate foster homes. The most traumatic separation comes when one twin dies.

But just as twins are exceptionally vulnerable to these common shocks, they are also often gifted with exceptional powers of endurance, recuperation and survival. It may be that twins who have survived the special risks of twin gestation and birth are like Mithridates, who drank enough poison to become immune. They are frequently able to rebound from tragedy in a way singletons can only envy. Many times twins say they sense that their "other self" is their second chance, providing a sort of immortality. The threatened one expects to live in his survivor; the survivor is prone to feel that his "vanished" twin lives in him.

Psychiatrist George Engel tells the enlightening and moving story of his own psychic history following the death, at age forty-nine, of his twin brother. He begins by recounting a number of significant dreams marked by "a profound confusion between myself and my brother."

Throughout their lives, Dr. Engel writes, the brothers had been aware of a "diffuseness of ego boundaries." That is, like many or most twins, they had never been sure who was who. Engel says wryly that they were *we*, not *he* or *I*. (No wonder that twins are reported to have higher than average difficulty with the use of pronouns. They simply don't always make the simple distinctions between persons that pronouns are supposed to make.) Once when George Engel saw himself from behind in the fitting-room mirrors of a clothing store, his eye "recognized" his brother Frank.

When Frank died unexpectedly of a heart attack, George

suffered chest pains en route to the funeral. Clinical examination showed no indication of danger to him, but he was convinced that he would die of the same affliction as his brother. Just one day short of eleven months after his brother's death, the prophetic intuition was partially fulfilled. George had his (their?) heart attack. "My reaction to the attack was one of great relief . . . the other shoe had fallen, so to speak. . . . I felt serene and tranquil; the waiting was finally over."

It was while he was recovering from this attack that the dreams began, "involving confusion between my brother and myself." Through the dreams—and his psychoanalytic interpretation of them—George Engel was able to reconstruct the lifelong relationship, including the rivalries and dissensions as well as the satisfactions of intimacy that being a twin had brought him.

Then, when George Engel approached the age at which his father had died, the dream figure of his brother was sometimes transposed with that of his father. "The question arises, had I unconsciously begun to fuse the images of my father and my twin?" The answer is that he had not done this in his dreams, he had done so in most of his attitudes, emotions and reactions throughout his life. The unresolved problems in his relationship with his father, the common resentments and rivalry of the Oedipal situation, had been carried over into the twin relationship with his brother. The point was that these classic difficulties became manageable when the brother figure presented them, serving as a kind of mediator or negotiator between the surviving son and his father. The "dissolving of egos" that is common to the twin relationship served as a pattern for dissolving the strong barriers between son and father. Thus, even in death, Engel's twin performed a mission of reconciliation, serving his surviving brother by furthering his understanding of the family relationships most important to him.

The special relationship which nature gives to twins often pushes the meaning of separation and loss into metaphysical territory and changes it into something rich and strange. "Twins are inseparable" is a commonplace observation, usually based on the fact that they like each other's company, but on occasion, as in George Engel's dream communion with his brother, the commonplace takes on awesome overtones.

Far into space range our probing satellites. When reports about them come in by television, our previous theories of what our universe is like are tossed to the winds. Deep into the terrestrial oceans go the famous mirror-image twins Auguste and Jean Piccard in their submarines and bathysphere. They find strange fish down there, strangely adapted for survival. And in our time, there are new techniques for looking into the womb to learn more about the hide-and-seek game of twins. Thus, the future holds new hope of solving mysteries about twinship that have persisted from the time the twin myths took shape.

How might the vanishing-twin investigations eventually affect the singleton world? The scenario of the future just might go like this:

The physician studies the intricate pattern of whorls and ridges in a patient's handprint and says thoughtfully, "The absence of some traits in your prints indicates a biological basis for some of your fantasies and emotions. The lack of these signs is found only in the handprints of identical twins."

Patient: "But, Doctor, I don't understand."

Doctor: "Simply put, when you were conceived, you had a twin, but at a very early stage of growth in the womb, your twin disappeared. We still don't know exactly why it happens. All we can be sure of is that it does."

4. Twins Meet the World

QUADS CREATE SCHOOL FUROR

Cynosure of All Eyes as Famed
Kentucky Children Attend
Class for First Time

Leitchfield, Ky., September 2 (AP)—Kentucky's famed Lashley Quadruplets started school today.

Martine, Mildred, Beulah and John Lashley created more excitement than usual for the opening day of school as they arrived to enroll.

Dozens of other children, teachers and adult residents of this Grayson county seat craned their necks to get a better view of the quads. . . .

Before you tell yourself that multiples are so rare that you'll probably never have much to do with them, ask yourself how often you have encountered such a story in the newspaper. How many times have you craned your neck to take a second look when a pair of identical twins passed by? In fact, beyond the people to whom the arrival of multiples is most crucial—their immediate family—there are many others who, at one time or another, are concerned about or are touched by them: the medical specialists involved with their survival and health, teachers, students, research scientists, spouses, their children, the press, the business community and the world of the arts. Of course, the larger the group of multiples—triplets, quadruplets, quintuplets—the greater the flurry of interest, but a pair of identicals nearly always stirs ripples of interest since, for one thing, their presence creates an eerie sense of optical illusion. *Not* paying attention to them is the exception.

Even twins have difficulty taking other identical pairs for granted. They, too, will whisper and make concerted efforts to distinguish one from the other, searching for slight differences in the tilt of a nose or slant of a brow. They will tell you that it is especially embarrassing for them to make an error in identification, since they feel they *ought* to know better. And most of them pride themselves on quickly learning the distinguishing characteristics of the individuals within a pair .

This ripple effect in the lives of multiples impinges on the society around them, but it naturally influences their lives as well. What sort of merry chase do twins lead the singleton world? Where does the influence they exert lead them? As twins grow through infancy, childhood and pre-adolescence, the interaction between them and the society around them leaves clues to these unusual puzzles.

In most cases, the furor begins either with the doctor's prediction or the unexpected birth of twins. Surprise (a crucial element not to be dismissed as merely amusing) is quickly followed by confusion. From that point, the family and societal patterns become complicated as they are not for those born singly.

For the twins themselves, however, the peculiarities of their condition have already begun to take shape, for they have shared the confined space of the womb in which enforced physical accommodation nourishes habits of mind and muscle which will exert incalculable influence once the occupants are launched, at birth, into the wider world.

The environment in the womb is strikingly similar to that which an astronaut experiences floating in the limited dimensions of a space capsule. For twins, however, there are two in a space meant for one. Both are attached to a life-support tube, or tubes, supplying food and oxygen. In the beginning, the two fetuses are relatively small and there is plenty of room between them. Each day, however, unlike the astronauts, their bodies grow, until finally the space between them has been consumed. Lack of space for living, growing and breathing sets up natural competition. If you have ever wrestled to get to sleep on a crowded plane, jammed in from both sides by other passengers also trying to get comfortable, you will recognize the situation that twins face in their prenatal confinement. An elbow nudges you here, an arm there. You seek a comfortable position for your head and neck. You shuffle your feet, shift your legs, flex your knees. The struggle of fast-growing fetuses goes on like this for months.

Try to imagine a couple of ballet dancers attempting the impossible feat of a pas de deux in a bottle. Some of the earliest medical ilustrations of twins in their prenatal environment depict just this, though the dancers are roly-poly cherubs and the bottle is upside down. As in any pas de deux, the necessity of supporting one's partner is crucial to one's own performance. For twins, however, there is a paradox: How far can one lend support without jeopardizing his or her own survival?

Within the womb, twins are competing for three basic things—space, position and nutrients. Some doctors believe the last element to be the most important. One doctor has discovered, for instance, that the difference in size between each partner in an identical set in the womb, during the middle of the gestational period, is often much greater than between those in a fraternal set. This, he believes, is due to the amount of nutrients each individual in the pair receives. This difference may be the decisive factor in the ultimate health and pattern of development of those who are born with a partner. The imbalance of nutrients may stem from (1) an insufficient supply from the mother, or (2) the fact that one twin may be linked in such a way that he is able to receive more than his share. Unequal amounts of prenatal nutrients can mean the difference between life and death for one or both of the twins. It may also set the stage for crippling ailments.

Position, of course, is also crucial, both during the gestational process and at birth. The need for space in the womb has brought about a sort of "pecking order," a dance of dominance and subordination practiced by both infants so that they can get what they need. If, at the time of delivery, one twin has been forced into an unusual position —or worse, if *both* twins have—then their lives and that of their mother can be gravely threatened.

Lack of any of the three basic elements—space, position, nutrients—necessary for the healthy existence of multiples in the womb can cause psychological as well as physical complications. While the physical anomalies are often apparent at birth or in the early months of growth, the psychological damage is seldom so apparent and is the subject of controversy, speculation and wonderment. I cannot emphasize enough the influence of early setting and conditioning on twins and other multiples. As the children grow and mature, the effects of these preconditions may show up in patterns that make assimilation into the singleton world particularly difficult. Traces of prenatal conditioning and birth trauma very probably last throughout the lifetime of twins, although, of course, such traces are modified by the particular environment in which the twins grow up.

It is hardly news that all children experience trauma at the moment of birth. From the warmth and comfort of a womb, each individual is thrust suddenly into a world of seemingly limitless space and confronted with an endless variety of challenging experiences. But the saga of twin gestation and double birth is more than a simple magnification of the trauma undergone by a singleton. While twins are, like all other infants, separated from their mother's body with shocking suddenness, they are at the same time separated from each other as well. This separation and its timing can be highly significant in the lives of most twins, although just *how* significant science has yet to discover. By the time of their births, after all, twins have already formed a natural partnership. In adjusting to the crowded conditions of the womb they have not just competed, they have learned to relate to each other and to make accommodations. Because they have survived numerous life-threatening situations, they have physically and psychologically adjusted to an array of special conditions. Then, abruptly, this first intimate relationship must be abandoned.

A particularly revealing example of what may have been occurring between a pair of identicals prior to and during the birth process is described by identical twin Dorothy Foltz-Gray.

Dorothy and her twin, Deane, shared a favorite fantasy of what it had been like for them in the womb. They imagined themselves having "a great time of it, laughing, talking, sharing secrets, commenting excessively on the dining services, arguing over who had the greater flow into whose placenta. We especially imagine[d] an enormous amount of discussion anticipating our birth—who should go first, when, why, etc." Dorothy always thought that the reason she has two curved fingers and a slightly curved spine was due to fights the two infants staged over these issues. "Deane maintains that since I was to go first, my reluctance to move was greatly disturbing, and only through long argument about the next world did she succeed in moving me. I imagine her thrusting her shoulder to mine, shoving furiously while I lay screaming my refusals to budge, quite furious that I would have to shove and kick my way out, while she lay comfortably observing, waiting for her chance to swagger on through."

In their fantasy, the twins hardly note their mother or what she must be going through. They realize that they are being supplied with food. That is what is important. The timing of their birth seems to have little to do with whether their mother's body is ready to go into labor and everything to do with whether the twins are ready or not to leave the cozy womb. "We see ourselves already possessing an advanced intimacy and friendship," Dorothy continues. Their fantasized conversation in the womb was the start of "a lifelong process of experiencing our environment by collaboration. If Deane was getting enough to eat, then I probably was, too. If she thought it was getting too crowded, then I could feel the pinch as well." This pair also recognized, subconsciously, that cooperation between them was essential for survival.

Birth order and all of its psychological and legal implications were a far larger problem in the past than they are today, unless, of course, the twins are born to royalty concerned with the choice of an heir to a throne. Naturally, we assume in our time that the one born first is the elder and consequently the legal heir, but it hasn't always been so. Luigi Gedda reports, "Jewish law considered the firstborn of a pair to be the first heir, while the intermediate law . . . stated that the secondborn should be the first heir because it was conceived first . . . both the Roman and modern law consider the firstborn to be the first heir." Still, for those secondborn (or who have been told they were secondborn when the parents didn't really know), it should be some consolation to know that the firstborn has not always been considered the elder.

Early in the saga of twins, some psychological aftereffects of prenatal rivalry may emerge, manifesting themselves as a traumatic and persistent sense of having been an intruder in the womb. A vivid example of this sort of special guilt is given in Amram Scheinfeld's book, *Twins and Supertwins*. A young man the author calls David had a twin, Daniel, who died at the age of eighteen. Throughout his life, David felt inferior to his twin. Being the secondborn, he believed his brother was more handsome and intelligent. When the two young men started college together, David secretly tried to surpass Daniel's accomplishments. The sudden death of his brother, however, intensified David's sense of guilt. Because he had always felt so strongly that he was an intruder, he immediately assumed that he had somehow caused the disaster. He developed "symptoms of hysteria, claustrophobia and various psychosomatic ailments," says Scheinfeld. These were traceable to his feeling that he had cheated Daniel by usurping a part of his brother's birthright, his rightful place alone in the womb.

Less traumatic evidence of this "intruder" notion showed up in my conversations with twins of all ages. Looking back at their lives, twins told me, "I know it sounds silly, but in a funny way I felt *in the way* when my sister fell in love and got married before me." "My brother and I agreed to stop laying guilt trips on each other—but not until we were twenty." "It's strange, after all those years living so close to one another, I suddenly felt my sister thought of me as a burden. Wherever we went, I was the fifth wheel."

The life-threatening elements that twins experience in the womb disappear for many a healthy pair at birth, but, the psychological problems that take hold during gestation are often nurtured by social attitudes toward twins, making adjustment for a young pair considerably more difficult than it is for a young singleton. Twins may be looked upon as freaks or showered with too much attention, or those around them may constantly compare their looks and abilities or attempt to thwart their natural closeness. Under these conditions, the twins' burdens multiply. Indeed, society is only now attempting to reach a more complete understanding of the deep complexities in the twin relationship in general, not to mention those specific quandaries that appear among identicals but not among fraternals, and vice versa. There remain many areas and levels of inquiry yet to be explored. In any of the above-mentioned situations—when twins are looked upon as freaks, given an overabundance of attention, are constantly compared and so forth—it is quite possible that one twin will not be affected until the other, perhaps the weaker or more sensitive of the pair, shows signs of consternation. The unaffected twin, out of guilt or because of the demands of their close relationship, will ultimately accept whatever behavior his partner has demonstrated as their norm. Whether their reactions are identical or complementary, the two will react in concert much of the time.

The Demand on Parents

"You just don't go out with triplets," says a mother of three identical toddlers. "We went to Europe before they were born. We couldn't even take a simple subway ride afterwards." "I don't think either my husband or I got a full night's sleep between us for those first six months after the twins were born," says another. Parents of single newborns who have problems getting baby-sitters or enough sleep to cope with the new addition to their household may be able to sympathize with mothers of multiples, but, according to these mothers, the parents of singletons cannot even begin to fathom what it's like.

Naturally, the first people crucially involved in the lives of any multiples are their parents. Since the birth of twins and their earliest days are often quite precarious, there is usually good reason for anxiety. A fair percentage of multiples are born into families already struggling to make ends meet. Two additional babies at once may even threaten the marriage. Whether this happens or not, there are many reports of the problems multiples thrust upon their unsuspecting parents.

Economics was, undoubtedly, the overwhelming problem in one situation in Angoulême, France. A father and mother were living with their eleven children in extreme poverty. Early one November morning in 1937, Julien Chatain learned that his wife had given birth to two more babies—twins. Mr. Chatain couldn't take the strain; his spirit broke. That evening he was found dead. He had hanged himself in despair.

Notoriety surrounding the arrival of his twins caused a real setback for Ronald Yinger. Back in 1950, he was labeled the "Mid-Century Dad" because one of his twins was born in the final minutes of 1949, the other during the first moments of the new year. Naturally, there was publicity—the couple was even offered three radio contracts for their personal story. Then Yinger was recognized by television viewers as a missing parolee—a bad-check artist. Police officials moved in and returned him to prison.

When, however, a twenty-four-year-old inmate in a state prison recently gave birth to twin boys, the enlightened authorities gave her at least temporary custody of the pair.

Producing a few sets of twins and then, perhaps, a set of triplets is unarguably a fast way to create a large family. Many women have told me that they prefer multiple births because they can have more children and fewer pregnancies. Or, they point out, fraternal twins of different sexes might please both parents when one is longing for a girl and the other wants a boy. Papa Dionne learned how quickly his family could be enlarged when his famous five arrived. Agnes O'Rourke of Brooklyn, a twin herself, said she always believed in having an extra name or two in mind, a practice which proved useful when she produced her second set of twin boys within one year. Back in the mid-forties, Mrs. John J. Walsh of Quincy, Massachusetts, had three sets of twins in three consecutive years—all born in the month of October.

The odds against having *four* sets of twins born consecutively to the same mother are said to be approximately 65,610,000 to one, but that didn't bother Mrs. Howard Morris of Powhatan County, Virginia; Mrs. Jules Rice of Seattle, Washington; or Mrs. Louis Hagehorn of Neillsville, Wisconsin. Mary Louise Morris offered a reporter the oft-repeated phrase of mothers of twins, "My doctor didn't even believe me when I said I could feel babies moving on both sides during my fifth month of pregnancy [with the fourth set of twins]." Along with her four pairs of twins (two fraternal and two identical duos) born in a twelve-year span, she also gave birth to five singletons. The other two mothers were working against even steeper odds, since Mrs. Rice had her four sets in seven and a half years and Mrs. Hagehorn had her four pairs in six years. Not only that, Mrs. Hagehorn, contrary to the majority of twinning evidence compiled by researchers around the globe, was only twenty-six years old when she produced her fourth set. Two other "twin families" of note are the Clarks who, as reported in Ripley's *Believe It or Not*, had four sets of twins, six boys and two girls, and won the National Family Basketball Championship of 1947; and Mrs. John Messing of Columbus, Nebraska, who is the mother of twins, the grandmother of four sets of twins, the aunt of two sets and the great-aunt of both twins and triplets. In addition, she is the foster great-aunt of twins and has a sister-in-law who is a twin.

Author David Lampe told me how, against the extreme odds of 80,000 to one, his brother and sister-in-law produced, consecutively, two sets of identicals—one pair of boys and one pair of girls—and thus joined the select group of people who seem to "collect" twins. The birth of their boys was a complete surprise, but before the girls were diagnosed to be on the way, someone suggested to the father that he take out insurance against having a second set. Unfortunately, he didn't take the advice, but in another case, a lucky St. Louis father did. When his wife presented him with two babies at once, Lloyd's of London paid up. In 1962, that same company coughed up $2,000 for Mrs. Joan Martin of Denver. She was pregnant for the first time, and her chance of having multiples was considerably lower than women who had already given birth. Nevertheless, she took out insurance for twins, then gave birth to a pair.

There are other cases, scattered throughout medical literature, of families collecting twins. In 1861, a pair of twin brothers married and each had ten children—all twins. Of these, four were female pairs and one was a male pair. Seven of these twins married, and the first children of four of them were twins as well. One of the male twins had three singleton children, while the other had four pairs of twins, all male, and three singletons. (While the sex of the pairs was reported, zygosity was not.) In 1896, the case of Dr. Mary Austin appears. This woman supposedly had thirteen pairs of twins and six sets of triplets.

The advantages of having babies in multiples are often reported humorously in the press. One account in *This Week* magazine back in 1948 described "a middle-aged Chinese named Chiu Shek-hoi who never does a stitch of work any more . . . the admiration of all Canton . . . the father of quadruplets." Why did he have life so easy? The government gave him a home and income for life.

The birth of large groups of multiples often elicits generosity from friends, local governments or businesses with an eye to good publicity. Author Joseph H. Satin gathered information about the Kasper quads of New Jersey who "retired" in 1938 at the age of two with $15,000 each; and the Zavada family of Pennsylvania for whom the Slovak-Catholic Federation put out a nationwide appeal when quadruplets appeared. Besides the cribs, layettes, toys and strollers the Zavadas received from manufacturers, gifts of all sorts poured in, including a $25,00 contract to appear in advertising for a milk company. The Perry triplets in Kansas received a year's supply of free milk; the Wilk triplets were given $150 worth of free weekly nursing as long as it was required; and a concerted neighborly effort helped Cleve Smith of Tennessee to build a home in record time. Smith had been attempting to get the work done before his wife delivered, but the work was going slowly, troubled by shortages of labor and materials. Then the obstetrician showed Smith the X rays that diagnosed his wife as carrying triplets. He rushed to the site waving the photographs. The problems vanished. That house was built way ahead of schedule, and the proud parents brought their three infants to it straight from the hospital.

Although one pair of twins—unless it is the second or

more consecutive set—seldom brings such compensation, help nevertheless, occasionally appears. In 1976, the *Fort Collins Coloradoan* reported how Michael and Timothy Diesslin were so small at birth that their parents used cotton balls for diapers. The twins fought for survival for three months, and as they did, the hospital bills threatened to bankrupt the family. "The births of the twins . . . prompted a financial crisis that produced a study in small-town closeness," the paper proudly reported. When the insurance company announced a cut-off point of $15,000 for medical costs for each twin, the people of the town started fund-raising events. Then the insurance company reversed its decision, paying for all but $2,000 of the medical bills. The twins' parents promptly placed the remainder of the money the town had raised into a trust fund for other infants in the county who might be in need of special medical help at birth. They thus placed their pair among the ranks of twins who, either as a result of medical problems or because they are thankful to have survived, and be in good health, take special pride in sharing with others.

One doctor, certain that a woman was not carrying more than one child, agreed to deliver any bonus babies free of charge. He discovered, to his chagrin, how wrong he had been, for the woman had triplets. The next time she was pregnant, he wasn't so quick to say she would not have multiple children.

Following on the idea that one is a "bonus baby" for the family is one way twins learn to counteract that "intruder in the womb" guilt. "Our parents always emphasized they were delighted they'd received a bonus when we were born," one pair told me. "I think it's the reason we never felt much jealousy about each other's accomplishments."

It may be, as some parents of twins assert, that "two babies are only about one and a half times more work than one." Parents with such views are, however, the exception. A first-time mother who is confronted with two unusually small and demanding infants will probably be difficult to convince. Uppermost in *her* mind is how, physically, she is going to care for two babies. A mother still has only two hands. There are only two parents. Each day contains but twenty-four hours. If the babies are particularly small or have health problems, the work is multiplied not by one and a half but by three or four times, according to some weary parents who have been through it. Looking back, many can't understand how they managed. Asked if raising twins is the same as raising two singletons of about the same age, Josephine F. Tingley, a nurse, mother of twin boys and coauthor with Rosemary T. Theroux of *The Care of Twin Children*, answered a resounding, "No, because you have two people who have a close emotional tie—a closer bond than two single children ever have." This closeness, along with the work overload that twins present, has ways of complicating and magnifying even the simplest of mother-child skirmishes.

The appearance of twins may overtax adult members of the family, but it very often, at least temporarily, puts any young singleton siblings in an untenable position. Although a toddler may have been prepared for mother to return from the hospital with one new baby, when she arrives with two and they grab center stage, he can hardly help being less forgiving. For one thing, he is obviously outnumbered. For another, the pair, because they are twins, receives far more attention from family members and strangers than any singleton baby. Even when a mother tries to soften the blows to the psyche of her other young child, there is very often little she can do to curtail them completely. Mothers of twins repeatedly described to me the efforts required to make certain their singleton toddlers didn't feel left out, given the constant flurry of attention surrounding the twin babies. "People are so careless," one said. "Twins become part of the public domain when they're out in their stroller. Strangers gush over them and completley ignore my son standing beside them. Even when I make an extra effort to spend time alone with him when the twins are napping, it still doesn't entirely take the edge off what he's going through when we are with strangers."

In an effort to preclude such problems, another mother admitted she paid as little attention to her twins as possible in the early months. "Of course, it was a mistake," she said, "but I was so afraid of spoiling them, and I was worried about ruining my relationship with my other child Meggie. With all the extra work the twins were giving me, the last thing I needed was for her to turn into a discipline problem."

As Marion Meyer, executive director of the National Mothers of Twins Clubs, observes, upstaging is tough enough, but when a singleton child comes *after* the twins, "there are two to beat up the kid." Twins uniting against the younger child, whom they see as an interloper threatening their special relationship, can create havoc.

Parents are faced with many quandaries: whether to give their offspring similar names; whether to dress them alike and if so, for how long; how to handle jealousies and rivalries within the twinship and the family. An extreme interdependence between twin children may also develop, whether or not they share such traits as boldness or shyness, aggressiveness or submissiveness. "The twins are far more shy than my other children were at their age," the mother of a three-year-old pair said worriedly. "They're all right when they're together. It's easy for them to make friends in preschool then. But when one of them is forced to be alone in a group, he tends to clam up and look around for his brother to play with."

Telling Twins Apart—Which Is Who?

One problem that is difficult for a parent of a singleton to comprehend, but that is commonly presented to parents of infant twins, is an inability to tell the children apart, whether they are identicals or look-alike fraternals. Rosemary Narimanian of Philadelphia had so much trouble identifying her five-month-old girls, Maryam and Shirin, that she eventually ended up at the police station asking for help. She could tell the twins apart at birth, she said, since Maryam, the secondborn, weighed eight ounces more than Shirin and had plumper cheeks. Over the course of a few months, however, Shirin's cheeks filled out as she put on weight, a common phenomenon of catch-up that identicals often go through. Mrs. Narimanian still thought she could tell her babies apart, but her husband disagreed. Finally, unable to sleep, the confused parent went back to the hospital where her twins had been born. The authorities there sent her to the police, to have the babies' footprints deciphered. Mrs. Narimanian was lucky enough to find a detective who also had a set of twins and sympathized with her plight. Specialists took new footprints, compared them with those taken at birth and discovered that the mother had, indeed, confused the twins. To avoid a repetition of this, she decided to have the babies' ears pierced and put different earrings on each child.

In Schenectady, New York, one September, a four-year-old boy was killed by an automobile while playing with his twin brother. The parents thought it was Richard who had been struck by the careening car and called their surviving child Raymond. It wasn't until the surviving twin said, "Me Richard," that the parents even questioned the name of the victim. Then they checked and settled the issue by finding an identifying chickenpox scar on the real Richard.

Young twins in North Carolina so confused their mother that, although they were baby boys, she decided to keep their toenails painted different colors until they were old enough for her to differentiate between them. Such color coding is not uncommon. Many mothers simply put a different color ribbon on each infant or deliberately dress them in a special color in an attempt to avoid confusion. I wasn't surprised occasionally to come across a pair who, in adult years, admitted that this early designation to them of a particular color had had its negative aspects. "I think I'll always despise that shade of green," said one. "It was wonderful when Mother finally let me pick my own colors to wear," said another. "We were just starting first grade, and I'll never forget the sense of pleasure at being able to put on whatever I wanted, never mind what my brother had chosen. Sometimes we chose the same thing, sometimes not, but I got to wear what *I* wanted." Mothers repeatedly admitted that it bothered them not to be able to tell their own children apart. "Don't tell *them* that," I often heard. "I'd hate it if they ever knew how confused I was about which was which."

Our father always said he never mixed up my sister and myself, even as infants. Yet that is difficult to believe, since now that we look at certain baby portraits, we can't even tell for sure which is Karilyn and which is Marilyn.

Stories of such twin confusion abound. In 1974, the Associated Press reported that against one in 550 million odds, five families out of six living in one block of an Ohio town had twins, all presumably keeping the rest of the neighbors mixed up for years as to who was who. Seventeen sets of twins attended one Brooklyn parochial school at once (six sets of boys, five sets of girls and six mixed-sex sets) in 1949, with twenty-one more sets living in the parish and preparing to enter the same school within the following six years. In this case, it was the teachers who had trouble distinguishing the individuals in the pairs, since all of the children at the school were required to wear identical uniforms. One of my favorite stories about confusion between multiples, however, is the one in which identical triplets Anthony, Bernard and Charles Harris of Muncie, Indiana, at six years of age all admitted they had trouble telling their own brothers apart.

On a sadder note, there is this story of the U.S. Army medic treating his first case during the Korean war. *The New York Times* reported, "Private Irwin Rietz, 21, Rock Island, Ill., did not recognize his twin until he and two other soldiers lifted the brother, Edwin, into a litter jeep." Irwin gave his brother emergency treatment in a shallow trench without a chance to look carefully at his patient's face. " 'I knew that I had done everything possible for him on the hill, so I followed him down in another jeep. I thought he was wounded only slightly. When I arrived at the collecting station, the doctor told me he was dead.' "

Naturally, parents of infant twins need to be particularly certain of the identities of their offspring, since feedings or, often, doses of vitamins or medicine are involved. After days of what seem like endless feedings and nights devoid of sleep, mothers are quick to point out that mixing up the children is the easiest thing in the world to do. Sarah Callaghan, a working mother of twins, eventually had to resort to meticulous organization. She found that only when she kept a very precise diary of everything that happened to each of her twins could she be at all certain of what she, her husband or her baby-sitters had done for whom.

The Unwelcome Pair

Most of these stories assume that twins are loved and cherished, whether or not they present their parents with unusual problems; and, of course, most pairs are. But what happens when they aren't wanted? There are no statistics regarding these unfortunates, but instances of abandonment are related by twin experts, obstetricians and, occasionally, the press. When twins are born into an abnormal home environment (as in the case of the pair born in prison), or to broken homes, their arrival puts even more pressure on the parents. Multiples, too, are often premature and in need of special medical attention. What happens when the costs for their care are staggering and there is no help forthcoming? One three-day-old pair was abandoned by their mother back in 1950 because, she told the doctors, "There were two, they were girls and too hard to bring up." The mother refused even to look at them. A child bride and a widow, she left the infants in the hospital a day after their birth. Another set of baby boys less than twenty-four hours old was discovered in a trash container in 1981. There were no clues as to their parentage, but, happily, many offers to adopt the pair came to the hospital authorities, who eventually assumed temporary care of the infants. Twins such as these are, of course, usually given up for adoption. Although it is now the general practice to place both of a pair in the same home, this hasn't always been the case. Scientists who discover twins reared apart are offered, as we'll see, a rare opportunity to try to find answers to the nature-versus-nurture puzzle: whether our heredity or environment plays the major role in determining what and how we learn and who and what we become.

Dr. Ian MacGillivray, twin expert in Scotland, discussed the problems presented by a case of soon-to-be-separated twins with Dr. Thomas Bouchard, an expert on twins reared apart, when they met at the Third International Congress of Twins Studies in Israel. MacGillivray wondered if Bouchard could advise him how to handle the situation he was confronted with. A pregnant mother had been told she was about to give birth to twins. She insisted she didn't want both of them; she would take only one home with her. This mother didn't want to see the other child after it was born. The father was willing to accept both children, but he either would not or could not convince his wife to do so. The doctors discussed the pros and cons of bringing both babies to the mother so that she could hold them. They eventually agreed that there were only two solutions to the problem, neither of which was entirely satisfactory. "To talk a mother into taking an unwanted child puts that child in considerable jeopardy," MacGillivray pointed out. "To separate twins immediately and permanently after birth may be the only possible answer, but the outcome may be only a little better."

MacGillivray's dilemma was real, since one of the twins was what medical authorities deem "at risk." Such "at risk" children in any population include a relatively high proportion of multiples. They may be threatened with asphyxia, or other respiratory problems, or the need for extremely delicate or early surgery. Also, a high incidence of child abuse— as well as failure to thrive—among premature and ailing newborns, a number of whom were twins, was described at the International Workshop on the "At Risk" Infant in 1979 in Tel Aviv. Dr. Margaret A. Lynch of Guy's Hospital Medical School in London reported on research that demonstrated "that the abused child, when compared with unharmed children in the same family," was "more likely to have been the product of an abnormal pregnancy, labor, delivery and neonatal period." Psychologist Serena Weider of the National Institute of Mental Health found a higher incidence of so-called "difficult" temperamental characteristics in "high risk" infants, including those who weighed less than 1500 grams (3.3 lbs.) or those who required respirator care. Consequently, it follows unfortunately that these babies are subject to environmental stress at the same time that their mothers may have a lower than normal tolerance for frustration. If the children and/or their mothers are separated for any reason, this lack of contact during the earliest nursery days appears to add to the adjustment problems of all. Obviously, mothers and children in such instances are on collision courses that all too often result in some form of child abuse. Not incidentally, the twins who must spend their early weeks in an isolet, fastened to tubes and dependent upon the attention of an intensive-care unit staff, with little or no contact with their parents, are in for yet another traumatic jolt on leaving the hospital, since they must break with those who have cared for them.

The Power of Names

All cultures have understood the power of a name and how it affects one's life. Many considered the act of naming a child a fateful practice. Some American Indian tribes gave a child a temporary name immediately after birth. Then, at the age of about a year, he received his real name. Just as his baby teeth, no longer fit for their job, made way for his permanent molars, so did he outgrow his birth name and take on another for life. Some tribes allowed a person to rename himself at significant periods of his life: at puberty, following the first ride with the adult warriors, for example; or after having had a vision. This allowed that person an opportunity to change his status in the tribe, since certain names referring to guardian spirits, brave deeds or other triumphs were to be earned. As a young man, a son might take part of his father's honorary name in order to live up to what it signified. Then, when the older man retired from active tribal life, he might reverse the process, accepting one of his son's honorary names, as if by doing so he could inject new vigor into an aging life. In both processes, each man was also trying to honor the other. The Pawnee Indians had a way of tricking fate with names, and those who produce twins might do well to take note of it. A Pawnee took a personal name or nick-name that alluded to a goal he had set for himself. For instance, he may have decided to become the youngest brave in the tribe to slay a buffalo. Accordingly, he would choose a name that indicated his ambition in a very general way. Although the name would be publicly announced at a special ceremony, the private meaning behind it was never divulged.

Onomancy (a way of forecasting fate by deciphering the omens surrounding a person's name) and numerology are so convincing to some people that they have changed the spellings of their names to ward off evil or to bring about happier circumstances in their lives. Followers of the philosopher Pythagoras counted the number of vowels in a name, calling an individual "enemy" or "friend," depending on whether that number was odd or even. The history of names abounds, too, with stories that tell of a person winning a crown or a loved one because of a fortuitous name.

Twins feel the confining influence of three types of names: their given names (often "twin type" names—similar or assonant); twin nicknames; and, occasionally, fantasy names. The last category of names often includes secret ones that twins take for themselves to help them reinforce their couple relationship.

When twin names rhyme or mirror each other, they can become an annoyance. Some twins told me they felt that either of their names was all right alone. It was that the two names together seemed "too cute" or "caused too much attention and confusion" later in life. A random extract from the International Twin Association roster reveals Marietta and Lauretta, Eirene and Eileen, Connie and Donnie, Marie and Maurice, Ophelia and Manelia, Sandy and Sindy, Marilyn and Carolyn, Ron and Don, Rena and Tina. Triplets have been named Tom, Dick and Harry; Franklin, Delano and Roosevelt; Uno, Segundo and Terzo. Back in 1967, twin expert Amram Scheinfeld surveyed 340 pairs of twins. He found that four pairs in ten had names that began with the same initial or were otherwise linked: Anne-Marie and Marie-Anne, Jack and Jill, Omer and Homer, Alice and Clarice are examples. This use of "twin names" was more true for girl twins than for boys, Scheinfeld discovered. Among the girls, 50 percent had similar names; among the boys, only one-third did.

While it has long been a practice to give twins twin-sounding names, there is currently a strong movement away from this. Many parents of twins and other multiples who belong to such organizations as the Mothers of Twins Clubs and Parents of Multiple Births Association of Canada tend to advocate not naming twins alike for fear of affecting the development of individual identities. In *The Care of Twin Children*, authors Theroux and Tingley suggest "following the practice of many parents who use unlike-sounding names for their twins, especially in the case of identicals or look-alike fraternals." As author Tingley put it during a television show, "I was distressed that the children couldn't recognize themselves when I held them before a mirror." She held one child and asked, "Who's that baby?" He gave his brother's name.

Still, there are other people who advocate the opposite naming practice. Twin expert Scheinfeld found a deep-rooted feeling on the part of many parents that they should emphasize twinship, since twins are "special." The one way this could be achieved was by giving their offspring similar-sounding names. Adult twins I spoke with only occasionally resented the similarity of their names, but this lack of resentment might be attributed to indifference, fatigue at answering questions about their lives, or a need to appear in agreement with their twin when questioned about anything to do with the twinship.

"Sticks and stones may break my bones, but names will never hurt me." The saying has a familiar ring to twins everywhere. Actually, rhyme is any child's shrewd way of relying on a sort of magic to ward off insulting taunts about a name or nickname, and multiples may have special need of it. Of course, incorporated in the chant is the admission that insulting names *do* hurt. Throughout their lives, twins hear such nicknames as twin, twinsie, twinny, two-fer, carbon copy, Pete and Repeat, Cycle and Recycle, clone and others with even worse connotations.

Tom Gullikson and his brother Tim, highly ranked tennis players, told twin photographers and authors Kathryn McLaughlin Abbe and Frances McLaughlin Gill, "One of our instructors called us Tim-Tom, because he could get either of us with that name." Jeff and Bruce Ellis, prominent caterers whose company serves the White House, said, "People used to call us 'dittos . . . carbon copy.' Now we get Mutt and Jeff, because of Jeff's name. They say, 'You must be Mutt.' "

Most pairs deal with the labels they receive without too much permanent damage, but all twins find such labels annoying at one phase or another (and usually early) in their lives. The young ones first venturing out into the wider world most especially do. Generally, people are given nicknames out of friendship or fondness, but twins receive theirs out of sheer expediency. It's easier to say, "I'm going to pick up 'the twins,' " than to say, "I'm going to pick up Mary and Margery." The suggestion here is of "things" rather than people, and identity boundaries are blurred by the use of one term for two individuals. Researchers at the Institute of Human Development in Berkeley who have been observing so-called "problem" children in general (not necessarily—or exclusive of—multiples) firmly warn parents not to allow their child "to be branded by labels." When parents do this, the child too often accepts the concept as fact, incorporating it into his idea of himself. Twins especially don't like labels. As one of a pair of toddlers told her mother after her first day in nursery school, "No one knows I'm me." This was simply because everyone had fallen back on the convenient label "twin" when talking about her.

Names have many associations, both public and private. Occasionally, they uncover personality problems. The book *Sybil* described a highly unusual case of a woman with sixteen names and sixteen personalities—four pairs of psychic quadruplets. The *Three Faces of Eve* captured the imagination of a wide reading public with the extraordinary story of a woman who was a sort of psychic triplet. She had three personalities—Eve White, Eve Black and Jane. Interestingly, the two psychiatrists who were treating Eve gave two of her personalities last names of opposing colors. These opposites, suggesting good and evil, are instantly familiar to many twins who have struggled to eliminate the notion in the minds of singletons that in all twin pairs there must be one good and one bad twin. Although this "Jekyll and Hyde" syndrome often amuses singletons, the repercussions on the personality of the twin labeled Mr. Hyde are not very funny at all. Even when picked as the good Dr. Jekyll, twins say they feel guilty for no reason other than that someone has decided they represent the "good" one of the pair. Many twins may not feel this to be a major annoyance, but when it is carried to extremes, some have been known to begin to act out their roles.

Since twins are so often a surprise (about 50 percent of the time), the astonished, unprepared parents usually flounder awhile before giving their infants any names at all. Sometimes pressure from relatives and friends forces parents to abandon the name they'd chosen for their expected singleton in favor of twin names. The usual procedure is for hospital staff to label the infants number one and number two, or baby A and baby B. Besides again subtly putting twins—or larger groups of multiples—into a "thing" rather than a "people" category, these designations delineate birth order and imply a grading system as well. I've spoken with twins who, although they laugh about it, admit that this is the reason they hate to stand in line or take a number in a store while waiting for service.

For twins who sometimes have to endure embarrassment or confusion concerning names they had no part in choosing, the sovereign remedy must be patience and common sense. Usually, the hurt or ridicule is a passing thing. As twins grow up and make their mark, so their individual names are welded to their personalities, the subject of distinct pride.

5. Life in Tandem:
Twins and Individuals, Too

Lemon, lime, butterscotch, vanilla; the cheery clerk in the ice cream store is used to dipping a different kind of cone for each kid in the gang, but when the twins walk in, he knows we'll both want strawberry, unless we both want caramel. All the world knows—or takes it for granted—that we share the same tastes. If we didn't, why would we dress alike, cut our hair in identical styles, go out for the same sports, ride matching bicycles, develop crushes on the same teachers and TV stars? Why, in the first place, did we choose to look so much alike if we're not, in all that matters, the same person spreading confusion by traveling in tandem?

What onlookers take all too easily for granted can add

up to an almost continuous obstacle course for twins as they
move out into the world. Throughout childhood, adolescence and adulthood, twins have to strike a balance between
the desirable aspects of their special situation and the
choices that make for individuality. Less frequently than
single children do they have role models immediately at
hand within the family circle—that is, unless they belong
to the rare families in which there is more than one set of
twins. Year by year, most twins have to reassess their
opportunities in the quest for personal fulfillment. It isn't
much help to them to be casually lumped together by those
they encounter.

Whether or not any particular identical twins look and
act alike, many singletons seem to expect them to. If those
singletons discern a difference, they pounce on it, playing
it up with amusement. Twins are expected to answer for
any difference between them. One question that irked my
sister and me as we became clothes-conscious was, "Why
are you dressed differently today? Are you mad at each
other?" Of course, we were only trying to express personality in a perfectly normal way; and, of course, our
experience on this one irritating point was not at all unique.
Those tedious questions have been borne by many twins
I've known.

The roots of such prejudice are obviously set in the conditions of twins' entry into the world. These surely color
the choice of tandem names, and the expectations of similarity are reinforced by all the good and practical reasons
for buying the newborns matching rattles, bonnets, teddy
bears and kiddy cars. Understandably, the parents are just
trying to be fair with such purchases. But surely their
generous impulses do not have to carry over into the later
years, providing a handicap reinforced by society at large.

In truth, I have never met twins who don't have a highly

developed sense of humor, at least about their situation—a good thing, since they have special need of it to counteract the foolish but widespread suspicion that they are as confused as is any onlooker about who is who. When my sister and I were in our late teens, we had a memorable encounter. We were trying on clothes in a department store, and I suspect that either of us alone might have worn out the patience of the harried clerk by rushing back and forth from the dressing rooms, flustering her with questions about colors, sizes, prices and alterations. Undoubtedly, we seemed to repeat inquiries she had already answered. We were close to spoiling her day. Finally, she threw up her hands in exasperation. "How can you tell each other apart?" At the time, we were left speechless by her question; I wish we had had the presence of mind to say, "We couldn't when we were tiny, but we're smarter now."

As twins get smarter, they catch on to the fact that the world would often rather deal with them wholesale than as individuals. So before we consider how twins succeed— or fail—in keeping a balance between bonds of twinship and need for personal expression, I feel the need to say to singletons, "Hold off on some of your prejudices until the whole story is told." As twin Donald Keith puts it, "Nature doesn't exactly duplicate anything. Only machines can stamp out exact replicas. Although my brother and I have recently discovered what most suspected—that we are identical, not fraternal, twins—we still have slight differences in our fingerprints as do all identical twins. If I committed a crime and wanted to pin the rap on him, I'm afraid I couldn't get away with it."

Dr. Gedda addresses the heart of the matter. Speaking to the question of whether twins surrender their identity to some hypothetical single entity, he says, "I have never heard this question from an identical twin. They never ask it because they experience their own individual personality as something authentic but special."

Having One's Cake and Eating It

Their special situation often pushes twins to introspection. As they grow up, they necessarily add up the costs and benefits of being so similar. In their earlier years, they are more apt to be lured back into the one gratifying relationship that requires no explanations—the twinship; they accept the idea that the devil one knows is better than the devil one doesn't know. In adolescence and later, they are apt to reverse their response as they feel the pressure to demonstrate their individuality. When asked if looking alike is an advantage or a disadvantage, adult twins Betty and Seraphina Alaimo told a reporter, "It can be both. In business, looking alike is advantageous since it is easier to get the attention and interest of business associates. Also, there are particular fields, such as modeling, where we can exploit and profit from our similar appearances. The disadvantage is that employers may fail to look upon us as two complete and separate personalities. Socially, the situation is almost the same. It's nice to draw people's attention effortlessly, but we consider it important to assert our individuality. That's why we stopped dressing alike."

Postponement of individual development in twins may often be the result of external pressures that overly encourage dependency. In common with other infants, twins are not as slow as has been supposed in gaining a well-defined sense of who they are. The older view, to the contrary, is expressed by twin expert Scheinfeld when he says that it is "normal for every infant to start off intensely self-centered, and it interferes with his ego formation if he finds another infant competing for his mother's attentions. Before a child

can know he is a distinct individual, or 'somebody,' he must
see and feel himself as separate from any other person."
New research at Princeton, however, leads scientists to believe that the human brain may somehow be programmed
or "prewired" to perceive the uniqueness of the ego. The
recognition of the self, distinct from everyone and everything else, occurs "much earlier than we thought," says
Princeton psychologist Michael Lewis.

In childhood, the temporary submersion of individuality
into a twin entity may provide a sort of psychic shelter
against the threats of the world. There is, for example, the
case of two identical toddlers who called each other by the
same name. Their given names were Kevin and Kenneth,
but they called themselves Kenneth. Their mother worried
about this and, in an attempt to help them assert their separate individualities, gave them name tags before they went
off to nursery school. At least for a short while, however,
they still called each other Kenneth. Another example of
temporary name bonding shows up in the story of Frances
McLaughlin Gill and Kathryn McLaughlin Abbe. They
received their unidentical first names from their father
Francis and mother Kathryn. But as a toddler, Kathryn
"changed" hers to Fuffy, presumably in an attempt to come
close to her sister's nickname, Franny. Sometimes even adult
twins find it advantageous to pass as only one person.
Edward and Ralph Fiori, both substitute teachers in Rhode
Island high schools, find this dodge helpful in their jobs.
"As a result," Ralph says, "the students stay pretty well
behaved. For one thing, they can't figure out how their
teacher can be so many places at once." "Since high school
kids like to try to fool substitutes, as twins we can turn
the tables on them," agrees his twin Edward.

Columnist Paul Harvey tells the story of a Miss Neef,
who was the executive's dream of a secretary. Through the
years, the amazing Miss Neef always did the work of two.

So much was she appreciated in the office that when the dreaded moment of her retirement arrived, her boss gave her a lavish send-off. As Harvey puts it, "Shortly after the guest of honor arrived, the guest of honor arrived." Miss Neef was, in fact, a pair of identical twins. The two women had been handling the same job for twelve full years without anyone being the wiser. Other identicals relate having pulled off the same trick, but never for such a length of time. The simple humorous point of all such anecdotes is that there are endless practical advantages in having a duplicate self to push onto the scene.

In a more serious vein, twin Dorothy Foltz-Gray describes the emotional interdependence of twins: "In [childhood] the validity of an experience was not assured until it was fully recounted to the other, and vice versa. To this day, I feel somewhat that I lead two lives, my own and my sister Deane's, and I am not fully comfortable until I am the informant of one and the informed of the other. This applies very definitely to my first memory of being apart from my sister. Our family was moving, and as there was no food in the house, we went out to eat in shifts, while the other shift stayed home to wait for the movers. I got to go to breakfast with my father. I remember being thrilled by the adventure of eating out with him all by myself. The best part of all was that he bought me a package of peanut butter crackers. However, the other predominant feeling besides the thrill was the urgency I felt to go home and tell my sister about it, to hand her a peanut butter cracker and to find out what in heaven's sakes she had been doing with my mother."

In their book *We Lead a Double Life*, twin authors Ruth and Helen Hoffman delightfully describe their discovery that there is safety in numbers and that there exists an extra margin of support that makes them more adventurous as a team than either might have been alone. Beginning risky careers as freelance artists, they split the tasks and disappointments. As they moved about the city, one would put through telephone calls for interviews, while the other would stand by watching over their bulky portfolios; then at night they reviewed the day together, sorting out the reasons for their successes and failures while they mapped new strategies. My sister Marilyn and I had a similar start when we went from college to New York to look for the jobs that would mark the real start of our adult lives. We came with the intent of declaring our independence and asserting our individuality—the start on that worked better because we could still draw on the old resource of our shared identity.

But the Hoffmans also report their growing awareness that the twin pattern can be a mixed blessing. They describe a shock they got early in life on a train ride through France. "We were suddenly startled by the sight of two old ladies who came into our compartment. Each was an exact duplicate of the other, and they looked like two aging, skinny birds. 'Twins!' we said quietly to each other. And then we became self-conscious, remembering how people had whispered about us. But we couldn't take our eyes from the other pair of twins until we had compared everything about them. Their severe hair . . . hats, long sharp noses, their . . . lips . . . their sunken eyes. Even the deep wrinkles appeared in exactly the same places. The two old ladies finally looked across at us . . . lifted their eyebrows and turned to each other. '*Jumelles!*' we heard one of them say behind her gloved hand. They turned back to continue staring at us, just as we were staring at them . . . 'Isn't it wonderful?' Mama whispered to us. 'They still dress alike!' Neither of us answered Mama. For suddenly we saw ourselves in the old ladies' shoes. And we were embarrassed at the thought of it. Each of us knew how the other felt." When the Hoffmans got off the train, they immediately made moves, slight though they were, to appear somewhat different. One wore her hat; the other took hers off and stuffed it in a suitcase. One wore her coat; the other carried hers over her arm. After that, they were both conscious of an ongoing need to distinguish themselves by some details of dressing. Such minor shifts of strategy may appear comic or inconsequential to singletons, but they loom much larger to twins.

Actress June Haver and actor Fred MacMurray adopted infant twin girls. Asked about the children's demands for parental behavior that demonstrated they were two separate but equal persons, Haver commented, "Oh my yes, they always insisted on two of everything. Birthdays especially were important. They had to have two different birthday cakes and all the rest." When twins were questioned about such celebrations, some reported that they had had to share one cake between them, a fact that they seemed to remember with a touch of bitterness.

At the same time that they are given the "two for one" treatment by casual acquaintances and are even possibly under pressure from family to remain alike and stay together, twins are often confronted with well-meaning schoolteachers, guidance counselors and psychologists who insist that they make an abrupt, definite break with each other in school. This is what happened to my sister and me, and many other twins report that they were confronted with similar dilemmas. In our case, it wasn't just the idea of enforced separation that annoyed me; it was the belief on the part of strangers that they knew what was best for my twin and myself. Such good intentions coupled with poor judgment may set the twin bond in concrete; some duos acquire an "it's us against the world" attitude and in the process ensnare themselves.

Unfortunately, a number of popular articles by psychologists fail to mention the need to rear twins as individ-

uals *without* a premature rupture of the bond between
them. Responding to one such article, an adult twin
heatedly stressed the values which are put at risk by push-
ing twins too quickly into separate ways: "Twins share
from birth. Twins consider at least one other person in the
things concerning them. The single child must be taught
sharing and consideration for others. To the twin it is a
way of life. As for naming twins, they have a right to
special names. They are special." Another letter to the
Center for Study of Multiple Birth suggests that twins are
naturally adapted to values that their parents' generation
has not yet caught up to: "The main differences I've seen
in twins is the early blossoming of 'Aquarian Age' characteristics: peer empathy, sympathy, group-mindedness and
egalitarian tendencies." The writer goes on to allay fears
that a twin may feel like "only half of something." On the
contrary, each twin may feel like "more than one," sensing
a strong individuality plus the reinforcement of the special
relationship.

This would seem to be borne out in the story of Lynda
Elson and her twin Jean Machlin. In 1979, according to a
report in the *London Daily Mirror*, Lynda and her husband
John made what they called their "priceless gift of love"
to Jean and her husband Roger, who were childless, by
offering them their third child at birth. As the stunned
and nearly speechless twin Jean put it, "not in my wildest
dreams could I imagine anyone making this kind of sacrifice for my happiness."

Certainly, it is true that when some identical twins grow
up and live separate lives they find themselves, often in a
subconscious rather than conscious way, "looking for someone to replace the other half," as twin Grant Mallett put
it. "Surprisingly enough," Grant Mallett continued, "the
replacement might be another twin. Since we 'separated,'
Gordon and I have had a number of close friends, both

male and female, who were also identical twins. In each case neither of us knew about the existence of our friends' other half."

Fraternal twin Richard B. Stolley, managing editor of *People* magazine, points out another feature particular to twins. "I think," he says, "twins generally are better adjusted, but perhaps more private because they have created a comfortable world for themselves. They don't need others; they grow up with love and understanding and companionship." This habit of retreating into twin privacy, or of respecting, without question, the privacy of others, may open to psychologists in the future new avenues of study.

Walking Into the Trap

The balancing act required of twins is threatened not only by intervention from outside, but by ambivalence on the part of the twins themselves. Periodically, duos may experience contrary and unsynchronized emotions. "As adults, we've had a difficult time trying to strengthen our sense of our individual selves without causing the other pain," one pair says. "It wasn't easy when we were young to do things separately, partly because we really didn't want to, partly because we were scared to try. But it was also because our parents didn't want us to. Whenever we started to go separate ways, someone insisted on pairing us up. That habit got ingrained in us. Now it seems we may be betraying one another, when we're only trying to outgrow a habit." Attempts to steer a separate course may also be felt as a betrayal of the loving parents who encouraged behavior that is perpetuated long after it has ceased to be appropriate. The long years as "cute twin children" take their toll. It's hard to grow while the old refrain of "I've

Got You Under My Skin" keeps reminding each twin of the sibling who seems to be left behind. Still, a long step toward maturity is taken when twins recognize and admit that they have helped to bait the traps they later want to avoid. Faced with stressful emotional problems—or the need to declare oneself independent of a strong personality—a twin must say: "Sure, all the attention we got in high school was great; sure, it was fun to play tricks and gang up against all comers; it was fine to rely on unquestioning sympathy. Now it's probably time to move on."

That "second self," no matter how friendly, can present problems in one's professional life. Helen Kirk Lauve, supertwin statistician, tells of a pair of identicals—one an orthodontist, one a psychiatrist—who as adults had lived in separate parts of the country. After years of living apart, the psychiatrist moved back to the town where his twin was practicing. He was quickly faced with a troublesome predicament. How was he gracefully to keep his patients from mistaking his brother for himself and carrying their psychiatric problems to his twin, the dentist?

The Seitz twins, actresses, found in 1959 that being twins was a drag for them both. Producers seldom had roles for sets of twins and, besides, seemed incapable of perceiving the women as separate individuals. They performed in several plays as a twin act but finally felt forced to restructure their careers. Their dissatisfactions, they said, became intolerable when a critic gave Caryl a rave review for a role that had actually been played by Caryln. At this point, they changed their names from Caryl and Caryln to Tani and Dran. One dyed her hair black; the other kept her natural color. They used not only makeup but all their skills as actresses to impress people with their differences.

Eventually, it is up to the twins themselves to decide whether the differentiations they make are to be only skin deep or more profound. The probabilities are that they can't settle this once and for all at any age. Charles Hildreth, whose identical twin brother Horace was a Governor of Maine, reminisced about their music lessons in childhood. "Horace was on clarinet and I was on the fiddle. We used to practice in adjoining rooms, and he made so much noise I couldn't even hear myself play. I switched to a slide trombone, but I never did catch up with him." The story plainly expresses a regret about something more important and long-lasting than being outdistanced in musical skills during childhood. The fear of never catching up with a twin who has chosen a diverging path is particularly acute for the twin left behind—and may be the source of guilt for the one who has achieved more success.

Twins are never quite permitted to lose sight of the price they have to pay for individuality. As they head off to school, one may respond to the enticement of group activities while the other shrinks from it. Then the unspoken oath of loyalty between them begins to tug at the more venturesome one. *I'd like to be on the softball team, but Don would hate it,* Ron thinks. Such thoughts may briefly pull the pair into retreat, to search for their own recreation, or they may be assigned to the unconscious, only to reassert themselves much later in Ron's life.

Such was the case in June 1981, in Columbia, South Carolina, when Lewis and Elliott Rowland, 16, were found dead in Lewis's room. Both had been shot in the head. While the family insisted it was entirely out of character for either boy to take his own life and believed it was just a horrible accident, the coroner ruled it was a double suicide. Lewis had suffered all his life from a congenital eye disorder that made him legally blind. All his life Elliott believed it was his duty to his twin to help him cope with his handicap. It was difficult for Elliott to live a normal fun-loving life when he knew that Lewis was depressed or unhappy. "He must have been trying to show Lewis how awful it all was," their mother insisted to a reporter. "He was saying, 'Lewis, if you do this thing, you will cause me to give up my life too.'" She believes that as Lewis's gun went off the noise startled Elliott who then fired his gun inadvertently.

At the very worst, unresolved tensions between twins can lead literally to murder. In 1950, fourteen-year-old Alice Richard of Fresno, California, ended a bitter argument with her fraternal twin Sally by killing her with a .22 caliber rifle belonging to their older brother. Two weeks later in the same city, four-year-old Kenneth Preston was drowned when his identical twin Jimmy pushed him into an irrigation canal. Undoubtedly, little Kenneth did not grasp the harm he had done his brother. The pair had always seemed close, and in telling his parents what he had done, the child said he was now looking for a pole to fish Jimmy out. But Alice Richard maintained consistently that she killed her sister because she hated her. Then in 1965, Tim Nicholson, twenty-two, on the witness stand during his trial for the fatal shooting of his brother, sobbed uncontrollably, "I didn't want to shoot Todd. I would never shoot him. I loved him." He claimed that his brother died as they argued and wrestled over the gun Tim had clutched at when his brother threatened him with it. These cases are mentioned not to illustrate a frequent outcome—in fact, their rarity should be stressed, the coincidence of dates in Fresno notwithstanding—but to point to the dense tangles of emotion that can snarl two closely adjacent lives.

Twins may mirror each other's faults and virtues all too vividly. Everyone knows how startling it is to encounter the reflection of a magnifying mirror. Suddenly your skin looks like the surface of a foreign planet; your eyes are enormous; a mole is like a boulder. For identical twins, all problems of appearance and behavior are enlarged when the mere presence of the other self emphasizes the awareness of personal shortcomings. There's no place to hide, no way to pretend the flaws are not there. Thus, one hears twins say, "I don't look like her, do I?" or, "Just because he messed up in the contest, I'll never hear the last of it." Most identicals truly like their partners; in the long run they will defend them against all comers, but they have to get through the short run—the bad days—too, and there are times when it can seem intolerable to have an ever-present, all-too-human reminder that one is far from perfect. Many twins joke to counteract the pain this causes. Having "one's own mirror," they say, is a decided advantage. "We can check to see if our ties are straight before we go out."

On Our Own

For twins, as for everyone else, growing up means gradually assuming responsibility for themselves. Twins come to understand that it is not so much a question of how their parents named or raised them, but of how they will handle what their parents gave them—how twins will make the very best they can of all the conditioning they received when they were too young to call the shots.

There are probably few adult twins who don't carry some psychological scars from the prejudices they have endured in their formative years. They may have been misled by counselors simply following fads in twin guidance; their companions may have encouraged them to play up the freaky or unusual aspects of their twinship; the confusions they caused from birth onward may have rebounded on them, causing personal problems which single children may never experience. All that matters less than it might seem, however, during moments of discouragement. In fact, twins and other multiples very often find that the seemingly unfortunate periods of their lives have

stood them in good stead. Helen Kirk Lauve tells how the
Badgett quadruplets, as adults, are completely unhampered
by their experience of growing up as four identicals in a
time when no one thought to do otherwise than dress them
alike and direct their lives along parallel paths. "Reporters
always are nonplussed that, although these women were a
unit as they were growing up, they have turned out to be
so normal. None of them has any emotional scars or abnormalities having grown up in such a way," she observes.
Thus, by reviewing their personal lives as wisely as they
can, twins can claim a very special sort of individuality.
They often have worked harder than singletons to define
paths they freely choose to follow. It is in that spirit that
most twins and other multiples participate in various kinds
of twin studies.

"Singletons who think—or say—to twins, 'Oh, isn't it
unfortunate to be a twin?' make me furious. And we hear
that a good deal," one twin comments. "They make it
sound as if we had something to do with being twins, as if
we had a choice. Biologically, we didn't, so I don't think
they should be so rude. But I wish they'd admit they have
no way of knowing how much good we've got from being
identicals. In spite of some minor problems, it's always
been fun."

Out of misguided pity, envy or unconscious malice, singletons perpetuate the notion that the native intelligence
of twins is below average. This is in spite of the fact that
as long ago as 1940 Dr. Horatio H. Newman tested twins
and came up with results that show this notion to be er-
roneous. As he reported in his book *Multiple Human
Births*, "Intelligence tests given to large numbers of twin
pairs taken at random from the school population and elsewhere indicate that the whole group of twins is mentally
the equal of the single-born individuals in the same
schools."

Twin expert Dr. Rene Zazzo concedes that very young twins do not on the whole measure up—but he asks: Doesn't this come from improper expectations and ways of measuring them? Twins will always come out "inferior" when measured by singleton standards. Turn that around—compare singletons by a twin measure, or twins by a twin measure, and the story may be significantly altered.

In school, a twin may—very properly—want credit for the individual effort he puts into any singly achieved accomplishment. If a professor gives Jack the same grade as his twin, the implication may be that nothing counts except whatever inherited talents Jack may share with his look-alike brother. Jack feels his own hard work has been discounted and, out of frustration, may turn his resentments against the brother. At such times it is all too easy for Jack to feel: If my brother hadn't got in my way, I'd have been recognized for what I've done. The competition for territorial rights began, as we saw, in the womb, and it usually persists at least through childhood. While they still share a single room in the family home, twins will squabble over invasions of shelf and drawer space. Later, when "territory" has been naturally expanded to mean all the paraphernalia and personal relationships gathered by the growing twin, the potential for disagreements multiplies proportionately.

Yielding "territorial" claims can be as intricate as the pattern of establishing them. (It's a lot like nations negotiating borders after a series of clashes.) During my first year of college, I was desperate to be called "Kay" rather than "Karilyn" or "Twin," as I had been up to that point. "Kay" would at least put two syllables between my sister Marilyn and me, redefining our territories to give us both some room to expand into new, more individual activities. I don't believe Marilyn disagreed with my wish for independence; she merely felt I was being too aggressive in emphasizing our differences. For her part, she was busy falling in love and wanted me to crawl back into the woodwork when her boyfriend was around—which I seldom did. In my turn, I was obnoxious enough to remind her of her continuing obligations to me. So the seesaw kept going up and down, though I believe that the long-term effect was to move us toward the individuality we both prized. Many twins I have spoken with report similar periods of tension.

We can see now that the passing hurts and resentments we felt had their positive consequences. We look back at a thinly veiled and continuing struggle for dominance, which was always balanced by concern for the other twin's feelings. We trained each other in competitions, and our competitiveness led eventually to new interests and achievements in fields where no distinction is made between singletons and twins. I have a strong feeling that our early life together gave us a real advantage in these later encounters.

Twins are less likely than their single siblings to compete with each other for the favor of parents or other family members. Having each other for emotional reassurance, they don't need extra displays of affection, and perhaps they even subconsciously fear that such unequal treatment would jeopardize their place in the family. There may be, however, some tendency for the more dominant twin to identify with the father, the more passive with the mother. To some extent, they may model their behavior with each other on the father-mother pattern they see in their home.

A particular strain is put on the twin bond when a pair is old enough to enter romantic or sexual relationships. Obviously, the emotions that are now called into play are sufficiently intense to disturb the demands of loyalty between twins. While the chances are very great that the sexual development and experiences of any pair will be nearly identical, the chances are just as great that the twins will not exchange secrets on these matters. Thus, they lack a vocabulary with which to deal with the strain of competing affections and enter the period of dating and courtship with more than usual naiveté, each with a distressing uncertainty as to why anyone of the opposite sex might prefer one twin to the other. A Bette Davis film, *A Stolen Life*, takes this to the extreme. One mousy looking twin and one beautiful twin are in competition for the same man. The beauty wins; the other is always envious. Then the beauty dies, trapped at sea in an accident, and the mousy looking one assumes her identity, only to discover the husband hated the beautiful one all along.

At this point, a twin has the acute need for individuality, along with sharp anxiety about its consequences. One twin admitted, "I wanted my boyfriend to like us both, but I demanded that he admit he liked me best. I wanted him to tell me he could never be interested in my sister—but I didn't want him to say anything derogatory about her, either." A teenager laments: "I don't see why boys always feel it's a compliment to me to say I'm thinner than she is. I'm not, and I wouldn't take it as a compliment if it were true."

It also comes as a shock to twins that many singletons seem to have a fantasy of having a sex relationship with both members of a pair—together or in succession. In one case I heard about, the fantasy came true. The results were painful to all concerned. A man fell in love with a girl before he knew she was a twin. Before he made any real progress, the twin had appeared and the man became involved with her. He continued to pursue his original love, while he secretly met the twin sister. The strain destroyed the sisters' affection for each other, and the man got neither one. Most twins would say: "The wish to possess us both is a real affront to our individuality. It's the worst possible example of that constant need of singletons to ignore the differences we prize in ourselves." Authors Ruth and Helen Hoffman describe a scene familiar to many twins, in which a very proper French gentleman friend invites them both for dinner at a hotel. When they arrive, they discover it is to take place in a private room and that the gentleman seems to have something more than dinner in mind. All along, they had thought that since neither one of them would be alone in the situation, it was undoubtedly on the up-and-up.

Something of the subconscious urge to flirt with such a twin fantasy must surely be lurking behind such books as Judith Rossner's *Attachments,* in which two young women—best friends and natural opposites—marry a pair of "Siamese" twins.

Singletons might be less bewildered by twins or other multiples if they just granted them the same amount of free will they assume for themselves. Twins are, after all, free to choose to emphasize or ignore their twinship in any given circumstances. As an adult twin puts it, "Sure, I still have vivid memories of a mystical childhood world peopled only by my sister and myself. I feel as if I can return to it in moments of emotional crisis and be supported by the memory. My sister and I still have our fund of private jokes and our codes that may cause some consternation when we use them in public. I know we sometimes sound idiotic, but that's just our little amusing twin conspiracy. We have other things to rely on when we want to."

Perhaps because so much has been written about the determining power of the genes—and because much of the most significant material has come from studies of identical twins—one may get the impression that identicals are more completely controlled by heredity than is the population at large. This is far from the truth, since twins are as much the observers as the objects of such studies.

Looking Out from Deep Inside

While discussing twin myths and the appearance of twins in literature in chapter 1, I did not speculate on the extent to which twins themselves contributed their insights to such lore. That is because my assumption was that most of the material represented the singleton's view of twins. Certainly, twins have much to learn from the figures they cut in the eyes of the world, but, of course, they also see everything from their own conditioned point of view.

Among the literary figures who have looked at the world from within the enchanted circle of twinship are the twin playwrights Anthony and Peter Shaffer. In a brilliant psychoanalytic analysis of their dramatic works, Dr. Jules Glenn has shown how many of their protagonists "manifest the personality characteristics of twins," even though these characters are not depicted as biological twins. One of Glenn's conclusions is that since a twin is inclined to see his partner as a near duplicate of himself, "he also pictures the world as populated by people almost identical with himself." In the case of writers like the Shaffers, this has led them to the creation of a range of works in which the special outlook of twins is projected onto a variety of human types, relationships and actions.

In Peter Shaffer's *Equus*, says Dr. Glenn, the two main characters who serve as "surrogate twins" in their dramatic relationship "are not merely similar. They *grow more alike* as they identify with each other." (The italics are mine.) The point is that however potent the biological determinants may be in shaping a twin pair, the twinship is constantly in the process of development. Within an unbroken and, in fact, unbreakable relationship, many permutations and paradoxes are permissible. The ebb and flow of influence between members of a twin pair will color all the choices either twin makes. Thus, if the choice is made for the sake of individuality to change a hair style, the decision as to how and when that change will be made is conditioned by the twinship. The dynamics of the twin relationship often actually encourage diversity of appearance even while the essential twin link is being reinforced.

The Royal Hunt of the Sun by Peter Shaffer dramatizes the deadly rivalry between the conquistador Pizarro and the Inca king whose gold he has come to steal. Dr. Glenn finds this also to be a symbolic representation of part of the twin's vision of his own relationship. In one scene, Pizarro ties his Inca surrogate twin to himself with a long rope. The act expresses the wish for closeness that coexists with rivalry. The rope itself is a symbolic umbilical cord like that which many twins imagine as the permanent invisible link between them.

Reviewing the rest of the plays by the brothers, Dr. Glenn notes as a common denominator the "desire to keep things even" between members of the fictional pairs. For every action there seems to be a compensatory reaction illustrating such fundamental twin formulas as (1) intense rivalry intertwined with intense libidinal attachment; (2) the lifelong identification of one twin with the other, and the use of that identification as a defense; (3) a fantasy of being half a person; (4) the wish to resolve antagonisms by keeping things even; and (5) a tendency to want to impose on marriage, friendship or the parent-child relationship the same emotional patterns established by twinship.

Dr. Glenn goes beyond his analysis of the plays to speculate about the creative advantages the authors enjoy by virtue of being twins. "The capacity of twins to identify, to put themselves in the place of others," he says, "must be a help in the creation of fictional characters." The very uncertainty about the boundaries of the individual psyche "can be adaptively used in the creative process;

projection of personal traits onto literary characters as well
as identification are facilitated by such uncertainty."

What is most striking to me about such analysis of the
Shaffer twins' dramatic work is how familiar it sounds,
how close it comes to my own psychic history and to what
I have heard from other twins from all walks of life. I
realize how easy it was for me to imagine that everyone I
met must somehow be like me—that is, would surely respond according to the formulas I as a twin had learned.
If I were to quarrel with someone, surely the "desire to keep
things even" would move him or her to wind up the quarrel
just as my sister and I would. When I tried to assess my
parents', my husband's or my children's feelings about me,
my standards were those that Marilyn and I used for each
other. Surely, I used to think, if I identified with someone
I admired, that person would (or at least would want to)
identify with me in much the same fashion. Such assumptions must have misled me many times—I am sure they did,
and I am embarrassed at remembering some of my naiveté—
but as compensation I believe that my creative sympathy
for a variety of people actually taught them something as
well. By briefly making them surrogate twins, I led them
to a point where they could enjoy the easy and intimate
sharing we twins are given as birthright.

It is a matter of record that my sister and I have lived
far apart in different cities for many years now. The
deliberate choices we made to go different ways mean that
with the passing years, our aquaintances and life-styles are
at last altogether distinct in every detail. Yet when we visit
each other's homes or meet each other's friends for the first
time, it is as if we had always known them and chosen them
ourselves. In ways we were not always aware of, my sister
has subtly conditioned her friends to welcome and like me;
I have done the same for her. Thus, in the most important

sense we have kept things even, though outward appearances might not always have indicated this.

Achievers and Superachievers

When asked to name famous twins, many people draw
a blank after they have mentioned the most familiar from
myth or the Bible. Yet history records two sets of twin
saints: Saints Benedict and Scholastica, founders of the
Benedictine order; and Saints Cosmas and Damian, famous
physicians in the third century A.D., who were beheaded by
Emperor Diocletian for stubbornly clinging to their Christian faith; as well as Saint Catherine of Siena, who was born
a twin although her sister Giovanna died shortly after birth.
Procles and Euristenes were twin kings of the Spartans.
Twins appear often enough in royal lineage down through
the ages: proud papa Louis XV was so pleased to have produced twin girls (dubbed Madame Première and Madame
Seconde by the royal household) that he had a medal
struck in honor of their births; and much of the speculation about the pending royal birth in Great Britain is fixed
on the possibility of twins. The list of famous parents of
twins is a lengthy one. It includes Ingrid Bergman, Joseph
Kennedy 3d (the eldest son of Robert F. Kennedy), Mu-
hammad Ali, Edward Asner, Marc Antony and Cleopatra,
Johann Sebastian Bach, Susan Hayward, June Haver and
Fred MacMurray, Dan Blocker, Jimmy Breslin, Joan Craw-
ford, Anita Bryant, Robert Burns, Bing Crosby, Mike
Douglas, Jean Kerr, Mia Farrow, Loretta Lynn, Art Link-
letter, Nelson D. Rockefeller and William Shakespeare. Far
rarer, because such multiples occur so seldom, are famous
parents of identical triplets. In late August 1981, however,
actor Richard Thomas, of "The Waltons" fame, and his
wife Alma became the proud and harried parents of three

identical girls. (As is so often the case, although the couple had been alerted to expect twins it was not until Alma went into labor that her doctor discovered a third infant's heartbeat.)

Why, then, does it appear that twins are noticeably absent from the ranks of achievers and of the famous? The obvious first answer is that twins are very definitely in a minority—they make up only 2 percent of the population. Further, if twins achieve renown not as twins but as separate individuals in separate careers and are seldom seen together, they become part of what one twin so aptly described as "the invisible minority." That is to say, they are invisible as twin achievers. Included in this category, too, are those people who rise to fame after the loss of a twin partner. In such cases, the surviving twin often feels an added sense of strength, as well as obligation to reach his goals "for both of us." Some of the eminent names in all of these groups may surprise you. They include: John Lindsay, Elizabeth Holzman, Ed Sullivan, Laraine Day, Henry Morgan, Anna Maria Pierangeli, Jim Thorpe, Heloise Bowles, John Mack Carter, Jackson Pollack, Peter Gimbel, Everett Dirksen, Eleanor McGovern, Randolph and David Hearst, Montgomery Clift and Elvis Presley. Author Elizabeth Kübler-Ross was one of a set of triplets, two of whom were identicals—she and one of her sisters— and according to her, not even their parents could tell them apart when they were young.

Nevertheless, it is also true that when a twin is in the news for an outstanding individual accomplishment or because of some twist of fate that would seem to have nothing to do with being a twin, the story is often expanded to include some comment on the twin relationship. The seeming irrelevance of this circumstance is evidently overridden by a vague, powerful notion that the destiny of twins is more significant than the facts would indicate.

For instance, when publisher Ross McWhirter was assassinated in England in 1975 by IRA gunmen, the report in *Newsweek* was illustrated by a photo showing McWhirter and his identical twin Norris in identical Scottish costumes, and the text dwelt on the partnership of the pair in founding the *Guinness Book of World Records*. Though there was nothing to indicate Norris McWhirter's involvement in the political crusade that had led to his brother's assassination, the reader was given the strong impression that the tragedy was the culmination of a life story shared, to the end, by twins.

The same may be said for the late Shah of Iran and his twin sister Ashraf. When the Shah was dethroned and moving about the world in a storm of controversy, his "other self" continued the battle in his behalf with a ferocity to be expected of a twin, perhaps, and also with a freedom of expression forbidden the Shah himself for diplomatic reasons. She published a memoir, *Faces in a Mirror*, with an obvious allusion to the twin relationship and, in the years of crisis, subordinated all other personal ties, including her marriage, to those with her harried brother. As an actress of some importance in a drama that held the attention of the world, she was newsworthy in her own right, but the reportage devoted to her role consistently (if inconclusively) fixed attention on the special bond linking her to her brother.

On the other hand, there was a pair who found fame by always being together. In the early 1800s, Moses and Aaron Wilcox led such synchronous lives that they were mentioned in Ripley's *Believe It or Not*. Their real contribution, however, was to put a town—the only one in the world named for twins—on the map. Lifelong business partners, this identical pair married sisters, fathered the same number of children and lived next door to each other. They were both stricken with the same ailment on the same day and eventually died within hours of each other. They are buried in one grave in this small town of parks, one of which the brothers gave to the community. Twinsburg, Ohio, about halfway between Cleveland and Akron, has seven churches, one appropriately named after Saints Cosmas and Damian. Each year the residents of Twinsburg spend one weekend celebrating twins with games, contests, sporting events and general conviviality. Twins have come from as far away as Lebanon and Poland to participate in these Twins Day festivities and to mingle with the twins who have come from Hollywood and elsewhere to entertain them.

During the 1980 celebration Jim and Jon Hager wowed their audience of doubles and were equally impressed with them. "It's great to be with so many others who know what it's like to be a twin," they said.

Another well-known set of twins is the Quaker pair, Albert K. and Alfred H. Smiley, who built and ran the Mohonk Mountain House and the Minnewaska Mountain House Hotel in upstate New York in the latter half of the nineteenth century. Both resorts were extremely popular and counted among their guests three United States presidents. In the same era, Francis and Freeland Stanley built their "Stanley Steamer" with such care that it was considered top of the line for cars of that time. They and the Piccards, Auguste and Jean, are probably the most outstanding twin pairs among inventors and scientists, but in those categories, as well as in the ranks of business, law, medicine, public service and the clergy, there are many achievers and superachievers who are multiples. Just a few: Alan and Manfred Guttmacher (physicians), Edwin N. and E. Malcolm Stevenson (physicians), Julius and Lasser Alexander (physicians), Judith Wright Hagedorn and Janet Wright Kizziar (psychologists), Horace and Charles Hildreth (attorneys; Horace, former Governor of Maine),

Charles Crail (judge) and Joseph Crail (congressman), James and John Onion, Jr. (judges). There are even triplets who are scientists: Robert, Wallace and Malcolm Brode. Robert, a physicist, and Wallace, a chemist, are identical twins who have a fraternal triplet Malcolm, a zoologist.

Some of the advantages that twins enjoy by virtue of their twinship—advantages that further their chances of success— have been mentioned earlier. Certainly, if we are to believe the findings of psychologists researching the creative process and the types of persons who succeed, innovative abilities are more often than not coupled with forcefulness, aggression, toughness and daring. As they resolve the contrariety of their relationship with their partner, twins often develop such traits as a matter of course. They learn early the skills required for successful collaboration and competition, in preparation for the rigors of achieving goals out of the ordinary. The crisis of identity and the impulse to forge a strong sense of self also strengthens the motivations of twins. Although there is often intense rivalry between them, there is almost always an accompanying sense of egalitarianism, a combination that provides the necessary strength to launch them on the road to success. Of course, there may be times when this is difficult to believe, as in the case of the Friedman twins.

Among the identicals with parallel careers and equal celebrity, two of the better known are columnists Abigail Van Buren and Ann Landers (both are pen names). They were born in 1918 in Sioux City, Iowa, Esther Pauline and Pauline Esther Friedman, and through their high school days were an extroverted, vivacious pair, well known and well liked in their hometown. At twenty, they were married in a double wedding ceremony and went off with their husbands on a double honeymoon. After seventeen years of domestic life and varied community interests, Ann began to publish her column in the *Chicago Sun-Times*.

Therein lay the seeds of a long and divisive feud between the sisters as well as between the vast readership both would claim. Eighty-six days after Ann appeared in the *Sun-Times*, Abby launched *her* own column. Before long, the famous sisters were sniping at each other through the press, which naturally exploited this manifestation of twin rivalry. Ann complained that Abby was "very imitative," and Abby rejoined by claiming that she had ghostwritten a great share of her sister's first columns. Insisting that Ann had shown her batches of the letters written by readers seeking advice, she said, "I provided the sharp answers."

Their public feuding lasted for eight years, fueled by so much press coverage that it might have been contrived for publicity purposes. Evidently it was not. In a 1981 article in *Ladies' Home Journal*, Abby confirmed that the feud resulted from competitive feelings engendered early in their lives. Be that as it may, the mutual sympathy so familiar in twinship never entirely failed, and at last the sisters and their husbands patched everything up by taking a second double honeymoon. The personal lives of these sisters never quite settled down, however; marital strains eventually caught up with Ann and her husband and they divorced after thirty-six years of marriage. The sisters would seem to have settled the major differences between themselves. Or have they? When Mort Phillips, Abby's husband, heard about the public verbal squabbling, he was quoted as saying, "If these are twin sisters, I'll take cobras!" Still, Abby says, "We are each other's best friend. I'd fight like a tiger for my sister and she'd do the same for me. . . . Oh, we have our differences—the anger, the hostility, the competition—but no one could ever come between us."

Of two male pairs who work closely together in their bid for fame the first are Jonathan and James diDonato, identicals known as the Tiger Twins. They hold a Guinness world record for a ten mile Atlantic swim doing the butterfly stroke, and in August 1981 came very close to crossing the English channel together the same way. Captains Bill and Buck Pattillo were, in the 1950s, famous aerial acrobats, members of the American air exhibition team, The Skyblazers. They were so attuned to each other that they flew in formation with a distance of only one and one-half meters between the wings of their respective planes while they clocked 800 kilometers per hour.

Conrad and Bonar Bain are actors and identical twins who experienced the familiar insult many twins will recognize. Their first grade teacher, discovering they had missed some answers on a test said, "Well, that's no surprise. We don't expect anything from the Bain boys because they have only half a brain anyway." As Conrad puts it now, "I guess if we could overcome that attitude we must have developed some resistance to defeat, but I don't think there's any question that it had its effect on us when we were very young. We both had a sense of inferiority then, and uncertainty about our ability to accomplish things." Recently, when he played the father to a pair of identical girls in a television film, *Raid on Short Creek*, Conrad spent a lot of time with the identical young actresses because "much of what they said about their lives as twins was so familiar to me. I have a special feeling about identical twins. I know they are going through something that no one except us—other identicals—fully understands." At the age of seventeen, Bain experienced an instance of ESP that he remembers as vividly as if it had happened yesterday. He was at a dinner party while his brother, Bonar, was somewhere else on a date. "Out of a clear blue sky I said, 'I wonder how my brother Bonar is doing?' Everyone around the table gave me a strange look because this was apropos of nothing. Although I didn't have any anxiety about Bonar, I did have a vivid general image in my mind of a fire. When I got home I discovered that Bonar and his girl had been at a

dance hall that caught fire. They barely got out alive. I
had happened to look at the clock when I mentioned his
name at dinner. The time coincided exactly with that of
Bonar's crisis."

The Morgan twins, Gloria and Thelma, were often fea-
tured in the press after their debut in New York society in
the 1920s. Then, as debutantes, they were called "The
Magical Morgans." Their romances typified the glamour
of the jazz age. In the next decade, they were internationally famous, Thelma for her close friendship with the
Prince of Wales, Gloria for a sensational court battle to
retain custody of her daughter. In 1934, Thelma had to
part company for a time from the Prince. As she did so,
she said to her friend Wallis Warfield Simpson, "Well,
dear, look after him for me while I'm away and see that
he doesn't get into mischief." Perhaps she should have en-
trusted him to the care of her twin sister because, as all
the world knows, the Prince soon afterward renounced
the throne of England to marry Mrs. Simpson. Gloria had,
however, married the chief heir of the Vanderbilt fortune
when she was seventeen. Soon after the birth of their
daughter, Vanderbilt died, and there began a long series
of squabbles about his estate and the custody of the child.
Garish testimony bearing on Gloria's unfitness as a mother
embittered her and led to an estrangement with her daughter that was never mended. But the two sisters remained
close. In 1958 they wrote their twin autobiography, *Double Exposure*, in which they describe several of their experiences involving the unusual psychic bond between
them. Like many other twins, they referred to their situation as "almost as if we were Siamese twins without the
physical connection." In their later years, they lived together in California. Even after their separate adventures,
Gloria could say, "We think alike, we like the same people,
we often interrupt each other and finish each other's

sentences. We're both very shy. Thelma always leads and I follow."

Performing comes naturally to many pairs who adapted early to the local spotlight. It's not surprising, then, that twins opt for careers related to the performing arts. Cherie and Marie Currie have had individual careers as singers, but they have also collaborated on a rock album, *Messin' with the Boys*. Ludmilla Lifschitz and Sophia Herman, twin sisters who emigrated from Russia recently, are concert artists. Sophia was a member of the famed Leningrad Symphony and plays the violin; Ludmilla is a pianist. Together they captured the prestigious Soviet Chamber Music Competition in Moscow in 1966. The Rainers, Alice and Clarice, are a pair of identicals and as professional pianists always perform duets. Ilia and Peter Kondove are high-wire acrobats from Bulgaria who debuted in the United States in 1979 with Ringling Brothers and Barnum & Bailey Circus. Following close behind are Matthew and Michael Houbrick of Orlando, Florida, a pair of five-feet-eleven identicals who were the first pair of twin clowns at the Ringling Brothers' Clown College. Magicians, jugglers and mimes, the two men have also been seen in commercials for Circus World and Samsonite luggage.

For quite some time now, identical duos have been frequently chosen by commercial advertisers to carry messages to the public. Few Americans past the age of twenty are unfamiliar with the long-running ad campaign for Toni permanent waves which pictured twin models in glamorous photos, one supposedly having given herself an inexpensive Toni home permanent while the other had a more costly treatment at a beauty salon. The reader was asked to guess, "Which twin has the Toni?" The indistinguishable features of the models emphasized the indistinguishable results of the hair treatments. (I remember with what glee my sister and I accepted our prizes of twin beds when we won the district Toni contest, one of several such "look-alike" tournaments we captured when we were younger.) In his way, the man who dreamed up that campaign and the coast-to-coast Toni Twin Caravans that carried it even to remote areas of the country in an effort to find Toni's "All American Twins" was also building a Twin Register, albeit not a scientific one. The barnstorming scheme worked so well that 154 sets of twins were turned up in Fort Worth, Texas, alone. Other advertisers, such as Wrigley, Lipton (Cup O'Soup), McDonald's and J. C. Penney ("Plain Pockets" jeans) among many others, have provided twin pairs with a good deal of visibility; some of it has initiated show business careers for such sets as Vanessa and Valerie Browne, Jeff and Greg Koontz, Michael and David Shackleford and Betsy and Carol Thompson.

Consuelo and Gloria O'Connor, however, got their start as twin fashion models, signing with the Harry Conover agency in the 1950s. This led to a glamorous marriage for one and a film career for the other. The girls, it is said, had been guided on their spectacular path by their "simple Irish mother." Mrs. O'Connor found them their first modeling jobs to help pay for their tuition at a fashionable New York school. As Conover models, everything opened up for them, from being cover girls to touring the country giving advice to teenage girls on matters of taste and grooming. Under mother's guidance, they also made a formal debut in New York and attracted considerable attention in the press. Later, their romantic involvements and marriages continued to bolster their fame. In all this they echoed a pattern set by Eloise and Genevieve Reed, who were tapped for the Ziegfeld Follies of 1907 and appeared on the stage and the silent screen for the next fifteen years. "We sang and danced our way across America," they recalled in 1979. "A lot of rich guys dated us. Some were millionaires. We had a good time."

Besides the fact that identicals make an eye-catching

idea for commercials, perhaps the other impetus for the
success of twins—at least the young ones—in show business
has been the child labor laws. These are so strict in California that producers of films and television dramas must
often resort to employing two for one role. Thus the "interchangeables" become one "star" to their public. Three
pairs who approached the Hollywood scene this way are
Sidney and Rachel Greenbush ("Little House on the
Prairie"), Joseph and Michael Mayer ("I Love Lucy"),
and Michael and Marshall Reed ("The Waltons"). Other
interchangeables who attained some fame by doubling up
include Mimi and Janet Kenan, University of Tennessee
coeds who won (as one entry) the Sweetheart of Sigma
Chi contest. They shared a trophy. The Cunninghams, Dorothy Jane and Jean, in 1946 entered the Miss America contest as Miss Chattanooga and Miss Tennessee, but when the
photographer snapped their picture, they had only one ribbon wrapped around both of them.

Scanning the Famous Twins List being compiled by
Helen Kirk Lauve, we find the names of twins, together or
singly, among those prominent in their art form. Thorn-
ton Wilder's twin achieved none of the eminence of the
great American novelist and playwright, but his presence
is interwoven in the text of stories and plays. The image of
the author in the public mind is that of a twin, with alle-
giances and intuitions significantly set apart from his singleton contemporaries. Hubert and Hobart Doublas Skidmore
were identicals born fifteen minutes apart in 1909. Hubert
won the prestigious Hopwood Award for the novel; Hobart received his Hopwood for drama. Paul and Dick
Sylbert have both worked for many years in film production, having both started out as artists painting scenery.
Paul's work has been with the Metropolitan Opera Company, and he has worked on fifteen films. Dick, former
vice-president of Paramount Pictures, has twenty-three

film credits. Most of their work has been in different productions, but they did combine talents in the films *Baby Doll* and *Face in the Crowd*. They have remarked, "We were always able to divide the work right, knowing who had talents in what direction." Ivan and Malvin Albright, Chicago painters of the macabre, created the paintings for the film *The Picture of Dorian Gray*. Artists Raphael and Moses Soyer, are also well known in the field of fine art. Artists and twins Margaret "Peggy" and Kathryn Prentice turned their talents from printmaking to papermaking for such other famous artists as Robert Rauschenberg, Claes Oldenburg and Robert Motherwell, saying that their work is "a result of a relationship." They particularly like the process of collaboration and discussion which their enterprise entails. The name of their company—Twinrockers, Inc. Among other sets of artists are Ida Libby Dengrove and Freda L. Reiter, both of whom sketch the primary figures in courtroom trials. Ida works on a freelance basis for NBC and Freda, who covered the Watergate trials, is employed by ABC. In Los Angeles, in 1980, photographers Kathleen and Colleen Kenyon had a joint show of their photographs in which they tried to capture the essence of twinship as they saw it. Unlike Margaret and Kathryn Prentice, however, Kathleen and Colleen attempt, in most of their work, to take separate directions.

Twins have frequently had spectacular careers in sports as well as show business, sometimes being of special interest to fans for their parallel performance and appearance. In 1974, the Big Ten basketball season was enhanced by the emergence of Kim and Kerry Hughes as stars of the Wisconsin team. At six feet eleven, that year they brought a lagging Wisconsin team back into the thick of the conference race. Their brilliance was all the more dazzling because it burst rather unexpectedly on coaches and teammates alike. Their quick growth in late teen years had given them the height they needed but was accompanied by problems of fatigue and growing diseases. A lot of hard work and conditioning on their part was required to bring them to the peak of stardom.

It is hardly a surprise that twins do well in those sports in which the coordination of two teammates is a definite asset. Thus, Tim and Tom Gullikson won the Miller Hall of Fame doubles title in tennis at Newport in 1978. Then, in 1979, Tim went on to upset John McEnroe at Wimbledon in singles play. Since one is a right-hander and the other a lefty, they make an extremely formidable combination to face across a net. Coordination is also the name of the game when pairs skate together, as have several twin sets over the years in the Ice Follies and Ice Capades, as have one set of triplets: Glena, Gladys and Gloria Burling.

Two sets of famous twins who have competed against each other in sports are Phil and Steven Mahre, champion skiers, and Mario and Aldo Andretti, auto racers.

Whether or not twins have risen to levels of fame proportionate to their number is a question that, like so many other twin quandaries, never can be settled absolutely. Too much depends on the definition of fame—and perhaps on the short attention span of a constantly distracted public. Suffice it to say that twins have made stellar marks in nearly all fields of human endeavor, whether or not they are recognized as twins when they do so.

6. Exceptional Twins:
The Ultimate Sharing Experience

Yorkshire, England, with its sparsely inhabited moors and dales—the region of *Wuthering Heights* and of the first version of Bram Stoker's *Dracula*—is a part of the world where the uncanny and the eccentric lurk. Its population, accustomed to some of the weirdness in the world, would seem unlikely to be thrown off stride by a couple of extremely unusual twins in their thirties. Yet it was in York in 1980 that the Chaplin sisters caused quite a stir. They were called "the mental twins"—a queer piece of slang implying a fearsome grotesqueness about them. In something similar to a reenactment of a medieval scourging of witches, children threw stones and jeered when the women walked down the street. Some adults spat at them. Because of their eerie similarities and strange ways, they received constant, low-level harassment wherever they went.

For fifteen years the twins shared a crush on a local truck driver, a man nearly twenty years their senior. A former neighbor, he used to pause to chat with the pair but halted the practice when he married. The women continued to pester him intolerably, following him to and from work, as well as lurking outside his home for a glimpse of him. As he paid them less and less heed, the twins' obsession grew. Eventually, they began to shout obscenities at him. When they threw themselves in front of his car, he brought suit to be relieved of their attentions. That was when the problems of Freda and Greta multiplied. A local disturbance suddenly became international news, and their story appeared in newspapers and magazines around the world.

The Chaplin sisters are mirror-image twins to a degree that baffles the medical profession. They dress *exactly* alike, unable to bear a difference of even one button or shoestring. If they are given pairs of gloves in two different colors, they simply swap one glove so each wears an unmatched pair. They walk and move their hands in unison. They speak at the same time in a stereophonic similarity of tone. It is not hard to see why the long-suffering object of their love, finding himself attacked by both of them at the same time, felt unusually put upon. His own sanity seemed under assault.

Doctors are forced to talk about "one mind in two bodies" in discussing the Chaplins' case. Further explanations, from medical and social workers and police observers, point to "an unusual amount of telepathy" between the Chaplin women, as well as to the possibility that they "may have practiced their act until it is perfected." On occasion, singletons are called "human echoes" because their hearing is so finely tuned that they can repeat the speech of another person with even more accuracy of tone and timing than a real echo. It may just be that the Chaplins combine this rare capacity with the natural duality of twins. Or it may be that the Chaplins came very close to being born conjoined.

Whatever the full explanation for the Chaplins' extreme likeness to each other, their closeness is seen as the basis for most of their problems. They may, however, have had no choice but to be extremely close. Born of working-class parents who dressed them identically and insisted they be constantly together, walking in step, the girls grew up fearing even the briefest moment of separation. This rigid environment conditioned them until they were in their late twenties, when they moved into their own apartment. By this time, they couldn't bear any separation whatsoever. They could not hold down jobs and were forced to exist on welfare handouts. Several years ago, in an attempt to help the women form more separate identities, the authorities sent the Chaplins to different hospitals. They rebelled by refusing to eat or to talk to the doctors. They set up secret meetings by telephone. After their brush with the law, the women settled into a more simple life. Their occupational therapist told reporters that they arranged flowers (in unison) and used the same ball of yarn when knitting, but that they were showing some interest in other people, taking tea occasionally with an elderly woman. In the past, the twins had had no social life whatsoever.

Another sensational twin disaster story, involving the Marcus brothers, surfaced awhile back. These twins were gynecologists on the staff of a New York hospital. At one point, their increasingly aberrant behavior so startled their colleagues and patients that rumors surfaced about their unusual closeness, possible lack of adherence to medical ethics and drug consumption. Suddenly, the two physicians died within a few days of each other. Police who broke into their apartment found two starkly emaciated bodies lying on an accumulation of garbage in a wreck of an apartment. Naturally, there was an outpouring of publicity. Patients and acquaintances were stunned. But as those who knew them best compared notes, a picture developed of increasingly afflicted schizoid personalities. Each twin essentially had another "twin personality" at war within himself. Twins within twins . . . a story of eerie permutations that would excite the writer of horror fiction. In this case, some writers were tempted. The story stemming from the unhappy doctors' situation presently went on sale, but it was fiction, not a documentary. Because the book focused on a grotesque predicament involving twins, other multiples naturally protested that it unfairly placed all of them in a bad light. Most duos who have grown into adulthood with strong, healthy individual identities are as stunned and mystified as singletons by the aberrations presented in the Chaplin or the Marcus stories. Both the aberrations and the attention the media gives them pose some threat to twins' equilibrium. Some pairs who have made highly satisfactory adjustments in adulthood find that occasionally they "have to start all over" convincing others that, though twins may be similar in a unique way, they are no more apt to have sinister deviations than singletons are.

In fact, a major discovery from twin studies conducted over the past few decades is that in some important ways the development of twins is very much like that of singletons. Twins are no more susceptible to retardation or emotional complications than singletons are. While it is true that in some IQ studies, twins scored several points lower than singletons, psychologists and lay experts now believe that this is as much the result of lack of parental attention during their most formative years as of anything else. These overworked parents may not have as much time to

read to their twins or give them that earliest of verbal encouragement that is suspected to be the best stimulus for
the child's developing mind. Since twins have each other
for company and are apt to relate to their twin sibling before they relate to their parents or other singleton siblings,
they may mislead their family. They may not appear to
need as much special attention as a singleton child. However, any slowness in twins' early childhood usually disap-
pears by the time the pair enters school.

Twins on Display

Twins are often accused, whether fairly or not, of exhi-
bitionism. In fact, parents may be tempted to treat them as
a spectacle. Researchers have found that some parents are
blindly enamored of the novelty of having produced identicals. The attention drawn by their offspring rubs off on
them—much to the delight of some, whose behavior can
be likened to that of stage parents. When the fame attached to being father or mother of twins is the most gratifying element in their otherwise restricted lives, parents
can be seduced into highlighting this attraction, encouraging their twins to dress, speak and behave alike. Then again,
it never occurs to some parents that there are any other
options. They take it for granted that for their own well-
being twins must be kept in a sort of twin-harness; otherwise, one could not get along without the other. This is
especially true if twins seem to be shy or emotionally backward as very young children.

To counter any anxiety their twins might have of being
an "intruder in the womb," mother or father or both may
implant the idea that the twins really are only one person,
or that it is bad for one twin to think and act differently
from the other. Their over-compensation may uncon-

sciously arise from the parents' awe at having produced twins. Then, too, when society places so much emphasis on the need for individual development in twins, some duos come to believe that their similarities are unacceptable. They should not be alike and like it. Their situation is comparable to that of women who feel guilty about being happy as wives and mothers when there is so much social pressure to have a career.

Occasionally, no matter how much parents and educators encourage twins to seek individual paths in life, the twins rebel against intervention and insist upon clinging to each other, or to their twinship, as the central core of their lives. This occurs particularly in twins who have been inseparable from babyhood and who have hence come to rely heavily on the twin-crutch. I believe that this is probably what happened, for a short while, to my sister and myself. Our mother died when we were infants. We compensated for that loss by an extra dose of closeness. Even into preadolescence, we reacted strongly against any attempts from the outside to steer us along different paths. Fortunately, when our father remarried, he and our new mother allowed us to follow our own instincts. They neither sided with teachers who wished to separate us nor put unusual pressure on us to remain close, leaving the way open for us to separate in a normal and healthy fashion when we were ready. Our new mother says now that the most amusing aspect of rearing identical girls was witnessing how we enjoyed confusing people. She believes such pleasures, as long as they are not carried to extremes, are the birthright of identical twins. Although separation later presented its trials for my sister and me, we have since progressed into successful individual lives. It was, however, we—and not the world around us—who chose the temporary postponement of our separation, and with good cause.

In a discussion of seriously maladjusted twins, twin expert Dr. Scheinfeld suggests that, in at least one instance, "there might have been more serious effects if they had not had their twinship to give them mutual comfort and security."

Maladjustment is certainly not the rule of twin life, but when it occurs, it receives exceptional attention from all quarters. While this rightly annoys multiples, the scientific reasons for a "twin watch" are valid; twins are the ideal subjects for comparative studies of many sorts. Although twins are no different from singletons in the great majority of ways, they are a different "species within a species," as some scientists put it. This difference very often stems from the particular social and psychological pressures they face. Consequently, they live through intense and continuing riddles which are unique to twins and which medical experts are just beginning to trace.

The Couple Effect

According to psychologist Rene Zazzo of the University of Paris, the biological roots of the "twin situation" need to be examined in light of: (1) the course of intrauterine life, including prenatal characteristics and risks overcome; (2) lifelong health patterns; and (3) long-range psychological and sociological formations, as well as family relationships and career developments. This mammoth undertaking is progressing through the work of many scientists around the world, thanks in large measure to the impetus provided by the formation in Rome, in 1974, of the International Society of Twin Studies. "As a matter of fact," says Zazzo, "twin psychology opens a new way to science." He notes that the twin pattern may serve as a paradigm for a study of what he calls "the couple effect" in all human relationships. The question Zazzo poses is: How does a couple's life and relationship with others determine psychic facts which heredity and general environment can't explain? By studying couple relationships of twins, Zazzo hopes to answer this question for all couples, twin or not. "In traditional methods, like Galton's and Gesell's," he says, "the twin partners were treated as *a double*, one same individual in two copies, but never as *a couple*." Then, eventually, others began to see that the twin couple's notion of *ourselves* came before their notion of *self*. "The conscience of the self" Zazzo says, "and the conscience of others form jointly and severally." More recently, studies of these primary attachments have allowed psychologists to set up tests to explore the effect on twin pairs of being a couple.

In the case of twins, this "couple effect" may actually inhibit the expression of hereditary personality traits, a likelihood suggested by the fact that twins reared apart often show more psychological similarity than those who grew up together in one household.

"Only a few of the remarkable peculiarities of twins' development are known for sure," Zazzo notes, "such as a delayed intellectual development, language retardation (with frequent special language development in its place), difficulties related to fragile self-consciousness and reduced sociability." He laments that psychologists have too long ignored the richness of clinical material available from twin study.

In the 1950s, Zazzo focused on such things as introversion/extroversion and timidity among twins. He looked at the restraints and social pressures on twin pairs by comparing identical twins, fraternal twins and single children. One result of these tests was the discovery that some singleton brothers, regarded as a bit backward socially, formed a tight couple and acted like twins. In a study of bisexed pairs, he found that the female of the pair was usually the dominant one. He reasoned that this role was established in very early childhood because the female was more socially mature. She tended to hold on to this dominance throughout her life.

Zazzo's investigation of the "couple effect" marks a change in the direction of his inquiries into twin psychology. This shift came about when he discovered that twins generally displayed a problem in respect to marriage. "In 1952," he reports, "I was Gesell's disciple and was very busy with twins' childhood, with the evolution of their intellectual capacities, with the classical questions of the relations between heredity and environment, maturation and learning." Suddenly, as it will for scientists in search of elusive answers, new light broke. As the longtime friend and confidant of more than one hundred twins, Zazzo began hearing them confess that they were, in one fashion or another, particularly disturbed when one of their pair decided to marry and thus break up the duo. The ways in which they described their dismay or concern, as well as the repetition of the stories from pair to pair, told Zazzo there might be something unique to twins here. These twin pairs had suffered and accepted and, in most cases, enjoyed their resemblance to each other, benefiting, too, from the perks that came from being something special in the eyes of society. All were to some degree dependent on each other in social situations. Along with that dependence, however, had grown an increasing need for a true sense of their individual selves. The symbol of release was seen as the ability to form strong, outside attachments, marriage being the strongest of all. The need for independence evolved gradually along parallel lines and had to struggle— almost as twins in the womb struggle physically, Zazzo thought—with the dependence on a firmly established, more or less satisfactory twin relationship.

Sensing the special quality of this struggle, Zazzo knew he was at the frontier of something big, something that would in time reveal much, in particular, about the nature of identical twins. He put aside his earlier research and embarked upon a tedious examination of birth and marriage records at a certain registry office in Paris. His quest was for twins of marrying age. He wanted to know the nuptiality rate among the pairs.

It was thought by Sir Francis Galton—who led the way for the use of twins in scientific research a century ago—and by his followers for some time after, that "twins do not marry so frequently as other people . . . I think they are less fertile." (How this view sharply contradicts the legends and myths in which twins so often appear as gods or goddesses of fertility!) Zazzo does not share this belief. "Nothing has ever proved that twins are less fertile, nor that there could be some relation between fertility and nuptiality," he says. On the face of it, his objections appear well taken. In how many cultures is it ever routine to test fertility *before* marriage?

His investigations to date have convinced Zazzo that the marriage rate among twins is psychologically determined. One study he cites shows the following rates of celibacy: 15 percent of male twins in opposite-sexed couples (fraternal twins); 25 percent of male twins in same-sexed couples (identical twins); 46 percent of female twins of opposite-sexed couples (fraternal twins); 47 percent of female twins in same-sexed couples (identical twins). In the population at large, 16 percent of all males and 26 percent of all females remain unmarried.

This much can be drawn from these statistics. Twins seem to have a higher level of hostility or at least indifference to marriage than singletons. What remain to be worked out, however, are the reasons for the hostility or indifference. Future studies of the divorce rate among

twins will be scanned for evidence of resentment of the intrusion that has "split up the twin pair relationship."

The subject of twins and marriage offers researchers
other interesting material for debate. Why do we choose the
mate we do? Or why are we chosen by our mates? Either
way it is put, the question of how random the choice may
be is a fascinating one. Apparently, there are both genetic
and environmental forces at work when a woman tells her
best friend, "Oh, I've just met the man of my dreams. He's
Mr. Right!" It turns out that it is not entirely a matter of
"free will" when a man gets up his nerve to propose to the
woman he's decided is for him.

Dr. W. E. Nance and his associates at the Medical College in Richmond, Virginia, have been looking into the
matter. Dr. Nance's investigations show that in some cases,
people may choose a mate most like themselves, while
others may pick a partner at random or even someone who
is least like themselves in environmental background or
genetic inheritance. However, in 1980 at the Third International Congress on Twin Studies, he reported on a study
he had conducted of twin marriages that attempted to determine how non-random the mating may have been. The
study involved 119 pairs of twins and their spouses; of
these, 72 twin pairs were females and 47 twin pairs were
males. For each trait examined, the material was partitioned
into four subdivisions: correlation between husband and
wife, correlation between a twin and the spouse of a co-
twin, correlation between both spouses of the twins and
correlation between each twin in a pair. Height as well as
verbal skill and vocabulary were some traits investigated in
this manner. "The factors which influence non-random
mating," says Nance, "may differ by sex." What he discovered was "a substantially higher correlation" among spouses
of male twin pairs than of the female twin pairs. In other
words, the male twins showed a stronger tendency than

did the females to choose spouses with backgrounds and physical traits similar to theirs. If this pattern holds for all males and females, twins or not, it certainly puts a melancholy light on our chances of finding what we want in marriage.

Twin expert Dr. Luigi Gedda also looks to twin marriages as an index of the greatest importance in any examination of the problem of individual development in twins. Far from believing solely in biological determinism regarding twins' development, Dr. Gedda stresses the importance of an individual's conscious effort, and how that may influence every marriage and its outcome. "It sometimes happens," he says, "that two identical twin brothers marry two identical twin sisters, but it is more usual for the identical twin brothers to marry women born singly in different families. In the majority of cases, the choice involved is *absolutely individual* [my italics] and does not raise any problems. Cases of marital competition—that is, two twin brothers who court the same woman—are exceptional and attract attention precisely because they are so rare. I know of no cases of the wife of a twin leaving him for his twin brother."

Nevertheless, there are instances in which a woman married to a twin has, on her husband's death, married his twin brother. During the Second World War, the widow of a jet pilot shot down over England did just that. Her husband, Charley, was at the controls of one plane in a squadron of F-84 Thunderjets, and his twin brother, Fred, was flying another. Suddenly there was a collision with another plane, a British Meteor hurtling out of control. Fred saw Charley's jet fall to the ground. The trauma was one Fred would never forget. The widow and the remaining twin, who had been the closest of friends when Charley was alive, turned to each other in their grief. Eventually, they married one another. "He's exactly like my first husband. We know it's the way Charley would want it to be," the widow told a reporter.

In *Gone with the Wind*, a pair of male twins love the same woman. In fact, they aren't content until they do. Brent and Stuart both fall in love with Scarlett O'Hara. As author Margaret Mitchell told it, "Just what the loser would do, should Scarlett accept either of them, the twins did not ask. They would cross that bridge when they came to it. For the present they were quite satisfied to be in accord again about one girl, for they had no jealousies between them."

A twin replaced her sister at the altar in Galveston, Texas, in 1939. Albert Kamens arrived in that Gulf town to marry Madeline Shamblin. Instead, he married her twin, Pauline. The bride's retort: "Well, my sister intended to marry him, but she changed her mind. So I married him instead."

Competition and confusion can invade a marriage to twins, as Mary Jane Swank and Margaret Jean Swank, a pair of dancers, found out. In 1937, a newspaper report told of a suit for annulment brought by Mary Jane against her husband, Harry Brown Cook III, scion of a wealthy Pennsylvania family. "It got so bad that none of us knew who was married to whom," she told the court. "He would come home and embrace Margaret Jean and ignore me completely."

One pair who apparently settled their marital difficulties in a way that satisfied all concerned were Willard and John Nichols and their wives, Eleanor and Mary. Both laborers in Missoula, Montana, Willard and John decided that they liked each other's wife best. The solution—they divorced and switched.

Marriage to a twin, for a singleton, unquestionably takes a special kind of understanding. Some have learned this to their dismay—and then gone on to make the best of a situation with unique opportunities as well as unique pitfalls.

The necessary understanding need not be ready-made before the marriage—twins need not wear a warning label: MAY BE HAZARDOUS TO MARITAL HEALTH— but it might be well for singletons to head into such a marriage with a checklist in hand, so that the areas of potential friction can be anticipated.

Are you ever jealous of your husband's twin brother? Do you believe that he has a part of your husband you can never possess or knows his brother in some ways you will never know? Have your wife and her twin sister developed habits of manipulating others to satisfy their private competitions and jealousies? Are you prepared to accept the fact that your spouse's twin may make subconscious emotional demands on you since you have married her twin partner? Between any members in a marriage, there may be problems of dominance and submission. When one marries an identical twin, however, such problems may become aggravated. One twin expert was told the story of a woman whose husband, a secondborn twin, married before his brother. The wife was troubled by the suspicion that the elder twin was still resentful of her, even after a number of years, for splitting the pair.

"I'm sure there's not a husband or wife—any singleton spouse of a twin—who hasn't had a glimpse of this at one time or another," says twin expert Donald Keith, referring to the intrusion of the twin into marriage. "The uninvited guest, a twin, comes and camps on the wife's doorstep, and the twin brother doesn't say, 'No, we're doing something else this holiday and you can't come.' Or the paths of twin brothers cross accidentally, and the wife feels, 'Oh no, can't I ever get away from this guy?'—her brother-in-law." Even Keith's wife, Phyllis, and Gail, wife of his twin brother, admit there have been rare occasions, however brief, when such twinges about their spouses' twin relationship occurred.

The habit of relying on a twin relationship often leads a twin, even subconsciously, to try to "twin" with others important to him or her. Neither the twin nor the singleton partner is quite aware at first of what is happening. This was apparently true in my own case; in the early days of my marriage, I heard my husband plead on several occasions, "I'm *not* your twin. Don't expect me to guess what is in your mind." Eventually, I realized that I was blindly expecting from him some of the synchrony of moods and enthusiasms I had long shared with my sister. He claims, without wanting to, I was falling back on emotional strategies I had learned in the twin relationship. I know it took a monumental effort to come to expect entirely different responses from my new partner.

The Quaternary Marriage

Twin marriages may have their frictions, but what marriages do not? Don't singletons also have bothersome brothers-in-law? Marriage to a twin, however, may also have some extraordinary assets that enrich what Dr. Zazzo called the "couple effect." To see what these may be, it's worth looking at the so-called "quaternary marriages"—those in which twins marry twins.

Researchers examining quaternary marriages stress the remarkable ability of members of such unions to withstand ever-increasing economic pressures and the problems of child rearing in contemporary society. These twin couples who marry other twin couples form natural communes, often living in the same or adjacent houses, sharing responsibilities, expenses and child care. Their divorce rate is far below that of the general population.

Those who have studied such twin-twin marriages believe that they may provide guidelines for other coupling arrangements. For instance, in the case of best friends marrying best friends, there may be potential for a type of quaternary relationship characterized by community of interest, values and personal affection.

Lois and Louise Coats married Roy and Ray Sebring, twin U. S. Marines, twice. The first time the marriages didn't take, and the couples divorced. Then, after a matter of months, all four decided that it was better to be married, and they went through the ceremony a second time.

Two sets of twins who are generating some excitement among researchers are those known as the Richmond "4." On June 5, 1976, LaVona and LaVelda Rowe married Alwin and Arthur Richmond in a ceremony that began to double many genetic and psychological elements in their already double lives. Everything about the ceremony was double: twin bridesmaids and best men, twins at the guest book, twins at the organ, twins in the audience, twins everywhere. In the wedding party itself, there were five pairs of identical twins. Naturally, there were two wedding cakes connected by a bridge. The Rowes, it seems, had had a premonition that things would turn out this way. At least they tell how all through their early lives, teachers, friends and even their mother tried to separate them. This produced the opposite effect. "We said, 'Don't worry, Mother, when we grow up, we're going to marry twin brothers and have twin children. Everything will be all right, just wait and see.' " The couples live together in Aurora, Illinois, and travel to all sorts of twin events side by side. They share everything, including a joint bank account, they say. They believe that they are expressing their individuality by *being* twins, since that's what they are, and by doing what they really want, which is to be together.

There are other quaternary marriages scattered throughout history. While these are rare, they seldom surprise twins, since many pairs admit to having longed for another pair of the opposite sex with whom to communicate, at least during early adolescence.

Twins may, in their marriage patterns, offer some novel examples to nontwins. But because of their special embodiment of the "couple effect," they may also be pioneers in the I-Thou relations that we all face in a lifetime. Twins must achieve self-differentiation without betraying the values of a deep-rooted partnership. As psychologists stress, every human must complete some processes before there is an adequate realization of the self. An infant's sense of himself comes bit by bit as he learns who is mother, who is father, who the strangers are—all distinguished from himself. The process of inclusion, exclusion and discrimination is a gradual one. In adolescence, there must be further concentrated effort to learn who one is by experimenting with relations to others, especially those of the opposite sex. There is a special cushion for twins during the years when self-differentiation is most important. Unlike singletons, they need not get involved in relationships just for company, or confuse sex and love in attempts to alleviate loneliness and fear.

On the other hand, the gropings toward others can be rendered more hazardous because the shocks come with less preparation and may also double up. I have my own traumas. I also feel my sister's. Often, it's harder to deal with hers because I have little control over them; there's so little I can do. Yet those who overcome such traumas can serve as models for others less severely challenged.

The Invisible Ligature

All identical twins narrowly missed being born attached to one another, as are "Siamese" or conjoined twins. "Siamese" twin births are statistically rare, true, but every identical has escaped this fate by still unexplained luck in timing. The thought of that narrow miss may well make twins shudder. Indeed, such a possibility is the stuff of twin nightmares.

Even those who do not reflect upon the chance of such a thing, however, frequently and naturally conjure up the image of "Siamese" twins to attempt to explain the psychological ties that link them to their partners. One of these ties (and many investigators have noticed a higher incidence of it among twins than among singletons) is Extrasensory Perception (ESP).

At first, it might seem all fun and games to have such power. How jolly to chat with your twin on a communication system no one can bug! What a saving on the phone bill! One has to remember, however, that much of what is transmitted between partners through ESP is shared pain and sometimes crippling anxiety. Many of the tales suggesting a telepathic capacity linking identicals describe tragic events. Dr. Louis Keith of Northwestern University was called as an expert witness when Martha Burke of California attempted to sue an airline for the pain and damage she suffered when her twin sister died thousands of miles away. Her twin was a passenger on one of the Boeing 747s that collided on the runway at Tenerife in the Canary Islands in 1977. According to Mrs. Burke's testimony, at the exact moment of the tragic collision she felt a great burning sensation in her breast and abdomen. She felt as if she had been cut in two.

In the litigation that followed, Dr. Keith went so far as to say that the constitution of twins could permit "the transmission over some distance of a complete image and, at the extreme, go as far as the simultaneous perception of a painful sensation." The federal judge who heard Mrs. Burke's complaint that she had suffered long-term damage in her own person from the plane accident refused to grant her damages, but he did not refute her claim. He merely pointed out that American law does not recognize this class of injury.

Just before he died in Heapham, England, Percy Black remarked, "I feel something is wrong at Sheffield." He was right. His twin brother Cecil had collapsed and died at his club in Sheffield earlier the same day.

Another setting, this time Indiana. The father of twin girls testified to the "sixth-sense qualities" of his daughters. Once, they had decided to go to a local carnival on alternate nights. On the night Della went, Stella was at home, ironing clothes. At one point, she carelessly burned her hand with the iron. At the same instant, she felt a cloud of terror, followed by dizziness and nausea. Overcoming this, she walked as fast as she could to the carnival grounds, feeling herself drawn there by something she could not explain. When she arrived, she discovered that the Ferris wheel was stalled and her terrified twin sister was swaying back and forth in the car at the top. Della was finally rescued. She rushed to her sister, hugged her and said, "You burned yourself again! Won't you ever learn how to iron?" There is no easily comprehensible way that Della could have known what her sister was up to while she was gone, for the girls had not discussed Stella's plan to iron clothes. What also defies explanation is how Stella knew that there had been an accident on the Ferris wheel.

It is possible to see how the "message" about Della's peril may have come in two or more phases. First, the "accident" with the iron may have signaled that *something* was wrong. Next, intuition may have been extended to become a conviction that the trouble involved her sister. Finally, the specifics were possibly supplied by third parties on the carnival grounds who knew about the difficulties with the Ferris wheel. To make such qualifications, however, is not to deny the reality of telepathic communication but to rationalize it as much as possible. By demystifying the process, we learn more about the whole network of codes, customs and "shorthand" verbal and nonverbal systems laced through the world of twins, whether or not they claim to have had experiences such as these.

Fortunately, there is a lighter side to some of the tales involving twins and their special forms of communication. In his book *My Twin Joe*, Judge Crail describes how he and his twin brother wrote such similar examination papers that the teachers separated them for the next such exam. Nevertheless, the twins' papers in Latin used the same words and the same grammar. They even made the same mistakes. At the start of the exam, one twin had felt unable to begin writing and could not explain why. It turned out that his brother in the other room had also been delayed, due to an administrative mix-up. When the snafu was disentangled, both men began writing at the same time. Is it any wonder that the astonished teachers were mystified?

My sister and I well remember the sense of injustice we felt when, after writing identical examination papers while across a school room, we received a note from the instructor saying, "Well, I guess two heads *are* better than one!"

The death of one twin leaves a surviving partner, who usually must face an agonizing period of readjustment. In some extreme cases, the survivor may not fully realize which twin has died. After the funeral of her twin, one woman complained of a weird feeling when she looked in the mirror. Was she not seeing her dead sister instead of herself? If she was, was it not she herself who was dead? Thinking that the shock was transient and temporary, her doctor gave her sedatives to get her over the pain of bereavement, but in the months ahead, her condition worsened; and always when she looked in the mirror, the worst spasms ripped at her body. Eventually, she had to be sent to a mental-health clinic. There, a physical examination disclosed that she had extra blood veins in the back of her skull. This correlated strangely with the fact that her twin had had a similar abnormality and had died of a stroke. However, the survivor's blood pressure and other vital signs were normal. Her problems were diagnosed as primarily psychological. The psychiatrist continually instructed her: "When you look in the mirror, call yourself by your name and not your sister's." Therapy finally helped, but even so, the doctors were not convinced that they had thoroughly solved the mystery. This twin's predicament has as a precedent the little-known story of Narcissus, who was in love with his twin sister. The sister dies. Narcissus consoles himself by gazing at his reflection in the pool, imagining it that of his beloved sister. Over and over, I heard from twins that their relationship with their twin was generally so satisfying that the one burden it put upon them was the inability to contemplate happily being alone for any period of time. The thought of losing their twin to death was particularly unnerving.

Knowing that your twin is about to call, knowing when the telephone rings what she has to tell you, knowing that whatever has happened to her is an event you will in some way share or even repeat—just what is this shared awareness called ESP?

Emphasizing a sort of primal psychic level, Freud went so far as to suggest that ESP might be a sort of leftover trace of ways in which all individuals communicated once, long ago. In his book *The Intelligent Eye*, R. L. Gregory observed, "In the evolution of life the first senses must have been those which monitor physical conditions which are immediately important for survival. Touch, taste and temperature senses must have developed before eyes: for visual patterns are only important when interpreted in terms of the world of objects . . . this requires an elaborate nervous system . . . if behavior is controlled by belief in what the object is rather than directly by sensory input." Both

Freud and Gregory are talking about a possible—but still controversial—notion, a hen-and-egg type question. Which came first, the eye or the brain? They are talking about something that predates the invention of signs, systems and languages—something that did not need any of the technology we possess today in order to communicate messages. When people are in a state of relaxation, at the threshold of sleep, say—or on the contrary, when they are so highly stimulated by some critical or traumatic situation that what they normally see is suppressed—they may be much more highly sensitive to these nonverbal transmissions. We are all familiar with the hypersensitivity produced by adrenaline in times of emergency. Children often seem to have psychic capacities until, usually, they are trained not to credit them, to give such notions up for more "adult" responses and behavior. People whose emotional lives are very similar or who have shared certain highly charged emotional experiences are, understandably, more likely to report ESP communications than are strangers of contrasting temperament.

Scientists generally agree that identical twins have the closest possible human relationship. Identicals are, therefore, particularly attractive to researchers who study ESP. In the Canadian city of Saskatoon, Dr. Robert Sommer and his associates experimented with thirty-five twins, fourteen pairs and seven who came in alone. At least one-third of these could report paranormal telepathy shared with their partner. They were, as one might expect, the ones who most conspicuously shared interests and abilities. Twenty-seven items in the test run by the Canadians demonstrated, under laboratory conditions, the twins' ability to "pass thoughts," either by pure telekinetic means or by codes imperceptible to the examiners.

Drs. Thomas Duane and Thomas Behrendt, ophthalmologists at Jefferson Medical College in Philadelphia, found two sets of identical twins with a sort of electronic

ESP. The physicians were exploring a phenomenon called photic driving. When a light is flashed on and off seventeen times a second, it causes, in a few people, a change in brain wave patterns. With the twins in question, however, when one twin brother closed his eyes, the other twin's brain waves changed as if he, too, had closed his eyes. The doctors claimed they had no idea how to explain this uncanny reaction.

Basic tests for ESP developed by Dr. J. B. Rhine of Duke University involve the identification of cards laid out face-down. In refining these tests to meet every conceivable criticism, the researchers administering them were careful to exclude any sort of hunting or coding—nonverbal sounds, body gestures, patterns of repetition in the dealing of the cards and so on—that might have tipped the subject.

Those who study twins are as interested in the whole range of nonverbal codings as they are in the so-called pure ESP. Such things as extraordinary sensitivity to timing (as displayed by the Chaplins in England), pace of breath, nuances of expression imperceptible to ordinary observation—all are common enough in the lives of highly sensitive twins.

No one knows for sure yet how thought transfers and other forms of ESP take place, but laboratory findings so far support and confirm what twins and their families have long been dealing with on a day-to-day basis. Parents who have tried conscientiously to guide their twins into separate activities report: "We wondered why Helen and Harriet wouldn't write to each other when Helen was away at summer camp. It turned out they didn't feel they needed to. When Helen won the canoe race, Harriet told me about it before Helen called to do so." "Maury knew that Mike flunked his chemistry test, though they were in different colleges two hundred miles apart. He drove over to cheer his brother up without talking to Mike first." "Edith and

Eleanor both arrived at the hospital at the same time when Eleanor's son was hurt in a car accident, though Eleanor hadn't been able to reach Edith by phone to tell her about it."

Twins are in some ways rather like mountain climbers roped together. If one loses his grip and begins to fall, he may take the other down with him, but it is more likely that the one who keeps his footing remains a firm anchor for the endangered one.

Even in the grim story of the Marcus brothers, there was an occasion on which their twin telepathy may have temporarily postponed the tragedy that eventually overtook them. Once, the superintendent in Cyril's apartment building became alarmed because Cyril hadn't been seen and didn't respond to repeated knocks on the door, and he phoned Cyril's twin, Stewart. "I think your brother needs help," he said. There was a long silence. Stewart seemed to be listening to another sort of communication. Then, amazingly, he replied, "Yes, you're right. He does need help. I'll be right over." Fortunately, the "message" didn't come too late. Rescuers forced their way into the locked apartment and found Cyril unconscious. They were able to summon an ambulance in time to save his life.

The Private Languages of Twins

As we have seen, the glare of the spotlight often has a negative effect on young twins venturing into the outside world. When the Kennedy twins were old enough to start school in the mid-seventies, they experienced the much too common reaction to pairs—they were quickly classified as "mentally retarded." Shocked as they were, their parents weren't entirely surprised. The girls had been a puzzle and a worry ever since their birth. They had been kept for a long time in the hospital for observation of unexplained seizures. At that time, the physicians had warned their parents that the girls might be retarded for life.

At about the time other children learn to say "Daddy" and "Mommy," the twins began to babble at each other. The sounds they made only vaguely resembled human speech. Their "words," intelligible to no one but them, might as well have come from the Martians. With Gracie leading and Ginny following, the twins' vocabulary grew. In their own language, they named the things around them in the house, chattering volubly with each other. In order to communicate with their parents and grandmother, they used a few English or German words—their grandmother spoke German exclusively—and a variety of nonverbal signals, the way any of us communicates our basic needs when confronted with a totally foreign language.

The parents had troubles of their own, so for a while they simply endured, ignoring the twins' language "problem." When the girls went to school, however, the problem came to the attention of school authorities and could be ignored no longer. Poto and Cabengo—the girls' names for each other—were the marvel of the neighborhood, as much for their extraterrestrial language as for their lively cuteness.

The first specialists who examined them called the Kennedy twins TMRs—Trainable Mentally Retardeds. The best that could be done for them, they said, was to send them to a school for retarded children and to train them in sign language. Once in the school, however, the twins showed a touch of genius by learning so fast. This startled their teachers into recommending further examination. At last they were seen by specialists in speech pathology, who recognized the twins' specific problem.

For an outsider, the Kennedy twins' language may

sound like a combination of Cockney, slang, baby talk and passages from *Finnegan's Wake*. At least one wonders what James Joyce would think of their babble. Now, as experts patiently analyze tapes made of the Kennedy girls' conversations, they are finding that the speech consists in part of German words, with about as many English words or sounds, and a very great many phonological coinages— substitutions of sound in patterns that are fundamentally like the English and German that the children have heard from their elders. Their sentences seem to have syntax, tenses, qualifiers and other parts of speech needed to make their meanings clear, at least to each other. Whether they *invented* the syntax and other refinements or *abstracted* them from what they heard around them is the question— and we can only guess at the answer. The Kennedy twins and a few others like them have accelerated scientific interest in idioglossia (sometimes called cryptophasia), the private languages that many twins develop to communicate with each other, at least for a limited time. Estimates show that nearly 40 percent of twins have their own private language, but to date no concentrated study has focused on this peculiar aspect of their lives.

"Cabengo, padem manibadu peetu."

"Pinit, Poto."

Twins everywhere may agree that that *could* mean: "Look out, the grown-ups are after us again."

Many identicals report that they vaguely remember having had a "twin language" as young children. Some, like Dorothy and Deane Foltz or the Flori pair, even remember a few words. (Interestingly, the Foltz women had private names for each other, both ending in the letters *us*. Another tantalizing echo of a twin's penchant for finding magical meaning in these letters and sounds is found in Peter Shaffer's play *Equus*, discussed previously. As this twin playwright put it, the mother of the principal character, Alan, reported that the boy became fascinated with the word equus "because he'd never come across one with two u's together before." Tell twins that story and they generally become as fascinated as was Alan.

While idioglossia remains the most spectacular illustration of some twins' problems of communication with the singleton world, there are others. Studies by Dr. Gabriel Levi and Dr. P. Bernabei of the University of Rome, presented at the First International Congress of Twin Studies, brought to light two afflictions that twins may experience regarding language. In the first, only one partner of a pair displayed difficulty in understanding or expressing himself, while the other was quite normal. In the second case, both twins were afflicted with the same form of language disorder. But in both of these instances, the doctors found no tendency for the twin pairs to use their own special language between them. Instead, the pairs talked considerably less to each other than the observers would have expected from "what is considered normal for the twin condition," as the doctors put it. These twins preferred to communicate verbally and nonverbally with adults or other children, nearly ignoring each other.

In the case of the Kennedy duo, tutors have tried to learn and use the twins' special language, but Gracie and Ginny have not cooperated. It is as if they think no one has a right to their language but its inventors. Other twins, looking back to the time when they relied on their special words, say that they felt the same need for secrecy.

Since idioglossia is, to some extent, a matter of habit and choice, its basis may not be entirely genetic. Twins learn through habit to complete each other's sentences, whether they compose a separate language or not, and whether they complete them aloud or not. Repeatedly, they will tell baffled outsiders that this is standard procedure in their lives.

Any serious study of idioglossia will consider how human pairs transfer awareness, since all forms of language are involved with other types of codes. A syllable may be expressive, but so is a wink, a grimace, a nudge or a poignant silence. As we habitually adapt to the personality of another, our spoken words get mixed into a potpourri of other means of communication. We all see how this works with two people in a tightly knit marriage or a pair of astronauts confined together on a long mission—or with a pair of twins. Now Ginny and Gracie Kennedy are patiently being taught to replace their exotic language with standard English. This is necessary, of course, for the sake of their schooling, but one cannot help but wonder what treasures, not to mention pleasures, will be lost in the transformation. Since language structures are inseparable from thought, what equally precious secrets of their twin relationship may be lost when they and others give up their language for the more practical tongue of their parents?

7. Twins Reared Apart
and the Bonds They Keep

Somebody was looking for him. For nineteen years the unusual search had been going on, but he hadn't known about it. Not, that is, until the first days at college.

Robert Shafran was a freshman, and all freshmen have a feeling of strangeness. A new phase of their lives has begun; often they are far from home; disorientation is part of the deal. Shafran felt his share as he walked out among the upper classmen at Sullivan County Community College in upstate New York, but he wasn't worried. He was an exceptionally bright young man. He was energetic and talkative. He had had his troubles. Now things were getting better. Most of all, his persistent sense of something missing in himself made him one of those people who strike up friendships actively, then quickly deepen them.

Still, for Robert Shafran, the strangeness of new surroundings was to develop with astounding swiftness into something more bizarre than his wildest fantasies. His easy and ready friendliness received disproportionate responses. It kept happening all day. Young men and women he had never seen before came on like best buddies. They hugged him, clapped him on the back and wanted to hear all about his summer vacation. The guys said things like, "You still dating the same chicks, Eddy?" That one threw him a bit. It just so happened that he was here in upstate New York in hopes of meeting new chicks, but his name wasn't Eddy!

When he pointed this out to his welcomers, they came back, "Sure. Same old Eddy. Anything for a laugh!"

Naturally, Robert Shafran thought he was being conned. Someone was playing freshman games, no doubt. But if this was the way things were done at college, he'd play along—at least up to a point. Then the get-this-freshman joke reached uncanny proportions. Was the whole student body in on it? He made some attempts to squelch it by producing his identification from his wallet. For a while this had an effect. People walked away confused but unconvinced—which only deepened the mystery for him and those who took him seriously.

Finally, a student named Michael Dobnitz began to ask the right questions. Had Bobby Shafran been adopted as an infant? Yes, by a Scarsdale doctor and his wife. Did he know where he had been born? Bobby did. At the Long Island Jewish-Hillside Medical Center. Did he, by chance, have a twin brother? Not, Bobby mumbled as the light began to dawn, to his knowledge. Suddenly, the lifelong intuitions of "something missing" in his situation came flooding back.

Dobnitz produced a photograph of his best friend Eddy

Galland. Eddy had been a student at Sullivan County Community College last year—and his face was unmistakably that of Bobby Shafran.

A photograph, however striking the resemblance, is not conclusive evidence, but this one was powerful enough. Bobby and Dobnitz made a phone call. Bobby said, the tremors in his voice quite audible, "Eddy, I think you're my twin brother." That phone call out of the night was not quite the total surprise to Eddy that it might have been. For the last few days, he had been hearing from friends on the Sullivan campus that someone up there was doing a great job of impersonating him. He had begun to wonder what was up.

Then came the midnight ride. Dobnitz and Bobby drove directly to the Galland home in New Hyde Park. When the door opened and the brothers saw each other face to face, any lingering doubts vanished. Not only were they alike in features and physique, their manners and even the way they greeted each other were a perfect match.

In the days that followed, while the brothers caught up frenetically on the nineteen years they had spent apart, a number of other singular resemblances surfaced: each had flunked fifth-grade math; each had undergone psychiatric counseling for mental disturbances; in each situation, the consultants had advised them that their problems stemmed from the fact of their adoption; they were both wrestlers with almost identical records in the sport; their tastes . . . you guessed it.

Up to this point, the story is certainly newsworthy, the stuff of headlines. Naturally, it was reported in the New York papers. The story was fascinating—twins who had found each other—but it wasn't the first time this had happened. It was just the latest—and very interesting—incidence of the phenomenon. Then the newspaper photograph of Bobby and Eddy came into the hands of a nineteen-

year-old student at Queens College named David Kellman. The revelation was to make medical history. David
Kellman, too, had lived his nineteen years with a sense of
something missing. Flunked fifth-grade math. Received
psychiatric counseling. Enjoyed wrestling . . . He showed
the newspaper photographs to his mother. "Mother, you're
not going to believe this. . . ." And why should she? It was
just too farfetched. But she did; and presently so did the
rest of the astonished world. The boys passed from notoriety into the annals of scientific research because they were
identical triplets separated at birth.

Identical twins who have lived entirely separated lives
present to researchers the best possible "human laboratory"
for the study of the differing influences of "nature" and
"nurture" in human lives. For the first time in recorded
medical history, identical triplets who were separated
shortly after birth and who grew up knowing nothing
about the others' existence were finally introduced to each
other.

According to some experts, the chances of identical
triplets being born are twenty-one in a million. Even so,
those births may cluster in certain generations since experts
report they know of many such living triplets. That these
triplets would also fall into the classification of multiples
reared apart is far rarer still.

Spectacular as the found-triplets story is, however, the
medical implications may be somewhat less valuable than
the personal ones. The very rarity of their case stands in
the way of an attempt to sort out the different influences
of heredity and environment, since scientists like to have
as large a sample of case histories as possible in order to
prove their theories.

Twins are fascinating, but more fascinating yet is the
study of identical twins reared apart. They are referred
to by the medical profession as MZA's: identical twins
(MZ) reared apart (A). In many cases, these MZA's tell—

sometimes long before they learn they have a twin—of having had that sixth sense of "someone else out there just like" themselves, or of being "special" without knowing why. The message in one twin's psychic "inner ear" has often been duplicated in the other's. Moreover, that message is often whispered at approximately the same time or under similar circumstances.

Pioneers in this field of research, seeking to solve the age-old question of the influences of heredity and environment, to date have had 121 pairs of MZA's to study, scattered throughout the Western world. The three major studies in the field were conducted first, in 1937, by H. H. Newman, F. N. Freeman and K. J. Holzinger in the United States; then, in 1962, by James Shields in England; and lastly, in 1965, by Niels Juel-Nielsen in Denmark.

One of the first scientific reports on twins reared apart, however, was made in 1922 by P. Popenoe. It outlined the lives of one set of twins—Bessie and Jessie. When Bessie and Jessie were two weeks old, their mother became ill. As a result, the twins were separated "temporarily." The mother died when they were eight months old, and the pair was then separated "permanently." The women wrote to each other occasionally from the age of eighteen and had three brief meetings when they were eighteen, twenty and twenty-four. Although one had only four years of formal schooling and the other completed high school and took some advanced courses as well, both had high IQ's; their scores were only three points apart. Like many twins, reared together or apart, these women had histories of illness so similar that they were noted by Popenoe. Both had tuberculosis, and the onset of attacks in one was synchronous with those in the other; one twin was reported to have suffered a nervous breakdown, the other one nearly did—again at approximately the same time. Their moods were nearly identical.

Popenoe's brief paper about the twins, and two fol-

low-up studies of the material by H. J. Muller in 1925 and
Robert Saudek in 1935, have established the criteria to be
used in later investigations of similarities between MZA's.
The studies took note of the pair's physical likenesses and
mental capacities, as well as the influence of the twin relationship on the individual women. Some researchers who
later analyzed the story of Bessie and Jessie believed that
the twins' backgrounds were not all that different. However, there is disagreement of some magnitude on this score.
Geneticist Muller, for instance, found that in some ways
the women were no more alike than unrelated singletons.
He believed, however, that this might be linked to less than
adequate personality tests, rather than to true differences
between the twins. Another observation Muller made has
been borne out by later studies of MZA's: The twins
seemed to become more like each other over a period of
time.

Another significant disclosure that appears in the story
of Bessie and Jessie: One of them ultimately married, but
not until after her sister had had an unfortunate love relationship. Thus, a significant degree of psychological closeness between twins reared either together or apart may
stand in the way of their forming other intimate relationships or, on occasion, may spur them on.

Although in most of the early studies of MZA's the twins
were pleased to have discovered each other and generally
got along well, in a few cases there was trauma. Psychologist Niels Juel-Nielsen presented this case: Robert, a quiet,
middle-class draftsman in his mid-forties, wanted desperately to find his lost twin. After finally meeting his
brother Kaj, however, he was gravely disappointed. Although in Robert's eyes he and his brother "resembled each
other in almost every respect," there were strong and
important differences which made him disapprove of his
twin. Kaj, for his part, wouldn't admit to sharing many

similar traits with his twin; those he did accept "were obviously unflattering" to him. To Robert, Kaj was suave
with women, something of a drifter and a hedonistic oppor-
tunist. When the two met, they went through painful
experiences of mutual identification and denial which eventually caused a break between them. Discussing his twin
brother with Juel-Nielsen, Kaj insisted that Robert had
made homosexual advances toward him, which he repulsed.
Although Robert never referred to these moments in the
same way, he did explain that he "always felt absolutely
certain that Kaj was 'the big brother.' " Because of this, he
had attempted to subordinate himself to Kaj from their first
meeting. According to Juel-Nielsen, Kaj "would sit afterwards for hours on end repeating to himself, 'We are
really like each other, but am I really like that?' During
one of the last interviews, he said: 'I hardly know, but
sometimes I am afraid that, in reality, we are much more
alike than I want to believe.' "

Roger Brooks and Tony Milasi, another pair of identicals
reared apart, were reunited in 1963, in their twenty-fourth
year. Their story, told in *The Twins Who Found Each
Other* by Bard Lindeman, repeats many of the dreamlike
details of other separated twins whom researchers have
studied. Before he knew it for sure, Tony believed that he
had a twin "somewhere." Roger as well, many miles away,
got the notion that he "probably was a twin." As the
psychology of twin fantasies would predict, Roger was
unhappy when this notion struck him. He felt the need
to be different, to stand out from the crowd. That was
when he concocted the story for his friends at school that
he was a "separated Siamese twin." To prove it, he showed
them a scar he had had since babyhood. Finally, exasperated
at Roger's unusual behavior, school authorities punished
him by forcing him to study the French horn and to play
in the school band. As the dean wrote in his report to

Roger's foster mother, "French horn players are as scarce here as separated Siamese twins."

Then it turned out that Roger, though not a "Siamese" twin, was indeed a twin who had grown up separated from his brother, Tony. When the two men got together, they were the surprised ones to learn that each, in separate incidents, had received very similar scars on their arms. Although Roger's playacting had turned the scar into the "place where we were cut apart as babies," in some ways it was closer to the truth than the school administrator could ever have imagined.

Their first meeting, predictably, was a dramatic one with which all twins will identify. The brothers had learned of each other's whereabouts through the assistance of social workers. Tony, living in upstate New York, ultimately agreed to visit Roger in Florida, but their reunion was postponed because of conflicting schedules. Finally, all the necessary details were arranged, and Tony, as excited as a child anticipating Christmas, boarded the Florida-bound flight. As Lindeman put it, "The plane rolled to a complete stop at ten-fifty P.M., and . . . Roger Brooks and Tony Milasi now began a game. Each was anxious to see his twin before the twin saw him. . . . Tony stayed in his window seat, having decided he would be one of the last to exit. In this way, he was able to see—and to study—his brother."

Both men were at pains to choose appropriate wearing apparel for this first, crucial meeting. Neither was dressed as he normally would have been, since his choice of clothing was based on what he imagined the other would wear. Tony remembered that his brother looked nervous and a little scared. "I *was* nervous," Roger later admitted, "especially when I didn't see my brother getting off the plane." Tony recalled looking out the aircraft window and spotting Roger. "When I saw my brother in that blazer with the crest and polka-dot ascot, I thought: 'Oh, no!' " Then

Tony descended, and Roger noticed that his brother was wearing dark slacks, a blue shirt with a black tie and a bluish-green tweed sports jacket. "Oh no!" he thought, realizing how wrong his own dress was. As soon as Tony and Roger greeted one another, however, all their anguish disappeared as each told the other about his earlier concern. The remainder of the visit was spent comparing every possible aspect of their separated lives in an effort to make up for lost time.

The Minnesota Project

Jim Lewis and Jim Springer knew that they had been born twins. When they were four weeks old, they were adopted by different families. Jim Springer's adoptive parents believed that his twin had died at birth and told Jim this when he was in his teens. Jim Lewis had survived, however. He learned when he was six that he had a twin brother "somewhere." His mother, Lucille Lewis, encouraged him to look for his twin even when he was very young. For some reason, Jim Lewis put it off. When he was grown and working as a security guard in Lima, Ohio, he began in earnest to look for his lost brother. In 1979, when he was thirty-nine, Lewis spent a month going over court adoption records. Eventually, he discovered that his twin was a records clerk in Dayton, less than one hundred miles away.

One spring evening in 1980, psychologist Thomas J. Bouchard, Jr., picked up his evening newspaper, the *Minneapolis Tribune*, and read about the reunion of the two Jims. The chance to study and to test thoroughly sets of identicals who happened to grow up separately was a rare and valuable one. For ten years, others at the University had been studying twins reared together. They had made in-depth surveys of a multitude of cases. The walls of their offices were peppered with photographs of more than 300 sets of identical twins. Within a few hours, Bouchard had raised the funds necessary to bring the two Jims to Minneapolis for a week. He quickly alerted the team of seventeen researchers in psychology, psychiatry and medicine who would be administering the various tests. The project, the *Minnesota Study of Twins Reared Apart,* includes Irving Gottesman, a behavioral geneticist recognized internationally for his twin studies with an emphasis on schizophrenia; psychologist David Lykken, who has a special interest in the brain waves of twins and the so-called ESP factor between them; and Leonard Heston, who has twin daughters and does the medical evaluations of the MZA's.

Since then, as a result of the publicity given to the two Jims, Bouchard and his colleagues have seen another twenty-eight pairs of twins, four fraternal and twenty-four identical, all of whom have been separated before they were three and were not reunited until they were at least in their late teens. (In every case except one, the separation took place before six months of age.) Out of their encounter with the Jim twins, the Minnesota team developed a standardized procedure for the week's stay in Minneapolis, during which they aim more than 15,000 questions at pairs of twins reared apart.

Scene: A laboratory of the University of Minnesota. Isolated in separate booths—a room apart and unable to see or communicate with each other—are two people who look so alike that no one can tell them apart. Yet these adults, when they aren't being tested for everything from their ambitions to their sex lives, are just now becoming acquainted. On arrival, they have been given fistfuls of instructions and a general rundown of the week ahead: a complete medical history including childhood diseases, complete cardiovascular examinations, a series of allergy tests, extensive pulmonary examinations, a psychophysiological assessment (EEG, or brain waves; EKG, or heart patterns; GSR, or galvanic skin responses); and a number of reaction tests, personality tests, psychological tests and measurements of psychomotor skills. Slumped over desks, chewing on the ends of pencils, gazing out the windows, they answer questions, sit through the medical exams, watch as machines monitor their brain waves and record them in wiggly lines on a screen, briskly stride on treadmills or discuss their phobias—snakes, elevators, enclosed places, bridges and so forth.

I am very slow at making up my mind—true or false?

I am afraid of deep water—true or false?

I prefer being chosen as a target for a knife-throwing attack rather than being sick for twenty-four hours—true or false?

A researcher appears and checks the steadiness of their hands under stress conditions and their eye-hand coordination. There are IQ tests and personality questionnaires: inquiries about reading habits; peculiar table manners; preferences in food and drink, television programs; and many other things. Another day there is a series of mental-agility tests with questions that make the twins giggle. Finally, another examiner appears and takes down more details of their life histories. The researchers find out not only when they had the measles, the mumps, various infections and broken legs. They ask about earliest memories, friends, schooling, vocations, outside interests, likes and dislikes—about almost everything possible. Typical coincidences, turned up during the interrogation of the Lewis-Springer pair, began to establish a pattern for what the project would later discover.

For the record, both Jims had:

Worked as law-enforcement agents, been employed selling McDonald's hamburgers and worked as filling-station attendants.

Married women named Linda, divorced the two Lindas and married women both named Betty.

Spent their holidays at the same 300-yard-long stretch of beach in Saint Petersburg, Florida, after driving there and back in their Chevrolets.

In childhood owned dogs they named Toy.

Grown up with an adopted brother called Larry.

Named their first sons James Alan and James Allan. (One wonders if a gene slipped here to account for the slightly different spellings.)

Hated spelling and loved mathematics in school.

Used the same slang words.

In addition, both have high blood pressure, "lazy eye" in the same eye, the same kind of cluster headaches which turn into full-blown migraines by evening. These headaches started to appear in both men at the age of eighteen. Both use almost identical words when describing the pain that the headaches caused.

During the interview, the cameras roll and a videotape is made. The camera picks up expressions and movements and peculiar actions—such as how the twins smile when they talk, how they slouch when they walk, the unusual way they pull their hair when they are reading a book or the twist of their wrists when they hold a pencil—things that otherwise would be missed in the pencil-and-paper tests. The videotapes verify what many people have recognized about most identical twins reared separately or together—their body language is extremely similar in spite of the fact that they have grown to adulthood apart. Sitting at the desks doing their tests, they will shift, cross their legs, lean back and run fingers through their hair or slump against the chairs when they are tired—in exactly the same manner.

All the coincidences may actually amount to little more than the stuff of newspaper headlines or gossip—until enough of them are tabulated to demonstrate whether or not there are genetic patterns that have initiated them. Although the Minnesota researchers have closely tested, to date, only some twenty-eight pairs of MZA's—a seemingly minute statistical sampling from the estimated 100 million twins (a third of them identicals) now alive— nevertheless, this figure is grander and more startling than it might seem. (The previous largest study, done by Shields, looked at forty-four pairs.) When the Minnesota study is completed, having scrutinized many more pairs, clearly it will be the most comprehensive ever made. Not only that, it is the largest likely to be made. "It may be the last chance," says Bouchard, since, given cultural changes in our society, the separation of twins during adoption proceedings is far less frequent these days.

The Minnesota group did not originally intend to concentrate on the genetic origins of personality traits. Says Bouchard: "I frankly expected many more differences [between twins] than we have found to date." Bouchard, who teaches a course in human individual differences at Minnesota, was, of course, familiar with the work of Newman, Freeman, Holzinger, Shields and Juel-Nielsen, and, having taught such a course, he naturally assumed that genetics influenced *some* things. His interests, however, did not lie either with genetics or with twins per se. "I'm a psychologist, not a geneticist. I want to find out how the environment works to shape psychological traits. But every conceivable trait we've looked at turns up some genetic influence. It doesn't seem to matter what it is."

Therefore, as good scientists should, those in the Minnesota group have conducted their investigations without any preconceived ideas about where the research might lead. Allergies have been studied, and though twin histories are somewhat divergent on this score, an interesting tentative finding is that allergies may be inherited after all.

Some twins in the Minnesota studies smoked, while their partners did not. Yet the condition of the lungs of the smoking twin was found to be *almost identical* with that of the nonsmoker. While this does not suggest that tobacco has no pronounced effect on the human lung, it tends to support the idea that some people may be genetically more resistant to the effects of tobacco.

The headaches that the two Jims experienced held considerable significance for the researchers. Certain kinds of headaches come in cycles and usually follow an intricate pattern. The Jim twins have headaches at the same time of day and the progress of their maladies is the same, suggesting that these, too, could hardly be environmentally based.

The record is not at all clear on the subject of exercise, but it is a fascinating avenue future researchers may well want to explore. Bouchard and his colleagues discovered that one pair of twenty-three-year-old male MZA's, though they were both extremely thin, shunned any kind of exercise. From this fact Bouchard thinks the team may discover that identical twins have a built-in penchant for a certain level of physical exertion—or lack of it. (Could this hark back to their early life in the womb?)

Part of the research efforts of the Minnesota team includes developing new ways to sort out the curious question of zygosity—whether twins are identical or fraternal.

Keith Heitzman and Jake Hellback of Louisiana are another pair the Minnesota group brought to the University for a week of tests. This pair had been adopted by different couples and had grown up on different sides of the Mississippi. They had attended rival high schools and knew nothing of each other's existence, although their adoptive family names were listed *almost side by side* in the New Orleans phone book. Keith was among those separated twins who, for most of his life, had been troubled by vague intuitions of "something missing." When he finally took a look at his birth certificate, he saw why—he had been born a twin. His adoptive mother was unable to give him more than that basic information and suggested he contact Dr. Bouchard in Minneapolis, about whose work she had read. On this occasion, Bouchard and his associates extended their usual services—they offered to help find brother Jake. From that moment on, it was inevitable that the twins would go through the tests.

To see if Keith and Jake were identical, the researchers looked, among other things, at their eyes and earlobes. Similarity of these features, Bouchard says, ranks among the most positive signs of monozygosity. Interestingly, they are the only duo by whom Bouchard himself was momentarily confused; he mistook one for the other during a lunch meeting. The men's brain waves were also monitored. The results confirmed the similarity of their physiology. This objective measurement corresponded to what was perfectly obvious to their acquaintances—the men thought alike. Though they were not familiar with each other's experiences, they tended to do what twins who have been through everything together do—they communicated with unfinished fragments of sentences, confident the other twin would finish the thought.

Although the mighty Mississippi divided these two physically, it could not separate their parallel lives. The welder from one side and the pump mechanic from the other found that they are both allergic to ragweed and dust. Both had done poorly in school. Both disliked sports and had cut their gym classes whenever they could. They are both addicted to candy. Their similarity of dress includes a penchant for wearing cowboy hats, which matches their parallel interest in guns and hunting.

Having noted all these correspondences, Dr. Bouchard turned his attention to what might account for some of the differences between Keith and Jake. They were the first pair to be examined who are, respectively, right-handed and left-handed. This suggested that they might be mirror-image twins and if so might have some—but not necessarily all—of the characteristics of mirror-image pairs. Then again, the difference in handedness might have been the result of childhood conditioning. Many children with a natural disposition to be left-handed have been forced to operate as right-handers. (Frances McLaughlin Gill of the McLaughlin pair, who incidentally was not separated from her twin Kathryn, reports that this happened to her as a child. Now, as an adult, she has returned to using her natural hand—the left one—for many things. As a result, she is ambidextrous, while her twin, Kathryn McLaughlin Abbe, is the born right-hander.)

From IQ tests, the Minnesota team learned some things that were well established by previous twin studies: Regarding intelligence, there is a remarkable similarity between identical twins. The one major discrepancy—between a twin raised in the family of a manual laborer and another raised by a CIA electronics expert—suggests to Dr. Bouchard's team that while environment usually has little effect on IQ, drastic differences in environment may produce drastic discrepancies in intelligence. The point at which the environmental influences on intelligence become critical might be compared to the freezing point in a liquid. Until this point is reached, there is no visible change; after it is passed, there is. Liquid changes to solid. The learning process stagnates.

Since the inheritability of intelligence has been such a fiercely debated subject in psychological research circles—especially since the British psychologist, the late Cyril Burt, was suspected of doctoring his research test results—the

Minnesota Twins-Reared-Apart Project employs outside investigators to administer and score the intelligence tests of the visiting MZA's. Nevertheless, the results of the twins' IQ tests occasionally are more similar than the results of two tests taken by one person at different times.

Bouchard and some of the pairs of twins in his studies have been interviewed widely by the media. One questioner asked the doctor if environment seemed to have anything to do with what we become. The answer, of course, is yes. Said Bouchard, "Our evidence does not exclude environment. There are quite a number of unique environmental effects. Nevertheless, across the broad range of behavior—interests, personality, one's expressive style and movement, general abilities—we do find a tremendous degree of similarity, in spite of the fact that the twins are reared in different homes."

New Emphasis on Heredity

The discovery that heredity seems to exert a somewhat greater influence on us than environment has naturally captured the imagination of many people. However, most doctors seem reluctant to draw final conclusions based on material gathered so far.

Those researchers involved in the three major studies prior to the Minnesota study all mentioned only very tentative theories about the influence of heredity or environment on our lives. Juel-Nielsen, in his 1980 edition of *Individual and Environment*, said, "I have never reached any general conclusion or definitive solution to the nature/ nurture problem." Shields remarked that some of the revelations about twins reared apart are obviously still in doubt when one considers such unexamined factors as possible adult manipulation, as well as economic and psychological conditions surrounding the separation. In some cases he examined, for instance, the twins did not want to get back together or long for their counterpart. Examining the reasons for this more fully, it was clear to Dr. Shields that in at least one case, one twin feared being kidnapped by the family of the other twin, because she had been told by her own adopted family that this would happen to her if the two were to meet.

Psychologist Susan L. Farber recently reviewed all of the published cases of twins reared apart. In Farber's re-analysis, she took pains to classify the twins reared apart into three distinct groups: those "somewhat separated" (that is, some with substantial contact); those with "mixed or occasional contact"; and those who had been "highly separated." In the major studies, 121 sets of twins were involved, but Farber believed that only 95 sets fit enough criteria to offer meaningful information. Of these, 45 were "highly separated," 23 "mixed" and 27 had had "substantial" contact. Three-quarters of the twins in Farber's selection were parted in their first year; one-quarter were considered mirror-image twins; two-thirds were reared by parents or relatives. Almost all were from lower-class families. Most of the sets were female. Only three sets were reared apart in the most conservative sense; that is, with no contact. It is Farber's contention, however, that if there are three sets of twins reared apart per million population, there could be 600 such adult MZA sets in the United States alone who might be available for study in the future.

A number of psychological and behavioral theories may be in for revision as the Minnesota studies continue. So far, these studies have shown that it makes no difference whether children are raised by men or women, since no detectable difference was perceived in twins. Phobias may not be caused by traumas, as practitioners of psychoanalysis have believed. In every case in which a twin reported an irrational fear, that fear was shared by the twin whose early childhood had not been marred by a traumatic experience. Claustrophobia (fear of enclosed places), agoraphobia (fear of open spaces), melissophobia (fear of bees) and the like seem to come to us through some channel of heredity.

Still, the first two might derive from the special closeness of the early moments of a twin relationship. Regarding twins and phobias, although all the phobias vary in degree of seriousness, they are still "remarkably alike," according to Bouchard. One pair of twins, for instance, is almost deathly afraid of escalators. One woman would absolutely never go up on one; the other would, but only with great trepidation. This pair has a whole series of phobias in common. It was true in every case, though, that one twin in a set was slightly less fearful than the other. One wonders if birth order, which sometimes influences the behavior of identical twins, has come into play here. Bouchard rejects the idea, feeling that twins are mixed up at birth more often than commonly supposed. "It's just a guess," he says, "but I'd bet there are many cases in which the parents can't figure out which is which or which was born first. They go back to try to discern birth order through hand- and footprints and such, but many records aren't accurate. Probably a significant proportion of the parents say, 'Forget it,' when the babies are a week or two old. They just decide which one is to be called the oldest from then on. It doesn't make any difference anyway until the children are systematically responding to names." (That is a singleton's response. Many twins do feel that it makes at least a subtle difference all their lives.)

Whatever information is uncovered in the Minnesota studies, however, the researchers seem to have found more uncanny details in the lives of twins. The "wiring diagram" of the genes can account for some coincidences in twins' reactions, but a blind spot remains. There is still no explanation for some of the arcane resemblances of dress and synchroneity of action reported by researchers around the world and well known to twins themselves.

Bridget Harrison and Dorothy Lowe are English twins in their late thirties. At their initial encounter, each woman happened to wear seven rings; each had two bracelets on one wrist and a watch and a bracelet on the other. None of the astounded team of researchers who greeted them has been able to get over this "coincidence." Certainly, no one is rash enough to suggest that it was entirely predetermined by the genes.

What psychologist David Lykken of the Minnesota team does conclude about these twins' behavior, however, is that "the case of the seven rings" may point to more information yet to be uncovered. "Fondness for rings is obviously not hereditary, but groups of unrelated genes on different chromosomes, producing pretty hands and other characteristics, may combine to result in 'beringedness.' " Psychologists call these idiographic traits—that is, traits particular to an individual but not necessarily to a group. It may be that these traits do not appear by chance, either. "There are probably other traits that are idiographic," says Lykken; "that may be almost inevitable given the combination of genes." He theorizes that there may be more unique characteristics in people that arise from their own specific genetic makeup than previously has been understood. He suggests that rather than becoming upset at such an idea— as many do—"to believe otherwise requires a naive dualism . . . an assumption that mental events occur independent of the physical substrata." Lykken believes that when all the data has been analyzed, proponents of both hereditary and environmental influence will be happy since there will be material confirming beliefs on both sides of that scientific fence.

Synchronous events in the lives of even temporarily separated identical twins may or may not, then, be related to the new information that the Minnesota team is discovering. I refer to those instances, common among twins, when one twin will call her sister to report buying a new beige blouse. The sister has bought the exact same style of blouse, at the same hour, though the two live in different parts of the country. Or a man talking on the telephone to his twin brother will mention having stopped on the way home from work to watch firemen battle a blaze, only to find his brother had, also. Recently, my sister and I were talking long distance. We were interrupted by my niece saying, "Oh, Mother, you let the cookies burn!" When I hung up the receiver, my son called from the kitchen, "Hey, Mom, are you trying to burn down the house or something? These eggs just exploded all over everything!" These occurrences were happening to my sister and me at the same moment in our lives, although we are not prone to such forgetfulness and we live 1,900 miles apart.

As we saw in earlier chapters, names and nicknames are a subject of great interest to twins everywhere. However, a look at the stories of some of the identical twins reared apart brings the topic of twins and names into the realm of idiographics as well. Bridget Harrison named her children Richard Andrew and Catherine Louise. Her twin, Dorothy Lowe, named hers Andrew Richard and Karen Louise. She chose the name Karen to please a relative. She told Bouchard's team that she really wanted the name Katherine. Clearly, genes cannot start fires, but do they help us pick names we like? The task for the researcher faced with such questions is to draw a line between meaningful coincidences and meaningless coincidences—without the aid of a soothsayer—which at times would seem no small order.

Identical twins reared apart present quite a paradox when their lives and behavior are compared to those of identical twins reared together. One would think that twins reared in the same family, side by side, with a mutual support system would be more alike than those raised in completely different settings. In most instances, however, the opposite is true: The twins with the least contact during their formative years are usually more alike than those who knew each other or had occasional contact. How is this explained? One theory suggests that, although it may appear that the lives of identical twins reared apart are different, they are, in fact, made more alike by the twins themselves. Their innate impulses force even disparate associates to treat them similarly. The same inner requirements appear to dominate twins reared together. Hugh Lytton, of the University of Calgary in Alberta, examined twins reared together and their families to see if identical twins received more similar treatment from parents than did fraternals. "Parents do treat identical twins more alike than fraternal twins in some respects, but not deliberately," he found. Parents don't initiate the duplicate treatment. It is required of them by the innate demands of the twins. They respond to, rather than create, differences. It seems that identical twins, because they behave identically, evoke the same response from the people they encounter. This idea assumes that the child exerts influences on those around him, rather than the contrary, as scientists in the past were too prone to assume.

The three major studies conducted prior to the Minnesota project focused on twins with similar backgrounds, a factor which psychologist Farber in her review of the studies believes must have influenced their results. Farber is one researcher who thinks that twins' similarities bring about similar responses from those people around them. She believes that if parents "alter or limit their 'seductability' out of a need to make twins different," it would naturally follow that such actions would affect the children, twin or not.

Although most researchers divide into camps which stress the influence of either heredity or environment— perhaps because it simplifies matters—both influence our lives. Future research may do well to look at the interrelationships of these two, rather than studying them in isolation.

Bridging the Separation

Not surprisingly, when twins reared apart get together under the auspices of the Minnesota group, they have one of the great experiences of their lives. As a twin myself, I don't find it hard to imagine most of these wonderful reunions. What twin who likes being a twin could not? For one thing, like any close relatives long separated, they are making up for lost time. But it seems to go beyond that. Having lived as singletons, these twins, now as adults, have the joy of discovering the amusements of twinship. The twins' greatest preoccupations for the week during which they are suddenly together is to match experiences. As they have talked with the doctors, they have learned a lot about themselves and the meaning of their lives, more than they ever imagined possible before being tested. But interestingly, what seems to astound the twins most is what is already well known to the researchers—that they are very often *more* alike than they would be had they known each other throughout the intervening years.

This extravagant likeness to another human—and a stranger at that—is primarily an entertaining interlude. English twins Barbara Herbert and Daphne Goodship, who were examined by the Minnesota group, certainly thought so. Known to the researchers as the "gigglers"—they both had very distinctive giggles and were the only gigglers in their respective families—they had so much fun during their evenings off from tests that they invented a drink they called "Twin Sin." All the twins seemed to revel in tracing the many ways in which their separate experiences coincided, but apparently reliving one's life so intensely in one short week has its aftereffects as well. When Jake Hellback and Keith Heitzman finished their time together in Minneapolis, they admitted to the researchers that it had been a physically exhausting and emotionally draining experience.

Probably no case of identical twins reared apart has received more attention in recent history than that of the male pair born in Trinidad nearly fifty years ago to a Jewish father and a German mother. Twin Oskar was taken back to Germany by his mother, while his twin brother, Jack, was raised as a Jew, first in the Caribbean, later on a kibbutz in Israel. Oskar was reared by a household of women; a father and other men were the primary formative influences on Jack. Oskar's stepfather suppressed part of the family history because he did not want it known in Germany that there was Jewish blood in the family. In his early adolescence, Oskar was involved in the Hitler Youth movement.

This pair met, very briefly, when they were twenty-one. It was not, by all accounts, the friendliest of reunions, one young man being fresh from a kibbutz in Israel, the other having remained in Germany after the war; the pressure of cultural differences was formidable. Nevertheless, the wives of the two kept in touch by mail, and eventually, at Jack's instigation, the brothers showed up in Minnesota to go through the testing program.

Despite the barriers that separated the twins, there was something stronger that linked them. From the moment of their arrival, their researcher hosts were struck by the similarities of their temperaments, their body movements and their behavior. When the men met at the Minneapolis airport, both were wearing wire-rimmed glasses and were decked out in two-pocket shirts with epaulets. Both men habitually fall asleep after eating, are similarly absent-minded, are fond of spicy foods. Both read magazines from back to front and have the habit of flushing the toilet before as well as after using it. Both have histories of being domineering toward women, though Jack uses terms that imply he is aware of the woman's liberation movement. Both wear toothbrush mustaches.

Bouchard says he can't help but feel that the press got carried away with Jack and Oskar's story, ripe as it seemed to be with such extreme opposites in upbringing. Looked at closely, however, their stories were not, according to Bouchard, as startlingly different as at first glance. "The twin who was reared in Germany belonged to the Hitler Youth, but virtually every young man in his community had to belong to it," he says.

"From the scientific point of view we're disappointed," Bouchard admits. Most of the twins whom the Minnesota group has studied so far have been raised in similar households after all, which is one of the biases in their research of which they are well aware. If a substantial number of identical twins are reared in totally different settings by totally different parents and still prove in adulthood to be so similar that they are nearly interchangeable, then more answers to scientific queries would seem to be available. However, "From a humanistic point of view," Bouchard says, "we are pleased we haven't discovered more twins who were exposed to those kinds of dramatic differences."

Because Dr. Bouchard and his colleagues have uncovered an unexpectedly large number of twins reared apart, they have attempted to increase the area of their investigation. Thus, part of their work involves devising new methods to test every possible aspect of the lives and behavior of identical twins reared apart. One set of questions they pose, for instance, is related to the pattern of sexual development in twins reared apart. With these they hope to focus new light on how humans view their own sexual natures and how they handle related problems. As always, the two sets of answers to these questions are startlingly alike. Certainly, when it comes to choosing spouses, one pair of twins who arrived at the University of Minnesota campus with their mates took the prize for multiple confusion. A secretary who met the two husbands of the twins, who were not blood relatives, thought *they* were the twins since they looked so much alike.

Nevertheless, says Bouchard, "It's very dangerous to generalize from one pair of twins or several. Once we've studied a large series of them, we can say much stronger things." Psychiatrist Leonard Heston of the Minnesota twin studies team says, "One can't expect to get absolute answers very often. It's rare to be able to come up with definitive information. The best you can hope for are strong, powerful clues that may help untangle the question of environment and heredity."

Perhaps the most startling material to come to date from the Minnesota Study of Twins Reared Apart is, according to psychologist David Lykken, something he calls "emerging traits," that is, traits that are not demonstrably familial but are some peculiar genetic combination that emerges only in identical twins. "The only time two individuals have the exact configuration of genes is when they are identical twins," says Bouchard. "When you see a trait in identical twins and you don't see it in any other relatives, there is a reasonable probability it's what we call epistasis." That is, the trait is not being transmitted within the family as are dominant and recessive traits—blue or brown eyes, for instance—because of a complicated interaction between genes which either masks the trait or superimposes another trait upon it. "The identical twins have identical 'clusters' of genes that result in a particular trait. Until another individual comes along with exactly that same cluster of genes, you'll never see that trait again. We haven't worked it all out yet. Sometimes a distribution of brain wave frequencies will act this way. You'll see identical brain waves in identical twins and then look at the brain waves of their brothers and sisters and find no similarity at all. Normally, such a lack of similarity between the twins' brain waves and those of their brothers and sisters would suggest there is no genetic effect on brain waves. But if that is true, how do you explain identical brain waves in identical twins? The only place you see them is in identical twins, and the only way you can be sure they are genetically influenced is by seeing them in identical twins reared apart." This way, scientists can be certain that similar brain waves are not the products of conditioning.

Speaking for himself, Dr. Bouchard believes that the Minnesota studies have revealed material of more general significance. "No matter what trait we look at—psychological interest, personality, temperament, across the whole spectrum—almost everything has a hereditary effect. Some psychologists concluded a while back from other studies that it looked like all traits were about equally genetically influenced. I always thought that was kind of foolish. But now, with these studies of identical twins reared apart, I'm starting to become a believer."

Does an early and long separation have its effect on twin pairs? Bouchard feels that it is too soon to say with any conviction. "So far I have no sense that the twins' separation affected their lives or these traits at all. I hear a lot of twins say they have a lot of time to make up for. They spend an inordinate amount of time together by choice. Some of the twins' wives report that after the twins were here, they were still spending that kind of time together. One pair spent every single day together from November to March. They said they were making up for twenty-four years apart! In terms of the twin bond, when these twins get together here on mutual territory, they become tremendously close. None of my training would have led me to expect it."

Are there signs of any jealousies or competition? "Yes, a little bit," he says. "But you can't generalize. It varies enormously from twin pair to twin pair, and, of course, it depends upon the twin pair's own traits. If, for instance, the pair is highly dependent by nature, then the individuals within it will be dependent upon each other, and vice versa."

The idea of being confronted, as an adult, with someone who is just like you has much potential for trauma, as was noted in the case of Robert and Kaj, studied by psychologist Niels Juel-Nielsen in Denmark. Although the pairs whom Dr. Bouchard has studied were delighted to meet, there was some apprehension, of course. Upon returning to their respective homes, a few of the identical twins reared apart have tended to lose contact, slipping back into their separated singleton worlds. Little by little, they loosen the bond that was so fascinating in Minneapolis.

The group of doctors at the University of Minnesota expects the Twins-Reared-Apart Project to extend over a five-year period. It will take them that long to gather and analyze all the informtaion about the pairs they have found and tested. Ultimately, they hope to have a total "picture" of each twin, with a complete case history and numerous specific traits studied so that these can be compared with those of the twin partner.

8. The Living Laboratory

The sun blazed down on the ancient streets of Jerusalem as tourists and worshippers from around the world swarmed to religious sites, rambled through the picturesque streets, paused to take snapshots or pick up souvenirs. Amid the buzzing of modern traffic, an occasional camel driver on his mount wandered past the street corners where peddlers offered bright-colored beads and postcards to the city's visitors. On the outskirts of the city, hundreds of scientists, doctors, twin researchers and students converged on the Diplomat Hotel, followed by ubiquitous reporters and photographers. In this ancient crossroads of the world where so many paths come together, the specialists from many nations had gathered. It was June 1980, and the

Third International Congress of Twin Studies was about to begin.

Also moving in and out of the conference rooms of the Diplomat were interested lay persons, since the planners of these conferences had recognized that twins and the parents of twins had a major interest in the topics to be examined. Not only that, but twins and their parents, who had provided precious data and statistical material for twin studies over the years, had come to pool their insights and experiences with those of the experts, in a mutual effort to broaden the base of twin research and to move that research ahead.

During this congress, more papers were presented than at any previous twin studies' convention. Some had been prepared by the lay observers. Between the formal sessions, friendships were made and renewed as questions about the abundance of theories, demographic studies and medical speculation sparked excited conversations. The groups, representing a wide variety of nationalities—American, British, French, Australian, Canadian, Italian, Scandinavian, Belgian, Japanese and African, to name a few—spoke their many languages. Woven through the jumble of tongues was the rather exotic terminology of science. For nearly a week in the hotel's meeting rooms, such words as *concordant, discordant, asymmetry, chromosomal abnormalities* and *methodological implications* filled the air. Overhearing the talk of seminar speakers, specialized groups or casual dinner companions might have given one the sense of visiting the Tower of Babel, but the tower actually being constructed was the structure to house nature's most convenient laboratory—twins.

Rather than excavating the ruins of ancient cities or sending probes to the outer planets, the scientists gathered in Jerusalem were those who were devoting careers to such questions as: What factors influence our selection of mates? Are certain behavior patterns genetically determined? What do the lives of twins reveal about which diseases are inheritable and which are not? What can the habits of separated twins tell us about the dangers of smoking and drinking? Why do some people age gracefully over a long period of years, while others decline seemingly overnight? Does the enrichment of education change the native IQ inherited by an individual? How is the onset of inherited diseases best predicted? Under what conditions do such maladies as allergies, alcoholism, myopia, depression or cancer appear to be inheritable? How much does a poor environment affect the course of creativity?

These questions are only a sampling of those probed and discussed during the exciting days and nights in Jerusalem. The sample, however, indicates clearly that topics studied in the living laboratory provided by twins have applications touching on the lives of everyone and on all branches of science dealing with human well-being. No wonder then that the scope of twin studies expands constantly. Psychologist and twin expert Frank X. Barron, who has examined questions relating to creativity through twin studies, is only one of a number of professionals who today claim that "a whole new era in twin research is opening up. We have never needed twins as much as we do now." No wonder that the twins who attended the congress felt that they were partners welcomed to a dazzling adventure.

The reservoir of specially coded information in the genes of all living organisms appears to be more readily decipherable through twin studies than by any other approach. Progress in understanding genetically transmitted diseases is accelerated by the work of those who came to the congress to exchange ideas. Some diseases recently thought to be passed on by the genes are, in fact, probably not communicated that way, while some never suspected of being inheritable appear to be precisely that. More than 5,000 diseases have been, as of now, labeled as genetically controlled, an advance of knowledge that will come as bad news to some who must now look forward to a high risk of affliction. If our grandmothers had diabetes or our fathers were nearsighted, it is fairly certain that these maladies are being passed on to us or our children through our genes. But the news is not exclusively bad. Although there has been a rise in the number of patients with genetically transmitted diseases admitted to the large children's hospitals, the number has grown partially because physicians now have the means to make earlier diagnoses and often provide the care that will blunt the effect of the inevitable malady. Add to this the fact that any one gene does not exist in isolation; it thus has the ability to interact with other genes to modify or even obliterate a programmed effect. As scientists begin to uncover the manner in which such occurrences take place, they progress toward a prediction about which of us in receipt of a genetically controlled malady will see it manifested in our lifetime and which will not.

Diseases passed on from one generation to another too often in the past have been treated like skeletons in the family closet. Knowledge about them was so fragmentary that they were often ignored, as if that would make them go away. In the new era dawning, the intensified studies of twins would appear to be changing all that.

On the other side of the spectrum, as it was laid out at the congress, are the approaches that can be broadly labeled as sociological, psychological and environmental. Delegates in Jerusalem heard a great deal both from specialists in these areas and from the twins and mothers of multiples, since their own experiences and observations are more directly related to environmental effects on human growth and behavior. Some who tried to fit together the wide range of approaches represented must have recalled Robert Frost's famous poem *The Road Not Taken*, in which he speaks of two roads diverging in a yellow wood, leaving the thoughtful person briefly but fatefully confronted with the need to decide which path to take. Like Frost's diverging roads, the two main avenues of twin studies tempt the student to concentrate on either heredity or environment. The first path is generally taken by researchers seeking to control disease. The second path leads on to studies of educational method, the learning process and psychological data on such things as depression, anxiety, motivation, creativity and the sense of identity. At some later congress, there may be a synthesis of these divergent lines, in which there will be a greater correlation than is yet possible between what is known about heredity and what is known about environment. At such a time, everyone will benefit, twin and singleton alike.

Unlike the two choices mentioned by Mr. Frost, however, there is available to scientists a third path in twin studies, called by Dr. Louis Keith "the step-child of medical research." Those who take this approach study gestation, birth and the early lives of twins with the practical objective of improving the infants' survival rate. The focus is on the care of twins. The principal benefit is to answer questions asked by parents, teachers and twins themselves. (See chapter 10.)

Methods in Twin Studies

The classical scientific twin study, says Rune Cederlöf of the Karolinska Institute in Stockholm, "rests on an assumption that the two members of any identical twin pair share their common environment to the same extent as do the two members of any fraternal pair. If this is the case, any greater resemblance between the two identical twins

as compared with the two fraternal twins should indicate
the genetic influence." An example of this method would
be a careful comparison of a trait such as motion sickness
between pairs of identical twins and pairs of fraternal
twins. If the trait is exactly alike in a pair, the twins are
considered to be concordant. If there is a difference between them in this trait, they are considered to be discordant. Whenever a characteristic is clearly more concordant in identical twins, scientists assume that the reason
for this is biologically determined. In a recent study in
India, for instance, it was found that identical twins were
100 percent concordant in their susceptibility to motion
sickness, while fraternal twins were only 27 percent concordant.

Within the two main categories of twin studies, a multitude of approaches has been devised. Some researchers, like
Dr. Bouchard, compile psychological and behavioral profiles of twins reared apart. Others tabulate the similarities
of a wide range of traits such as eye color, tooth structure
or blood pressure in many sets of twins, correlating these
when possible with their known genetic background. The
so-called longitudinal studies are compilations of important
items of information gathered systematically over an extended period of time. These often, though not always,
involve a large number of twin pairs. Such sweeping longitudinal surveys have been under way in Italy and California for some time, and other areas have begun to accumulate statistics on significant numbers of the twin population. Longitudinal studies are particularly relevant to the
understanding of continuity and discontinuity in patterns
of growth and development. Unique among them is one
reported by Noel W. Smith of the State University of
New York at Plattsburg, New York, which "took advantage of continual observation and recording by a parent
in the home situation." Information that could not be ob-

tained by outside observers was dutifully recorded for a period of thirteen years by the mother of an identical pair of twins.

Some scientists choose to set up tables of comparison between twins and singletons to measure variables in personality traits or levels of perceptive and cognitive ability. But Dr. Zazzo and others concentrate first on twin psychology and the relationship between members of a twin pair before generalizing about psychological structures common to all kinds of human pair relationships. Then there are studies of the families of twins, in which the parents and kin are scrutinized for biological and behavioral factors that influence the twin pair. A refinement of this is the partitioned twin analysis, in which groups of fraternal twins are divided—"partitioned"—into subsets according to the number of Mendelian dominant traits they have inherited from their parents. This method has cast some hitherto unexpected light on the effect of chromosome structure on genetic variations in all humans. Dr. Walter E. Nance of the Medical College of Virginia at Richmond is a leader in this type of twin research and one who is particularly interested in the offspring of identical twins, calling them "a unique class of human half-sibs who provide an unusual opportunity to resolve and measure several additional potentially important sources of human variation including maternal effects, the influences of common environmental factors and assortative mating." By studying these relationships, he has come up with as many as sixteen different equations which can be used to estimate a number of possible variant genetic components within human beings. The research has been applied to such things as birth weight, dermal ridge count (in hand- and footprints), blood pressure, serum cholesterol and uric-acid levels, as well as several psychological traits.

In co-twin studies, one twin is systematically trained or

conditioned in a specific way for a certain length of time, while the other is not. This method was introduced by K. Elasasser, who in 1905, watched newborn identical twins as they slept. His objective was to learn how sleep positions might affect the head shape of an infant. Subsequent co-twin studies have involved putting one twin on a special diet, submitting one only to a program of exercise or measuring the results of different modes of treatment for a physical handicap shared by the twins. J. Theodore Schwartz of the U.S. Public Health Service describes a study in which one twin received the standard treatment for myopia, the other a special pair of glasses. The difference in the progression of the twins' nearsightedness wasn't statistically impressive, but Schwartz is convinced that further study will lead to a much improved treatment of this visual problem—one which, incidentally, may be of more value to twins than to the general population. A recent sampling shows that an extraordinarily high percentage of fraternal twins of opposite sexes wore glasses to school when they were five and six years old. The sampling is not definitive, nor is its significance fully grasped yet. It might mean only that the control group was not truly representative of twins at large. Perhaps other twins with even more severe ocular impairment didn't make it to school at all. The high incidence of ocular defects could be an indication of the risks of sharing the womb or undergoing the twin birth process. Or it might indicate the genetic determination of physical growth processes.

The Role of Conditioning

Back in the late thirties, one twin study startled many experts; from it, the Woods twins, Jimmy and Johnny, became famous. Dubbed by the press "The Scientific

Twins," this pair seemed to threaten long-held scientific theories. When they were a week old, a child psychologist at Columbia University picked them for use in a series of co-twin studies. The psychologists wondered how education improved upon experience and which kinds of environment in a child's early years were most beneficial for learning. Johnny was given the benefit of what was considered at the time to be the best possible encouragement to a child's mental development. Jimmy was left alone to learn skills or not. The twins spent evenings at home together with their parents, but during the day they were ensconced in controlled environments at the Normal Child Development Clinic of the Columbia University Presbyterian Medical Center. After four years, the twins "graduated" from their extraordinary school setting and returned to a regular nursery school.

What was the outcome of this unusual experiment? Early reports left many surprised and perplexed. It turned out that untrained Jimmy was the self-reliant one. He handled his problems and Johnny's, too. Teachers noted that he was more helpful, putting away materials used in class. He was definitely more talkative than his brother. Johnny didn't finish tasks, though he obeyed when teachers asked him to do something. He seemed to enjoy himself most of the time. Both twins had a habit of inverting syllables in words. When Jimmy was corrected, he learned from the experience. Not so his brother. Jimmy, the "untrained" twin, had forged ahead of his "trained" brother. He was the child who didn't have a toy until he was twenty months old, while his brother, through careful instruction, had learned to swim without fear when he was seven and a half months old, dived when he was a year old, rollerskated at sixteen months.

The press continued its periodic coverage of the "scientific twins." *The New York Times* even returned to them in 1953 to note that they had turned twenty-one. But the story of this particular co-twin control study was ultimately invalidated when researchers discovered that Jimmy and Johnny were not, after all, identical but fraternal twins. They were even less alike than many pairs of singleton brothers.

This use of twins as "guinea pigs" raises serious questions, of course. Is it fair to deny a child—specifically a twin—an accepted benefit just for research's sake? Might this approach also deny a cancer cure to one twin in order to compare the progress of the disease in the other? Undoubtedly, the answer is "no," but the question is worrisome.

While researchers made no real advance with Jimmy and Johnny, psychologist Arnold Gesell of Yale University had better luck. In 1941, he used a group of twins whose zygosity was definitely determined to be identical to confirm that education and an improved environment is advantageous in a child's formative years. Gesell and his colleagues concluded that such early training not only helped children learn certain skills, but enhanced their general growth and development and improved their behavior as well. The conditioned twin was more independent, resourceful and disciplined than the unconditioned twin, after all.

Progress and Continuity

Scientific progress often seems to follow the halting pattern common to the beginning knitter: knit two, purl two, rip out four, knit two, rip out two. Over the years, interest in twin studies has waxed and waned. As Dr. Gordon Allen of the National Institute of Mental Health reminded the delegates at the First International Congress of Twin

Studies in Rome in 1974, twin research was expected by its critics in the 1940s and 1950s to become obsolete. Instead, it has flourished. It is also true that scientific conclusions have not always furthered knowledge about twins. Some statements made by scientists, when taken out of context or misunderstood by the public, have increased the problems that twins face. For instance, in his study of twins reared apart, Dr. James Shields found slight evidence that there was a hereditary relationship between IQ scores. Although Shields himself admitted that this question was open to interpretation, his results are still used widely out of context to support specific biases.

Looking back, however, the correspondence in thinking between some of the early researchers and today's scientists is amazing. Before medicine was truly based on science, many serious thinkers were weighing the evidence that twins presented in order to unravel mysteries of our universe. Dr. Luigi Gedda, who for nearly thirty years has been surveying the entire twin-related literature, sums up this early scientific probing in his book *Twins in History and Science.* "Hippocrates believed twins were conceived by the division of the sperm into two parts with each part penetrating one of the two uterine horns. Andreassi observes that in ancient times the twin phenomenon was associated with double formations. Empedocles believed them to be due to an excess of sperm emitted at one time, while Democritus ascribed them to sperm emitted at different times, each time corresponding to an embryo."

Consider the antique theories about "Siamese," or conjoined, twins. It was believed in Aristotle's time that immediately after conception, combined twins were separate. Then somewhat later they fused, or grew together at least partially. Another idea was that multiple pregnancy was brought about by "excess heat in the uterus." Astrologers believed that twins were conceived under certain conditions in which the stars were in a particular alignment. Of course, some of the conclusions about twin conceptions and the connections between twins' lives in these ancient theories are now known to be in error. But some of them are amazingly close to what we now accept to be true.

One thousand eight hundred sixty-two spontaneous abortions recorded by medical researchers at a New York hospital between 1933 and 1940 were looked at in relation to the signs of the zodiac. There were interesting revelations. It was discovered that June conceptions, under the Gemini—or twins—sign, had fewer miscarriages than September conceptions, under the sign of Virgo, the virgin. Strangely enough, twin pregnancies had a lower incidence of miscarriage, and unwed mothers had fewest. The peak months for spontaneous abortion were April, July and November. The low months were June, September and December. Also, "the mating of animals at the time of the vernal equinox may not be a happenstance," according to this same study. Most of us won't take all this information too seriously; it comes as an addition to other more familiar pieces of folklore, old wives' tales and astrological calculations that still surround modern obstetrics and gynecology, such as the relation between the moon and menstruation and the new moon and the onset of labor, or the calculation of the duration of gestation as ten lunar months.

As far back as 1671, a medical paper suggested that monozygotic twins—that is, uniovular or one-egg pairs—are always of the same sex. Only in rare cases has this ever been challenged. In 1865, a Scottish doctor, J. M. Duncan, observed that there seemed to be some connection between the age of a mother and her chances of producing twins—and this was at a time when twin studies as we know them today were essentially nonexistent. In the latter part of the nineteenth century, Sir Francis Galton took a much closer look at the facts surrounding twin births. He examined twins who looked alike and those who did not, and surmised that the reason for such variance was that the look-alikes must have come from one egg, while those who did not must somehow have come from two separate eggs coincidentally fertilized at the same time. The conception, gestation, births and lives of identical twins had something important to tell us, he reasoned. They could contribute to the study of comparative influence of heredity and environment on human development. Initially, practitioners in many different medical disciplines received Galton's idea with enthusiasm. Later, it came under strong attack by those who, for political and social reasons, were fearful of some of the possible conclusions to be drawn from the studies. The racial theories of the Nazis cast a massive damper on enthusiasm for genetic studies. In some instances, one can still find physicians who contend that the use of twins in research is waning. Anyone attending the International Congress in Jerusalem, however, would have been hard pressed to believe it.

Even during those periods when the interest in twin studies flagged, isolated reports of new conclusions reached through such research continued to appear sporadically in professional journals, from investigators working in medical, anthropological and psychological areas. Then, too, during those periods of lukewarm scientific interest, the general press continued to provide stories about multiples and their unusual lives, which have contributed to the wealth of information now available to today's scientists and interested laity.

The Genetic Connection

A century and more ago, the prevalent popular notion about "madness" was that "it ran in the family" or was "in the blood." Royal families and minor nobility vanished from the public eye when such a mysterious taint produced mentally aberrant kings or queens. Melodramas—onstage and in real life—frequently hinged on the renunciation of a lover on grounds that he or she "carried a streak of madness" that would blight the lives of any offspring the fated couple might produce. Then Freud and Jung and their followers mapped more sophisticated theories of psychology, tracing the effect of childhood traumas and repressions in crippling the mind.

While the role of heredity in pathological psychology was taking a back seat, however, certain details continued to emerge over the years in study after study. In 1936, Dr. Franz Joseph Kallmann organized a research team at the New York Psychiatric Institute, using twins in the study of psychoses, mental deficiency, suicide, male homosexuality, aging and longevity, deafness and tuberculosis. At the time, Kallmann had to bear accusations of bringing back medieval prejudices as he developed evidence that severe mental illness is determined more by heredity than by environment. Kallmann's research with over 2,000 twins brought him to the conclusion that a chemical imbalance in the bodies of the mentally ill may be the cause of certain kinds of schizophrenia and manic-depression. These disorders, he feels, are hereditary and, if they are not the "triggering" cause of mental illness, they are at the core of many such problems which respond to pharmaceutical treatment.

Kallmann did not set out in the beginning to demonstrate any such thing. In fact, in the twenties, when he was a young doctor in Germany treating schizophrenics, he set out to prove that heredity was *not* a prime factor in the genesis of the disease. The weight of data, however, had to be respected. Slowly and laboriously, he gathered the material that discounted the importance of environmental causes, the effects of experience and other nonbiological reasons.

Another disease that surprised Dr. Kallmann was tuberculosis. It *seemed* to fall clearly into the category of environmentally caused disease. The specific bacilli of tuberculosis had been identified a long time before. Observation confirmed that poor diet, climate, bad sanitation and bodily exhaustion favored the onset and progress of tuberculosis in its classic forms. There seemed nothing else to be said about its causes. And yet, as Dr. Kallmann and his associates found by a persistent scouring of the records in numerous hospitals treating tuberculars, another factor asserted itself. Sixteen percent of the twin partners of dizygotic twins treated also were afflicted, while 87 percent of the twin partners of monozygotics developed the same disease. As a consequence of these and related studies, some scientists then began to recognize that a genetic factor was making the ultimate difference when all the other familiar conditions were present. The earlier major studies of twins reared apart revealed this same threat of similarity, as have studies of the genetic components affecting polio, diabetes, epilepsy and some forms of blindness and deafness.

Nevertheless, while evidence piled up on the side of heredity as a determining factor in disease, many still balked at the idea that it played a major role in psychological or behavioral destinies. Debates that raged in professional journals and the popular press were often based on fear and misunderstanding. The either/or quality of such discussions fueled the flames of dissension and tended to obscure what scientists are now beginning to recognize: Neither our genetic heritage nor our environment is alone reponsible for the quality of our lives. Although under certain circumstances one may be more a controlling factor than the other, it is also true that genetic and environmental influences tend to complement each other. Saying that any disease is genetically guided is not the end of the matter. When the cause of a mental disease, say, can be clearly recognized as a chemical disorder hereditarily determined, then the appropriate chemical treatments can supplement the other psychiatric approaches, offering a far greater chance of success for the total treatment.

Studies of twins, adopted children and patients' relatives have long suggested that depression is hereditary, but until very recently no test has detected physical differences among depressed patients. Some University of Iowa researchers now have found an abnormality of the nervous system in persons suffering from hereditary forms of simple, severe depression. The symptoms and severity of the disease are the same among all patients, but when the sufferers are given a certain cortisone drug, doctors can tell which patients are suffering from inherited depression and which are not. The conclusion to which the doctors came was that there are two or more separate diseases of depression, each with a different sort of inheritance pattern and response to treatment.

Doctors have demonstrated that the hormones from the adrenal glands of schizophrenics differ from those of mentally healthy people. It is the adrenaline system which governs and reinforces the body's defenses against all kinds of traumatic shock. A defect in this system lowers the defenses necessary to sanity, which permits the progressive disorientation observed in schizophrenic behavior. By correcting this adrenaline imbalance, doctors have seen some results in the treatment of advanced cases of depression, and they foresee that this kind of treatment may help hold off the most damaging effects of the illness in others.

Manic-depressive psychosis—the uncontrollable and rationally inexplicable vacillation between moods—is the other major nemesis that eventually may be avoided because of Kallmann's original twin research. He found that when one twin was manic-depressive, the other shared symptoms of the disease 95.7 percent of the time, a fantastic correlation. These statistics not only emphasize the potency of the hereditary factor, they also help clarify the distinction between schizophrenia and manic-depressive illness, a considerable advance in diagnostic detail. None of the evidence in Kallmann's or later studies, incidentally, suggests that any form of mental disease occurs more frequently among twins than in the population at large. It occurs, indeed, at very much the same rate as among singletons.

Alcoholism is another affliction that has been given intensive study and about which much is still to be uncovered. Results of twin studies have revealed, however, that when one of a set of identicals becomes an alcoholic, there is more than a 50 percent chance that the other may as well. The concordance between fraternal twins on the subject of alcoholism is considerably lower. For these pairs, if one is an alcoholic, there is a 28 percent chance that the twin partner may also become one.

A Laboratory As Big As the Earth

Past and current twin studies are as diverse as the puzzles which human afflictions and human development present to the minds of the men of science. Even a cursory glance at the subjects that have been approached through the careful study of twins' lives and health leaves one with the impression that no area has been left untouched. Since the "laboratory" that twins present is immense—there are estimates of 100 million twins in the world today—and the riddles that scientists continue to hope to solve may be even more numerous, a look at what is being examined and concluded through twin studies is akin to examining the proverbial iceberg's tip. These days if you plug in any medically oriented computer asking questions about twins and twin studies, you will come away with literally pounds of printouts leading to these innumerable studies.

Some of the most comprehensive twin research has been conducted, of late, in Italy, Sweden, Denmark, France, Germany and the United States. In Italy, twin studies are being led by the eminent twin-research pioneer Dr. Luigi Gedda and his colleagues. Much of their focus is on chronogenetics, discussed in the next chapter. In Western Germany, a major research emphasis has been on dermatoglyphics (the study of hand- and footprints), as well as the study of similar and dissimilar twins. England, Scotland, Norway, Finland, Spain, India, Nigeria, Argentina, Canada, Australia, Switzerland, Japan—nearly every country in the world has contributed important data to the mounting scientific study of twins and other multiples.

The existence of twin studies furthered the early development of genetic research and contributed to the fields of medical, biological and behavioral sciences in the United States, beginning with a pilot project in 1905. Universities with human genetics centers include Chicago, Columbia and Michigan State, among others, and ongoing twin studies of significance are being undertaken at the universities of Louisville, Minnesota, Colorado, and Virginia at Richmond, among others. Of all countries, the United States has led in promoting twin research through the establishment of social organizations for twins and supertwins and their parents.

What is more obvious than this? In order to study twins, scientists must have twins to study. One of the problems that besets twin research is locating the necessary twin population and then tracking the members through time. Twin registries tend to divide into two categories, neither of which is entirely satisfactory in the minds of some researchers. Either they are large, with information available relating to many sorts of scientific inquiry about a great number of twins but based on public records, mailed questionnaires and sketchy personal data; or they are small and specialized, aimed at answering only a limited number of specific questions.

The first sort of registry may come about almost by accident. Both Sweden and Finland have studied twins since as far back as the 1650s, with material collected from parish records and other sources on multiple births. One of the primary reasons for this is the fact that until recently, these countries had one of the highest twinning rates for any white population in the world. In Sweden, for instance, the twinning rate in the latter part of the eighteenth century was almost double what it was during the period of 1966–1970, and the triplet and quadruplet rates "were about three to four times as high as they are today," according to Dr. Aldur W. Eriksson of the Free University of Amsterdam, who made a retrospective study of the records. He suggests that the degree of relationship between the parents of the mothers of twins had more to do with the rate of fraternal twinning in these cases than the degree of relationship between the parents themselves.

The Finnish Twin Registry, established in 1974 to study various aspects of chronic diseases, had a basic file of 32,000 like-sexed twins by the opening of the First International Congress of Twin Studies in 1974. In Sweden and Denmark, all citizens have long been included in a national register. Vital statistics on the populations of these countries provide a vast store of information for its researchers. The Swedish Twin Registry, for instance, now includes nearly 10,000 twin pairs born in Sweden since 1886. Along with a series of studies dealing with questions of how smoking and drinking habits affect health, these researchers have devised a special method for using twins in environmental research. Denmark has had a national twin registry since 1954. At the Gregor Mendel Institute in Italy, a Twin Registry of over 17,000 pairs exists, and the material gathered there is one of the most detailed data banks for genetic twin research. At the Third International Congress of Twin

Studies, researchers from Belgium reported on The European Twin Registry, a joint effort of scientists at approximately forty teaching hospitals from the European Economic Community. Their primary aim is an accurate recording, at birth, of the zygosity of a large enough number of twins, so that they may study the rate of concordance and discordance of the most common congenital malformations found in twin pairs. In order to participate, the doctors must record a number of points of vital information, such as the number of multiples, the type of placenta, the blood types as they appear in an examination of the umbilical cord in like-sexed dichorial twins. They must also sample and deep-freeze placental tissue corresponding to each infant. The registry will be used for other twin-related studies, as well as for monitoring the quality of perinatal care, definitely a leap forward in the area of the third avenue of twin studies. As twin studies progress, the collections of names, locations and specific information on twins multiply accordingly.

In the United States where there is no national registry of all citizens, there are several twin registries, some obviously more formally maintained than others. In 1967, the National Academy of Science-National Research Council set up a Twin Registry with data on 16,000 adult twin pairs, all white male veterans of the armed services born during 1917–1927. There is also a large twin registry at the Northern California Kaiser-Permanente Medical Care Program in Oakland. This center has accumulated data on 8,000 pairs of twins, all ages and races, both fraternal and identical sets. Information included consists of longitudinal medical records ideally suited for follow-up research on over half of the pairs. It offers, as well, a large group—nearly one-third of the pairs living in the San Francisco Bay Area—that is available in a relatively small region for interview and examination by medical researchers.

Another registry (a population-based survey) is located

in Richmond and is known as the Virginia Twin Registry. To locate twin pairs, researchers there have been scanning birth records in the state since 1915 and so far have obtained current addresses for 4,812 like-sexed pairs: However, they consider their work far from completed. According to them, "population-based twin registries are of particular value for the ascertainment of twins with rare traits." The Universities of Louisville and Minnesota also have specialized twin registries; the former is known as the Louisville Twin Study and the latter, the Minnesota Twins-Reared-Apart Project. Specialized registries are instituted, too, to further certain investigations such as the study of environmental and genetic factors in multiple sclerosis and Parkinson's disease conducted by National Institute of Neurological Diseases and Stroke at the National Institutes of Health, Bethesda, Maryland.

A Potpourri of Discoveries

A study described at the conference in Israel had tracked 656 twin pairs for infectious childhood diseases such as whooping cough, scarlet fever, measles and chicken pox. Its findings led scientists to believe that susceptibility to whooping cough or scarlet fever is not inheritable. In apparently 25 to 46 percent of those studied, however, susceptibility to measles, chicken pox and rubella did seem to be inheritable. In another study, MPD, a syndrome of muscle tenderness manifested by a clicking or popping noise and limited jaw function, was closely examined. This malady is thought to be related to reactions to emotional or physical stress and occurs in about 10 percent of the male population and nearer to 30 percent of the female population, a ratio similar to that for twins. The doctors found that environment and not heredity probably governs this stress-related occurrence.

Since coronary heart disease is such a prevalent problem, twin studies related to it are of considerable significance. Opinion about the extent of hereditary influence sways back and forth. It was in 1939 that famous cardiologist Paul Dudley White became interested in what the lives of twins could tell him about the causes and forms of certain heart diseases. The doctor participated in a study of electrocardiograms of identical twins. Twenty-two years later, one of the twins in his study wrote to him for help when she learned that she had contracted a heart disease. Doctors told her that she was suffering from something called mitral stenosis—a narrowing of the heart valve—while her twin seemed in perfect health. Dr. White then examined her twin and discovered that the twin had the same condition, although as yet she had none of the gross symptoms of her sister. Why did one twin have the heart condition so much more seriously than the other? The twins wanted to know, and nothing in Dr. White's records could provide the answer, so he found himself appealing—as more and more doctors have done since—to the press and the twin organizations to help him find identicals with certain traits who would be available for medical observation and study.

Dr. Kare Berg, of the Institute of Medical Genetics at the University of Oslo, joined researchers at the University of Virginia in a joint study of heart disease in twins. He reports that genetic factors "are particularly important in coronary heart disease" among young people. Corroboration of these findings is found in the work being done at the University of Minnesota on twins reared apart (both of the Jim twins had high blood pressure, and both had had two instances of supposed heart attacks) and elsewhere. These discoveries point out the importance of genetic factors in heart disease and will doubtless require some revision in the thinking about the role played by such factors as high cholesterol, obesity, lack of exercise, smoking or emotional stress.

Any number of behavior traits have been carefully observed in twin studies around the globe, and the concordance between identical twins as opposed to fraternal twins or singleton siblings remains constant in most traits. Drs. Frank X. Barron of the University of California and Paolo Parisi of the Gregor Mendel Institute studied sixty-one sets of twins between the ages of eighteen and twenty-five in an effort to assess heritability of creative ability. Their findings found a strong concordance between the identicals and less between the fraternals, pointing to the part that our genes play in regard to our musical or artistic capacities. On the other hand, there is still considerable scientific discussion and differences of opinion about how firmly can be established the genetic components of such factors as obsessiveness, neurotic tendencies, impulsive hysteria and compulsive behavior. Dr. Robert Plomin of the Institute of Behavioral Genetics at the University of Colorado is one who believes that when these traits are assessed by the methods generally used (answers to questionnaires either by the twins in the study or by their parents), there is little to suggest that personality traits are inherited. But he did discover, in a study conducted with Dr. Joseph Horn of the University of Texas, that one trait—the ability to speak freely to strangers—seems to have a genetic basis.

One study of twins from five to eleven years of age used other methods—videotape observation, mechanical measures and objective tests—to assess twins' attention spans, physical-activity level and aggressive traits. The researchers found considerable concordance between twins for height and weight, but not nearly so much for the personality measurements. While Svenn Torgersen of the University of Oslo found a high correlation between identical twins for some of the personality traits he looked at—the "so-called general neurotic and obsessive factors"—he concluded that there remains considerable doubt about scientists' abilities to separate the hereditary and environmental influences on personality structure. Nevertheless, some studies are looking at such traits as emotionality as well as nervousness and are thus opening up a new avenue in this research, since, as one psychiatrist who is also an identical twin observed, "too many psychologists and psychiatrists forget the human element of emotion" in their research into the human personality.

Dermatoglyphics

Dr. H. Warner Kloepfer reminds some of his colleagues of a sort of modern-day Paul Revere of twin studies. Whenever he can, he hops on his motorcycle and heads to gatherings of twins and mothers of twins around the country. His mission is to collect the finger-, hand- and footprints of 4,000 twins and other multiples, and as many prints from their immediate families, as possible. Kloepfer is one of the first of five persons in the United States ever to have received a doctorate in human genetics and is the only one with extensive training in the highly technical field of dermatoglyphics.

Dermatoglyphics is the study of finger-, hand- and footprints. It consists of a thorough analysis of the loops, whorls and ridge counts that show up on these human extremities. Kloepfer's current study of these markings in twins has a twofold purpose. He hopes to devise a method of determining zygosity of twins with at least a 95 percent accuracy. It is also his wish to calculate the degrees of penetrance certain genes display. Penetrance is a quantitative measure which describes the amount of time any given gene will take to produce actively and uniformly the trait it governs. That is, it is a calculation of the frequency with which a heritable trait is manifested in the co-twin when twins are identical. Of course, the effect is also present in

fraternal twins and singletons, though not so easily meas-
urable. Kloepfer now has some hundred different features
which are usable in the twin zygosity test. All of our genes
do not have 100 percent penetrance. In fact, only a very
small number of our relatively rare dominant clinical
genes—about 10 percent—are expressed 100 percent of the
time when present. Estimates of penetrance are important,
says Kloepfer, because by discovering the variations in the
extent to which a given gene is expressed scientists can
more easily determine how that trait is being transmitted
and the extent to which it may be conveyed to successive
generations.

The use of dermatoglyphics as a diagnostic tool was
developed in large part by Dr. Harold Cummins, called by
many "the father of dermatoglyphics." Cummins discovered a way to describe the patterns on the skin which has
become universally accepted by the scientific community.
Kloepfer joined Cummins at Tulane over a quarter of a
century ago at Cummins's urging. The elder scientist hoped
that Kloepfer would carry on his pioneering work. At that
time, the study of dermatoglyphics was aimed almost exclusively at demonstrating how frequently characteristic
features were found in various ethnic groups. But in order
to outline his study of specific genes expressed in ridge
features, Kloepfer discovered that he was confronted with
the matter of the degree of penetrance of the genes. Although in the past scientists believed that all that mattered
was whether a gene was a dominant or a recessive one,
there is, it turns out, a wide range in the expressions of a
given gene from earlier to later onset of first symptoms,
or to various levels of severity. "Genes express themselves
differently in different people," says Dr. Kloepfer. "Doctors say to me, twins must be fraternal if a gene isn't expressed in both twins. What they're saying is they don't
know anything about penetrance."

At the beginning, Kloepfer was able to use Dr. Cummins's collection of 2,000 prints to facilitate his study. In these, he found 30 percent penetrance for a gene controlling what is referred to in scientific terms as "the absence of the c-triradius" in palms. (Triradii are points where ridges converge from three directions. The c-triradius is located at the base of the ring finger.) With this data, he presented his findings to the other scientists gathered at the First International Congress of Twin Studies in Rome in 1974. As he finished his presentation, he mentioned his conviction that many more prints from twins would be necessary to track accurately the genetic information he was seeking. Fortunately, Mrs. Joyce E. Maxey was in the audience. She had been sent to Rome as a representative of Mothers of Twins Clubs, to report the latest developments in twin research. For several years she had demonstrated her abiding interest in the subject through her own newsletter, "Twin//Lines," which had achieved worldwide circulation. Mrs. Maxey approached Dr. Kloepfer and offered to help him collect additional prints of twins. He admits that at the time he had no faith that much would come of the offer, but he painstakingly demonstrated the printmaking method required for his scientific analysis. (Prior to this time only Dr. Kloepfer and other trained scientists had the skill to make the prints properly. While the method is not unusually difficult to follow, it is necessary to be extremely accurate and thorough.) What Kloepfer discovered was that a dedicated mother of twins with "tremendous organizing abilities" had come his way. Mrs. Maxey developed a printmaking kit that could be distributed to Mothers of Twins Clubs. Without it the task of collecting the prints from twins and their families would have been far slower and more tedious. Dr. Kloepfer was so impressed with it that in 1975 he designated Mrs. Maxey his international coordinator, and she has helped him to collect over 3,000 of the 4,000 sets of prints he is seeking.

There is another factor, however, that makes the dermatoglyphic study different from other scientific research. Every six months Mrs. Maxey, in consultation with Dr. Kloepfer, distributes progress reports in her newsletter written in laymen's terms to mothers of twins clubs. This is important since, in the past, participating organizations have had little or no feedback from scientists regarding the results of twin research. "Dr. Kloepfer is in great demand as a speaker," says Mrs. Maxey, "because he has made his study a model in creative communication. His twin zygosity test is going to open up all kinds of medical research and those who participated in his dermatoglyphics study truly will have been pioneers."

As Dr. Kloepfer has been analyzing the data received from the prints, he has discovered a number of previously unidentified genes. His work offers hope that scientists may eventually be able to identify a carrier of a trait even though that person may not show signs of the trait. Dr. Kloepfer studies the range of ways a particular gene expresses itself, as well as the frequency of its occurrence in a population and how often it is visible. This is no small task since, for example, as many as 139 different genes may be responsible for the disease muscular dystrophy. Once these newly found genes have been described, Dr. Kloepfer expects colleagues to look into the relationship between them and the onset of particular diseases. Other researchers have discovered that there are fifty diseases known to date to be revealed by markers in handprints; nineteen congenital diseases can be located on the "map of abnormal palm prints; and Down's syndrome leaves its clues in the print of the sole of the foot. Already, researchers know that anemia, arthritis, diabetes, heart disease, high blood pressure, insomnia, stress, thyroid trouble and congenital abnormalities may provide some early warning of their existence in human handprints. Since Down's syndrome is known to leave its tracks in prints before it can be diagnosed by other means, newborns' hands are routinely studied for traces of this condition. Dr. James Miller of the Children's Hospital in Vancouver, Canada is one of a growing number of physicians who believes a more thorough study of infants' prints should be part of their every physical examination.

It may come about that the footprints of identical twins hold some of the most interesting information determining zygosity. Even if a pair of twins were to have truly identical handprints, down to the last little whorl, loop and triradius (which, by the way, has never happened), there might still be enough difference in their footprints to determine that they are fraternal rather than identical twins.

A Medical Puzzle

Back in the mid-sixties, a twin pair dubbed "The Memory Twins" had scientific observers baffled. Charles and George were identical twenty-five-year-olds, clearly retarded. They spoke in unison; much of the time they behaved like small children. Yet when it came to dates and numbers, they were geniuses. Ask George what day February 15, 2002, would fall on, and he would instantly give the correct day. Or go backwards in time and ask if he knew what day August 28, 1491, fell on, and his reply—which would come almost as soon as the question was asked—might be "Wednesday"—again correct. He could play this game ranging over 6,000 years. Neither twin could count up to thirty, but on learning your birth date, they could tell you how many days or weeks it was before that date would come again and how many since your last birthday. Charles knew the birthdays of famous Americans. He could tell you instantly how old George Washington, Abraham Lincoln or Thomas Jefferson would be if he were alive at the time you asked.

These twins were born prematurely and had had an unfortunate home environment, a story not unfamiliar to many unlucky pairs. Their father, an alcoholic, beat them. Whether they might have had a chance for a normal life under other circumstances will never be known, of course. By the age of three, they were diagnosed as retarded. When they were six, George, the quicker of the two, was so fascinated by calendars that he was given a perpetual one, the sort that covers many years. Apparently, he memorized it. After the twins were put into an institution, both boys became fascinated with the calendar, treating it as an all-absorbing game they could share. They were classified as "idiot savants," a condition long known to medicine but still little understood. That both twins showed the same defects and the same capacity for memorizing appears to point to hereditary components in human intelligence.

Ronald S. Wilson, head of the Louisville Twin Study at the University of Louisville, might agree. He has made studies of how our genetic heritage affects our early childhood development. To analyze the growth of both mental and motor skills, he tested 261 pairs of twins during their first two years of life. Although there seemed to be no pattern by which the youngsters learned, there were times when they grasped these skills quickly and other times when their learning abilities appeared to be slowed. Nonetheless, in identical twins, the patterns of learning and those spurts and lags of activity were nearly identical, while those of fraternals were not nearly so similarly correlated. Wilson's study data was so convincing that he was able to predict what stage the identicals had reached merely by examining one of the pair. Then he gave 350 pairs of twins IQ tests. The correlation between the identicals was nearly twice that of the fraternals. "Evidently," Wilson says, "the course of mental development in the preschool years is heavily dependent upon the genetic blueprint" of each twin. An extremely abnormal environment may affect a child's early development, but without that deterrent, it is the genes that are the primary influence.

The Question of Handedness

The subject of left-handedness is one that receives a considerable amount of attention from time to time both in medical-research circles and among twins and parents of twins as well. What, if any, is the relationship between the appearance of this trait and the phenomenon of twinning? Do twins tend to be left-handed more often than do single-born children? Is there any relationship between left-handedness and the appearance of other deviations from the norm? Part of the confusion stems from the old wives' tales that hover around the subject. Eventually, scientific investigation may put some of them to rest.

It is not clear whether right- or left-handedness among twins is caused by the same factors that produce 5–10 percent of lefties among the general population. In 1978, M. A. Annett put forward the theory that left-handedness is attributable to a single gene. There are, however, competing views of the perplexing question.

Some doctors believe that crowding and positioning of the fetuses in the womb may affect hand preference after birth, but this is extremely hard to prove. Doctors would have to know how much shifting or rotation had taken place during gestation, how crowded or restricted the babies were in the womb. They would also need to find out at what stage of fetal development handedness is determined, if, in fact, it is not genetically decided at the time of conception. Since the great majority of twins are born right-handed, the theory of prenatal conditioning for handedness is shaky.

According to another hypothesis, some form of prenatal cerebral damage takes place. Since the left hemisphere of the brain controls the use of the right hand, the damage in question would necessarily be to the left hemisphere. Again substantial evidence for this theory would be difficult to accumulate.

Yet another idea—and a fascinating one—suggests that mirror imaging may account for the left-handedness of one twin. This seems to imply that one ambidextrous "person" has been split by the original division of the egg cell, leaving instead two individual people in his or her place.

Far more prosaic are the studies using twins who are discordant in handedness—one left-handed, one right-handed—in tests attempting to find a correlation between handedness and cognitive performance, or intelligence. In 1975, Louise Carter-Saltzman and others tested 399 pairs of twins and two sets of triplets recruited from the Philadelphia public schools. The zygosity of these twins was determined by an elaborate set of blood-group tests, dental measures, photographs, finger- and footprints and questionnaires. Their handedness was verified by first asking each one if he or she was right- or left-handed and then observing which hand was used in writing. The twins were then arranged into groups of ten sets each, all pairs of twins being separated from co-twins so that there would be no collaboration in responses. Various 35-mm slides and taped instructions were handed out. Under the guidance of an adult instructor, all those being tested answered a battery of questions, none of which depended on reading skills. The adult leaders watched carefully to see that each twin understood the questions and followed directions precisely.

What was discovered? When the answers were categorized for (1) both left-handed twins, (2) both right-handed twins, and (3) one right-handed twin, the other left-handed, it was found that: The performance of Group

1 was below average for identicals, above average for fraternals. Group 2 showed no significant difference between identicals and fraternals, while Group 3 showed the identical left-handers performing at a higher level than their right-handed co-twins.

Still, the mysteries remain. Such findings clearly deepen them, tantalizing some observers with evidence that there are some elusive connections. As Charles E. Boklage from East Carolina University School of Medicine, Greenville, North Carolina, puts it, "Students of the genetics of left-handedness consistently find that twins give them more problems than solutions." Boklage adds yet another complication: In his study, the parents of twins have the same excess frequency of left-handedness as the twins themselves. This leads to the conjecture that the different twinning processes involved between monozygotics and dizygotics "may have more in common than previously recognized."

But what, then, do we do with Dr. I. C. McManus' critical review of all previous work in the area of handedness and twins? He concluded in 1979 that since most of this work was done "prior to the time when zygosity determination was sufficiently refined to preclude errors, the evidence suggests that neither identical nor fraternal twins tend to be left-handed any more than singletons do."

Is this really progress, you may well ask, when each step forward seems to muddy the waters that were clearing? The answer must be a qualified and optimistic "yes." The best scientific endeavors more often than not follow a labyrinthine path through the wood, and although no major medical quandary has been absolutely settled, scientists are finding a way to narrow down the number of infinite possibilities. Borrowing Frost's words, nature—through twins—"takes the path less traveled by." It may well turn out that "that has made all the difference."

9. The Time Clock in Your Genes

On May 4, 1975, John and Arthur Mowforth, former Royal Air Force pilots succumbed to heart attacks. Not only had the two men died of the same cause, they died at approximately the same hour. Perhaps the only thing that made their deaths different was the fact that they had been taken to hospitals in different cities. Each grieving family was unaware of what was taking place in the other emergency room. The stunning coincidence was revealed only when the families shared their bereavement. Then they had to admit the eerie parallelism that had haunted the twin brothers all their lives. The two had moved toward the moment fatal to both along corresponding paths of physical development and subsequent decline. The same invisible clock had measured out the span of their days.

In an equally disturbing instance, one Saturday morning in March 1981, the parents of nine-week-old twin boys awoke to discover their babies dead of what doctors call the Sudden Infant Death Syndrome (SIDS), or "crib death." This was probably only the fourth or fifth time in recorded medical history that twin infants had died of SIDS at the same time. A luckier pair—defying one-in-a-billion odds, according to the *Guinness Book of World Records* (incidentally, started by identical twins Norris and Ross McWhirter)—recently ended parallel lives at the ripe age of one hundred years, dying within a brief time of each other.

Such startling coincidences can hardly be dismissed as mere chance. Because there seems to be no other plausible explanation for the coincidental timing of death or illness in the case of twins, a genetic explanation has been formulated. The current theory—called chronogenetics—describes the effect of time on genetic patterns. Until this theory was introduced to the scientific community, time was the neglected factor in genetic studies. No one had systematically examined the possibility that genes function on a schedule controlling not only *what* an individual will be like, but *when* certain genetically directed processes will act to support an individual life and when they will be withdrawn. Chronogenetics modifies all the established views of the role genes play.

Every living thing is distinguished from every other living thing by the arrangement and type of its genes. Sets and combinations of genes determine not only the appearance of an individual, but the quality and fitness of his organs. The genes we inherit are essentially storage banks of information defining the multitudinous shapes and functions that human tissue will take in the complete organism.

What is deposited in the storage bank by our parents at our conception is what makes us different in greater or lesser degree from our own brothers and sisters and from other family members. It differentiates us most particularly from people outside our families.

To imagine how minute genes are, consider this: If all the genes that have ever existed and that have made up everyone who has ever lived could be gathered together, they would all fit nicely into one small drop of water. But in this case, small is mighty. A gene is extremely powerful. It not only dictates our physical characteristics but, to a degree, our dispositions. The genes we inherit from our ancestors each have their own particular story to tell, over and over again, down through generations and centuries. Like the compulsive storyteller in the famous poem, "The Ancient Mariner," by Coleridge, the genes are compelled to tell their story, whether it has a happy ending or not. As Loren Eiseley put it in *The Immense Journey*, "The door to the past is a strange door. It swings open and things pass through it, but they pass in one direction only." However, he also observed that man is constantly devising new ways to see behind the door and to infer the design that brought us through into the present. As we have seen, twin studies have been a powerful instrument for decoding the instructions of the genes and, with the passing of time, will tell us more about which are benevolent and which promise misfortune.

As things stand, we seldom know if we are carriers of harmful genes. If a child has a hereditary disease, it can be taken for granted that the disease was passed on by the parents. By the time the first symptoms appear, however, it is often already too late to help. Genetic researchers do not yet entirely agree as to what anyone's genetic story foretells. Some hypothesize that all the crucial data are coded in the genes at the time of conception. Others focus on the interaction between our inherited tendencies and the possible modification of them by varying elements in the environment. (Genotype is the primal forecast printed in the genes themselves. Phenotype is the result of that forecast as it appears in subsequent life.) Happily, most researchers believe that we are approaching the time when it will be possible to postpone or sidestep an inherited tendency through early warnings of health problems predetermined by our genes.

The death or disintegration of cells, normal in the scheme of nature, is the mechanism which orchestrates the growth and then the subsequent decay of our bodily organs. Genetic disease or a predisposition to it must be seen as a process of a dwindling immunity. The disease manifests itself when the resistant powers are obliterated. This would seem to answer the question of why some people get diabetes in youth and others show no sign of it until they are adults. (Much about diabetes is still a mystery.)

It is not only in disease, though, that the pattern of timing asserts itself. Some types of cells are useful only in the early stages of the life of the embryo. Their production is discontinued when they cease to have a function. Other types of cells are demanded for later phases of the development of a human being or for activities that begin as the fetus takes shape. Through animal studies, scientists have learned that as the embryo develops, the death or disappearance of certain cells is crucial to the emergence of such items as fingers, toes, arms and legs. The programmed death of one kind of cell at an appointed time coincides with the development of organs requiring another kind.

There are many puzzling cases, however, in which the normal patterns falter. Take the rare disease progeria, or premature aging. Almost overnight, and for no apparent reason, a young child's body turns into that of an old man or woman. Doctors see bald, wrinkled children with senile conditions of the blood vessels and heart. Although they have lived only a few years, these unfortunates eventually die looking as if they had lived for seventy or more. Physicians still don't know what causes the disease. All they understand is that the aging process has been greatly accelerated. Somehow the genetic "clocks" in the genes that control the body's life span have gone awry.

Twins, like their singleton counterparts, come into being carrying a mixture of the genes inherited from both their mother and father. The age of the parents at the time of a conception affects the pattern of genes transmittted to the infant. All twins receive their directives from the genetic code at the same time. Identical twins have received identical codes at the same time. It is now believed this means that any hereditary disease carried by identical twins will appear at approximately the same time in each of them. The theory that there is a sort of time clock built into the genetic code leads geneticists to twins—with their time clocks identically synchronized—as ideal subjects for study.

The theory is borne out by the case of twin housewives back in 1954. Two Cleveland doctors reported in the *Journal of the American Medical Association* that the sisters had contracted the same disease only a few months apart, although for most of the time they were separated by 3,000 miles. The malady, called sarcoidosis, is a chronic infectious disease affecting the eyes and face. A glimpse into medical literature turns up several other sets of identical twins with such identical disorders. In another example of this synchroneity, sixty-nine-year-old American twin women both had cataract surgery on their left eyes in mid-June 1980. The operations were performed in Des Moines, Iowa, on the same day by the same doctor, who must have had a strong sense of déjà vu as she performed the

second, identical operation. Of course, the date for the
operations was elective, but the exact physical maladies
and the timing of their progress were not.

It is only natural that such a "coincidence" makes headlines. Such stories seem to toy with our notion that individuals naturally have entirely individual fates. While it has
been said that our world and all that is in it pulses with
rhythms and repetitions, still, most people tend to believe
that human life is individual at its core. They tend to see
each of us marching to our own drummer, biologically and
hereditarily, a strain which scientists have traced to an
individual's unique combination of genes. To anyone acquainted with twins, however, and especially identical
twins, conformities suggesting a certain kind of predestina-
tion are not unusual; in fact, they tend to the norm.

Chronogenetics Comes of Age

To the ears of Dr. Luigi Gedda, pioneer geneticist and
leading authority on twin studies, the stories of such "coincidences" ring with scientific significance of a profound
order. For over thirty years, Gedda and his colleagues have
been studying questions of genetics as demonstrated in the
lives of twins. His voluminous records covering those three
decades hold the scientific documentation that points to
the role that time plays in all genetic blueprints.

Gedda's unique contributions to science follow from the
long-accepted discoveries of the Austrian monk, Gregor
Mendel, who demonstrated that our genes are the carriers
of important and specific information. Mendel's work with
sweet peas explained the process by which dominant and
recessive characteristics were passed on from generation to
generation. His theory uncovered the proportion by which
the dominant characteristics—brown eyes, for example—

would spread in successive generations, overcoming any recessive characteristics present in an individual's genetic code.

As a young physician in Rome, Dr. Gedda studied under the prestigious professor Nicola Pende, whose work in endocrinology and how it related to disease fascinated the younger man. At the same time, Dr. Gedda took a job in an orphanage to supplement his financial resources. It was there that he came across the first set of twins he would study—eight-year-old identical boys, Romolo and Remo, named after Rome's most famous pair. At one point he had occasion to give them tests that held a mystery. Much to the doctor's surprise, the boys' glutathione—part of the body's red-cell structure—was found to be identical and always constant in quantity. That two individuals, no matter how much alike they might look, would have identical readings simply couldn't be explained statistically. The only plausible answer, Dr. Gedda concluded, was that the two boys had identical hereditary makeups, and these included the time when certain physical characteristics would appear.

With a growing sense of excitement at each new examination, the doctor monitored more and more details of the twins' physical lives. After Romolo and Remo, he continued, both during and after the Second World War, to concentrate on other pairs of twins whenever they crossed his path. He gathered data about twins' eyes, ears, noses and teeth. He monitored their cardiovascular, nervous, endocrine and respiratory systems. He studied their bone structures, skin, hair and handprints. And all the while, his data on twins mounted until he had an overwhelming vision of the part that the forgotten element in genetic research—time—played in all hereditary functions.

The study of heredity is an exacting enough science when researchers attempt to decipher information from

plants or animals; to unravel this data from the study of
human beings is far more difficult. It is never certain enough
to satisfy scientists who the father of a child might be,
although the mother can be identified with assurance.
Added to that, longitudinal studies involve the monumental
task of looking backward and forward over a series of generations. Twins, with their identical heritages, offer the
scientist a far more convenient laboratory than singletons
do. "It's not that we couldn't find out the same sort of
information from single individuals if we had time enough
and knew where and what to look for," says Gedda. "Of
course we could. But the study of twins gives us a decided
advantage because we have two people exactly alike to
study side by side at the same time." Science has already
identified a family tendency to baldness, for instance,
which is passed on from father to son. By studying identical twins, the scientist's job of proving such a theory is
made much easier. He doesn't have to outlive three or four
generations of one family to find the interrelated patterns
in any particular family's genes.

According to Gedda's theory, when doctors look at a
DNA molecule to attempt to translate its recorded message, they should look for an explanation of the variability
in the length of time the molecule maintains its hereditary
information There are three parameters possessed by the
DNA molecule—one is the presence and arrangement of
the paired structural units that make up the molecule; the
second is redundancy, that is, how many times these pair-
ings are repeated within the molecule; the third is the
amount of resilience, the molecule's ability to repair itself.

Gedda describes a birthday cake with candles of varying sizes and lengths to show us how chronogenetics works.
These candles are lighted at our conception. The candles
represent one's genes, each with its own strengths and
weaknesses. They will burn up, or be used up, according

to their individual physical characteristics. "From the number and the importance of the candles which are extinguished, one can see both the length of life and the condition of health as well," says Gedda. "If nothing unnatural forces the extinction of the candles, or genes, before the end of their natural life span, these genes will be consumed and extinguish themselves spontaneously at different times according to their length." Senility is just one example. Compare a tiny piece of skin from an older person to that of an infant, and you'd see that the cells in the older person are very different. That is because for each of us, there is an aging rate built into our cells at the start of life. These "aging cells" have a blueprint for a certain time span, at the end of which they no longer function and senility sets in. Interestingly, the "memory" in these genes remains active under all sorts of unusual conditions. If you took that same small patch of skin and froze it in a storage bank for months or years, it would not matter. Defrost it, and the growth pattern remains the same. Scientists know this, but so, too, does anyone who has planted a seed in the winter but had to wait until spring to see it bloom. Seeds have been found in Egyptian vases that begin to bloom after centuries, and in the desert there are seeds that have lain dormant for seasons, maybe for many years, until the first rain comes. Then they blossom.

The outcome of Dr. Gedda's early and voluminous study of twin pairs was a 1,381-page medical tome, the *Studio dei Gemelli* (the *Study of Twins*), published in 1951. It dealt with case histories of over 5,200 sets of twins and had more than 600 illustrations, tables and charts. Researchers described it as the entire world literature on twins since Galton's first observations back in 1876.

A year after the book appeared, Dr. Gedda founded one of the most prestigious journals in the field of medical genetics and twin studies, the *Acta Geneticae Medicae et*

Gemellologiae. The following year, he opened the doors of the Gregor Mendel Institute in Rome. It was dedicated to the intensive comparative study of twins. On the twentieth anniversary of its founding, this Institute became the site of the First International Congress on Twin Studies. This meeting, in the fall of 1974, brought together hundreds of scientists from around the world.

The unpretentious but completely modern three-story building is situated in the heart of Rome's hospital district, south of the Tiber, a short distance from the Porta Pinciana and the Porta Pia. Housed within its walls are examining rooms, a library of literature related to multiple births, a medical museum with many examples of pathological cases of twinning meant for geneticists to study, meeting rooms, an auditorium and chapel. All who visit are struck by the Institute's unusual doorknobs. These sport its symbol, a modern emblem showing the egg split into two equal halves. A tapestry, depicting the creation of man, and the chapel are visible demonstrations of Dr. Gedda's deep religious convictions, which he easily combines with life as a scientist. The Institute has a full-time medical staff devoted to research and treatment. It offers free medical, gynecological, dental and psychiatric care to all twins and other multiples who request it. To date, the staff has provided this care for over 17,000 sets of twins. The information the doctors gather, a by-product of this free treatment, is used to advance mankind's knowledge of genetics and hereditary diseases.

The doctor's pioneering work has been so successful and has captured the imagination of so many researchers that twin studies have now blossomed about the world. In the summer of 1980, the Mendel Institute's "twin," The Luigi Gedda Institute, opened in Jerusalem on the Mount of Olives. Dr. Gedda, proudly presiding over the opening ceremonies, referred to the ecumenical philosophy of service to all mankind behind the work of both Institutes.

There was a triple objective in extending the work of the Mendel Institute to a new site in Jerusalem. Dr. Gedda sees the location as a meeting point for the races of Europe, Africa and Asia. As such, he expects it to draw on an even broader group of people with more varied ethnic and hereditary backgrounds than those who have come to the Mendel Institute in Rome. The Jerusalem facility will build an information bank for medical records relating to twins and genetic studies everywhere on earth, all of them stored in the most up-to-date equipment available to computer science. Given such a centralized information depository, physicians, clinicians and researchers will be better able to serve twins of all races and to correlate the data needed for genetic research. Finally, this central location, with its international conference-center facilities, may well become the primary meeting place for future generations of scholars who need to exchange information about their work.

Theory and Practice at the Mendel Institute

The work of Dr. Gedda and his staff is a combination of clinical medicine with extended research and a continual flow of publications. On the Institute's staff are many doctors with a variety of specialties, as well as some senior-level medical students from the medical school at the University of Rome. The genetic counseling carried on is quite similar to such work done elsewhere. Basically, doctors take information, make tests and advise patients or their relatives how to deal with problems stemming from the occurrence—or possible occurrence—of genetically influenced diseases. Blood samples are tested for chromosomal abnormalities. A detailed family history is assembled, noting the diseases of family members, their onset time, causes of death and so forth. The doctors are composing a picture that is both a cross section of the current health status of the whole family and a longitudinal patterning that shows the distribution of abnormalities through generations. Risk factors are assessed for the twins under examination, but the overall purpose of the quest is to find clues that may lead to the eventual eradication of the genetic diseases they carry. "With chronogenetics we can rebuild the past through the children and foresee the future through the parents," says Dr. Gedda.

The study by Dr. Gedda and his colleagues of over 17,000 pairs of twins is by far the most comprehensive survey of twin couples in the history of genetic research. Many pairs have been coming to the Institute periodically ever since it opened, and those who have moved away continue to respond to questionnaires about their later medical history, so that the value of the material automatically increases with the passage of time. The Institute has, in a word, an ideal population for studying normal and pathological heredity in the conditions of actual life. The original groups of twins are nearly all still alive, their average age in the mid-thirties. Since many of them have grown up in the company of Dr. Gedda and his associates, they are naturally very fond of the staff, seeing them as extensions of their own families.

Usually a twin is not tested alone if both of the pair are alive and available. The examining rooms of the Institute are unusual in that there is always two of everything—two beds, two tables, two dental chairs, two sets of instruments for the doctor's use, two X-ray machines and so on. Thus, the records are begun in pairs, and that is the way they pass on into the massive files. This parallelism in testing also has a direct benefit in the clinical care of the patients observed. When a malady shows up in one twin, there is strong reason to suppose it will be followed shortly by a similar affliction in the partner, so prophylactic or preparatory measures can be taken to benefit a twin who has not yet displayed symptoms.

One exception to this rule was made in a recent study at the Institute when the researchers wanted to learn how twins develop an awareness of their own individual ego. For this study twins were separated and interviewed in depth in a cordial, relaxed atmosphere when the co-twin was otherwise occupied. The doctors were interested in how the twin recognized the differences and similarities between himself and his twin and whether he accepted or rejected the "twin condition." The answers to the latter question would help them evaluate the influence of the twin condition on each twin separately. They found that most fraternal twins as well as identical twins consider themselves to be different from their co-twin in terms of over-all personality, although they speculated this may reflect a wish to be—rather than an awareness of being—different. In the few cases in which a twin defined himself as identical to his twin, his twin did not do so.

According to Dr. Gedda, it is insufficient to compare the health profiles or table of trait resemblances of twins at any single point in time. After all, they are not twin statues that will remain unaltered, but living, growing, developing beings whose life span is a process of continuing change. This patent truth applies to all organisms, but in the case of twins, the variations will be synchronous at every level, for they demonstrate the temporal schedule derived from heredity. Their lives scan in parallel. They are like two violins playing the same music and keeping time to the same metronome. Identical twins are, according to Dr. Gedda's findings, isochronic—which means simply that genetically, their time clocks are set the same. When a difference between identical twins appears with the passage of time, scientists can attribute the difference to environmental factors.

Einstein, in order to explain the theory of relativity, used the idea of the "twin paradox," describing it thus: If one twin stays on earth and the other twin is launched into space and returns after a certain period of time, the second twin would be younger than the twin who stays on earth. In realistic genetic terms, however, Dr. Gedda points out that twins who live in similar environments show "a very special phenomenon called 'twin synchronism.'" He is talking about the parallel times in their life cycles, of which anyone who knows identicals is well aware.

Examples of this synchroneity are numerous in the files of the Institute. Some of the cases are particularly interesting, genetically speaking. For instance, there is the pair of identical twin sisters who, at the age of ten years and ten months, experienced the onset of menstruation on the same night while they were asleep. Both menstruation and menopause are predictable events in the life of every female. They seem to be controlled by an inherited mechanism, one with its own time schedule. Doctors believe that the onset of menstruation does not occur until a certain time in a woman's life because the genes programmed to hold it off are vital for a prescribed length of time. When they become inactive, the process of menstruation begins. Among their many conclusions, the researchers have found, for instance, that the onset of menstruation in all women is determined by heredity about 80 percent of the time and onset of menopause about 70 percent of the time.

Another dip into the Institute's voluminous files revealed the cases of a pair of seventy-three-year-old identical males who died only ten days apart, both from circulatory problems caused by senile diabetes; a pair, sixty-three years old, who turned up with pernicious anemia; and still another set, sixty-four years old, who had adenocarcinoma in the right breast. In this last case, the disease developed in the same place and at close to the same speed in each twin. In yet another pair, the researchers discovered that both twins were afflicted with a form of myopia called anisotrophy. That is, the two eyes do not see in the same degree; the afflicted eyes are doubly refracting and have a double polarizing power (they create abnormal vibrations of light). One twin had this defect in the right eye; the other had the same defect in the left eye, suggesting that this pair were mirror-image twins. Looking at all the data on file, one is reminded of a photograph made with a stroboscobic flash, the results are so repetitious and overlapping.

The overwhelming evidence of similar genetic timing both in natural phenomena, such as menstruation or aging, and in the development of diseases confirms for Dr. Gedda—and an increasing number of converts to chrono-genetics—that our hereditary structures decidedly have an encoded chronological message. The clock influencing each tiny gene determines the appearance and the disappearance of a wide variety of traits throughout our lifetime. "All genes are present in the egg at birth," says Dr. Gedda, "but they reveal themselves sooner or later in the life of an individual. The active life of the gene can cease early—and does in some instances. Or it may be programmed to become inactive later in an individual's life. When it ceases, it gives the clinical geneticist an area of prediction. With the concept of time affecting the genes, we can predict the date of the appearance or disappearance of an hereditary illness. For instance, if a doctor knows a person has certain hereditary antecedents, he may predict the time a genetically transferred illness will probably begin. If one twin has an allergy, for instance, the other twin at least has *the potential* to develop the same allergy, although it has not yet appeared in his medical examinations."

This is, obviously, extremely important in cases in which one twin develops a more serious, life-threatening malady. Its diagnosis alerts physicians to search for clues of the same disease in the other twin. By this early sleuthing, says Dr. Gedda, "the possibility of a cure is doubled and the risk of failure is cut in half."

Once again, twins turn out to be each other's keeper, like George Engel who spent much of a year dreaming of and expecting his own heart attack after his twin brother's death from that disease. The twin who was haunted by her dead sister's image in the mirror found she was rattled by an annoying psychic echo she couldn't explain, one that subconsciously alerted her to her own physical problems before there were any clear symptoms that a doctor would recognize. Twins everywhere speak of the knowledge that their destiny is imprinted in their twin's life, and vice versa. What they marvel at is how long it has taken the scientific community to grasp what they have known all their lives. Certainly, I've often noticed that though I offer a doctor information about my twin sister's medical condition as well as my own, the data has seldom been noted as relevant. With a more widespread understanding of chronogenetics, perhaps this situation will change dramatically in the future.

The Promise of Chronogenetics

Although so far, over 5,000 different types of hereditary diseases have been identified, Dr. Gedda believes that future studies in chronogenetics may demonstrate that some of these may have been either misidentified or mislabeled or both. A few already thought to be hereditarily transmitted include sickle cell anemia; pernicious anemia; breast cancer; mongolism; dwarfism; diabetes; glaucoma; silicosis; numerous types of allergies; and phenylketonuria, an inherited metabolic problem producing mental retardation. Some mistaken identifications may have been made because one disease can closely resemble another in a different stage of its progression. Says Dr. Gedda, future pathology may lead us to discover that because of their chronogenetic variability, different names were given to the same disease.

How does chronogenetics affect humanity at large? Does it mean, for instance, that if your mother had Parkinson's disease or a rare form of diabetes at the age of thirty-two, you and all her other children might also expect to see symptoms of it in your early thirties? Not necessarily. Genetic mysteries aren't quite as simple as that. For one thing, since the genes weaken as time goes on, much may depend upon the age your mother was when you were conceived, as well as which genes you received from which parent. Dr. Gedda tells this story. "One woman who gave birth to nineteen children passed on a kidney disease to them. The onset age was, however, in an inverse ratio to the age of the mother at the time of their birth. That is, the later the conception, the earlier the age of onset of the disease in the children. The fourth-born contracted the disease when he was fifty-eight, the seventh-born at the age of forty-eight, the ninth-born at the age of forty-six and the eleventh-born at the age of forty-two. That is because the gene is strong when the mother is young, keeping the disease away. Later in the mother's life, the gene has gradually become weakened or may be entirely exhausted, which brings on the disease."

There are yet other complicating factors. Hereditary diseases affect different families at different times and in different ways. It is important, therefore, to keep in mind that what is true for one family's genetic inheritance is not necessarily true for another with the same disease. The gene's demise is slower in one and faster in another.

Here is an example: A woman was affected by Fabry's disease, a corneal problem; she passed the susceptibility to both of her sons, the age of onset for both being thirteen years, although, of course, they were conceived at different times. Another woman, over a longer period of time and with twenty conceptions, showed a progression in time of the onset of the disease in her own progeny that corresponded with the sequence in which her children were born: Number seven, onset age twenty; number fourteen, onset age twelve; number fifteen, onset age eleven; number sixteen, onset age nine; number nineteen, onset age five.

Some diseases tend to repeat themselves within certain families (but not all) as if keyed to a recurrent calendar. Doctors can chart this calendar. When they have perfected the method, they can predict subsequent calendars for future generations of that particular family. As an example, Dr. Gedda points to the fact that the onset of diabetes is early in some families, delayed until adulthood in others and shows up much, much later in still others. A variety of other diseases, too, such as epilepsy and progressive muscular dystrophy, occur at different times in different families with different genetic patterns. With so much variation, it is continually amazing that researchers come to any definite conclusions. Still, when a geneticist discovers a certain genetic disease within a family tree, he is in a favorable position to predict its occurrence in future generations.

Happily, there are some optimistic discoveries being made through the study of chronogenetics. Research shows, for instance, that in certain families with a history of diabetes, not every member will necessarily get the disease. Let's say you are the third child born to your mother, and she was thirty-five when you were conceived. If you do not have the symptoms of the disease by a certain age—the age when diabetes would be expected to appear in your family and in you, the third-born—it is probable that you will not get it at all.

Once the "time clock" of a certain inherited abnormality

is known, it might be possible in the future for scientists to predict that a couple with such an inheritance might be freed from passing it on to their children through wise counseling. If a couple knows for sure that having more children will inevitably subject those born after the mother reaches a certain age to a debilitating disease, they will be in a position to decide against having a larger, but inevitably sicker, family. At the very least, they and their physicians will be more fully prepared to deal with the inevitable problems ahead.

What else has been uncovered in the genetic studies encouraged by the Institute? Because it has been observing and treating sick twins, the Institute has learned a great deal about the patterns of concordant susceptibility to infectious diseases between identical pairs. In certain infectious alimentary problems, there is a surprising similarity in the way twins display symptoms. This is highly significant from a scientific point of view, since it demonstrates how heredity is affected by environment.

In a look at the genetic influence on allergies and immunities, Dr. Gedda and his colleagues at the Mendel Institute surveyed 400 twin pairs. Half of these were between the ages of six to eight years and half between the ages of sixteen to eighteen years. Among these twins, they found that heritability of allergies accounted for 78 percent in the younger age group and only 19 percent in the older group.

Another study of 153 twin sets, again in the two above age groups, the scientists studied the sleep and dreams of the twins, analyzing the length of time the pairs slept and the content of their dreams over a period of seven nights. They found that the older twins slept less and dreamed more, and that the inherited conditioning regarding dream content increased with age and decreased with respect to sleep duration. In other words, while they slept less, their dreams were more alike.

Another Kind of Clock Watching

Chronogenetics should not be confused with chronobiology. The latter focuses on rhythms of hours, days, months and years and the influence certain such cosmic rhythms exert on human beings. Chronobiology, for instance, looks at such rhythms as sleeping and waking or patterns in seasonal diseases. With the help of this science, doctors have been able to define such things as jet lag and personal body clocks as they affect us in certain stressful situations. Chronogenetics, on the other hand, is the study of hereditary biological time. Hereditary biological time is nonrhythmic and begins in the genetic structure of all living things. It deals with the amount of time a gene needs to give off its information in a person's lifetime. The scientific study of this process—chronogenetics—looks at the element of time built into our genetic structures, rather than the external element of time on which chronobiology concentrates. Interestingly, according to Dr. Gedda, chronobiology has helped to demonstrate the existence of chronogenetics by showing that environmentally induced biological rhythms also relate to certain hereditary characteristics. Chronogenetics studies a continuum of time as it is produced and controlled by genetic information. That is, it attempts to see the picture built into the genes of a family over a number of generations. Dr. Gedda's theory gives the study of genetics a longitudinal view up to now not closely examined by scientists. "It opens up the scope of research," he says, "and allows for a continuous profile of the individual's life cycle.

"The often simultaneous onset of a genetic [pathological] condition in a pair of identical twins proves that the disease as well as its time of onset are the result of their identical inheritance," says Dr. Gedda. There are abundant documented examples: John and Jim Sullivan, identical twins in their forties. Each had to have surgery for a thyroid condition. Both wear glasses with the same correction. My twin sister and I had a series of dental visits when we were preadolescents. No one, not even the dentist, paid much attention to which teeth were being filled when. Then a curious newspaper reporter asked if there was a pattern to cavities that had appeared. Looking back in his records, the dentist was flabbergasted to discover that we had had identical fillings in exactly the same molars within days of each other. When we were adults, we each had operations on the same disks in our spines. Although they were performed a year apart, the dates were very close to the same day in the same month.

A huge assortment of diseases is currently being studied through the use of the double genetic history of twins. "There is no question that, among identical twins under the age of seven, the appearance, for instance, of leukemia in one would almost be a sure sign of its subsequent appearance in the other," says Dr. Louis Keith, who supervised the translation into English of *Chronogenetics*, coauthored by Gedda and Gianni Brenci, published in 1978. "Under the age of two years, in particular, the appearance of certain types of leukemia in one twin is a virtual sentence for the other, as far as we now know."

A particularly poignant display of the truths behind Dr. Gedda's theory of chronogenetics was the story of John and Joseph Smith of Baltimore, Maryland. At age forty-nine, the identical pair lived within a few blocks of each other. Twenty years previously, they had developed high blood pressure and kidney problems at the same time. They had to undergo kidney dialysis at the same time. They developed renal failure at the same time and had kidney transplants at the same time, becoming the first pair to receive kidneys simultaneously from the same donor. Then, almost like clockwork—indeed, by an internally controlled genetic clock mechanism—both twins experienced a spell of transplant rejection, which the doctors managed to stop. The twins, athletes who had starred at track in high school, inherited the disease that killed their father when he was fifty-two years old. Called glomerulonephritis, it is described by physicians as the most common reason for kidney transplants.

There was no doubt that this pair was identical. Before the operations, the doctors kept discovering that they had trouble telling the two apart. Although one twin had distinctive gold work on his teeth, it would be little help in distinguishing between them since during surgery, the patients' mouths would be closed. To ensure that they made no errors between the duo, the doctors eventually decided to put the intravenous tubes in the left side of one twin's neck and in the chest of the other.

A Glimpse of the Future

Trick paintings or photographs often use the device of a person standing next to a series of mirrors. The repeated images of the person are identical to the model, except that they become smaller and smaller in reproduction as, to the naked eye, they recede into infinity. If we imagine ourselves as that person by the mirrors and the reflections of ourselves as our ancestors, we get an idea of the duplicating power of the genes with which we have been endowed by the many generations before us. What the mirrors cannot show but which chronogenetics attempts to describe is how long any particular trait we have received —such as the color of hair—will remain. Even researchers such as Bouchard, whose intensive study of twins reared apart has revealed so much about the synchroneity between twins, have come to the conclusion that there must be a fourth dimension in the genetic patterns we inherit. "There is no question about it," he says. "There are many instances that prove it. Take the two Jims and their cluster headaches—same kind of headache with the same kind of intensity, appearing at the same time in their lives, occurring at the same time of day and even described by them in the same way. Also, they both quite suddenly and without any explanation, such as an abrupt change in diet or physical activity, put on ten pounds at approximately the same time. And these are twins who were reared apart."

With Dr. Gedda's discovery—the element of time that affects our genes so overwhelmingly—we have a more dramatic view of that door to the past which Eiseley mentions. We now have a broader comprehension of what the future may hold. As Dr. Gedda defines it, with Mendelian genetics it is as if we are viewing a series of slides, but these are static, discontinuous stages. With chronogenetics it is as if we are looking at a motion picture: dynamic, continuous stages in sequence. He sees chronogenetics and twin studies offering the area of preventive medicine a rare gift for the health and well-being of all mankind.

10. New Directions

The registration clerk at the Four Seasons Hotel in Colorado Springs wore the familiar expression of absolute wonder. As she stared, the joke about seeing double was multiplying in geometric progression around her, and like her, everyone who walked into the lobby, the restaurant and the meeting rooms stared, too. Everywhere you heard the whispering: "I don't believe it. I've never seen so many twins before in my life." This pleasant discombobulation was heightened as flashbulbs popped and banks of television lights were spun on to first one group of multiples, then another. Duplicate smiles faced almost mute reporters. Over and over the same questions (What is it like to be a twin? Do you ever have disagreements about what to wear? Which one is the leader? What's the biggest worry about having a double?) were asked, and similar replies (We like it a lot. Of course, but not as often as you would think. I am. I don't know what I'd do if my twin died.) were given. The Forty-seventh Annual International Twins Association was underway.

The first recorded reunion of twins took place back in 1931, when Edward M. Klink and his twin sister of Silver Lake, Indiana, played host to thirteen other sets. This meeting eventually developed in 1934 into the International Twins Association, Inc., a nonprofit organization with the aim of promoting the spiritual, intellectual and social welfare of twins throughout the world. At first, the group held its meetings in Fort Wayne, Indiana. In 1939, it had its largest gathering to date: 2,500 pairs of twins appeared to set 25,000 spectators agog. Since then, every Labor Day weekend, the group has met in one city or another around the country and in Canada. With a mailing list of over 3,000 names, the group has members scattered as far away as Switzerland, England, South America and China. The convention moves from city to city to give as many twins and other multiples as possible an opportunity to participate in a unique organization, whose members are chosen by God.

In many ways, it is no place for singletons. Even if you are a twin, you can feel momentarily out of place if you arrive without your sidekick. All offices are held jointly by pairs—co-presidents, co-vice-presidents, co-secretaries. There are twin contests. Since there is no age limit for membership, those attending range in age from a few weeks to the high eighties. Although during the rest of the year, some twins may shun matching clothes and a life led too tightly in tandem, during this weekend, surrounded by so many others who understand what it is really like to be a twin, they have a wonderful time highlighting their similarities. "It's the greatest experience of my life," one previously reluctant twin admitted after his first visit to the gathering. "I never expected to enjoy this. I was just going through with it because *he* wanted to," his brother added with a grin. "But now, I think we'll attend the meetings whenever we can."

Of course, as at most other conventions of fraternal or social organizations, the emphasis is primarily on amusement, but occasionally scientific twin studies and related subjects are the focus of seminars. Scientists seeking twins for study have attended to record blood groupings, personality traits, the shapes and sizes of heads, hand- and footprints and extrasensory perception. Other experts have addressed the mothers of multiples who may have come with their young twins. Helen Kirk Lauve, supertwin statistician, goes to the conventions to gather more information for her files and to entertain and inform her audience with many little known facts about multiples. At Colorado Springs, informal groups talked about the lives of twins with actress Lily Tomlin, attending to gather background material for a show dealing with multiples. Others tried out for a stint on a television game show featuring twins. Interestingly, possibly because the subjects of twins and twin studies have become hot items, such gatherings also attract singletons, who might be compared to camp followers or sports groupies in that they are simply fascinated with twins and other multiples. In light of the emerging information about the "vanished twin," one cannot help but wonder if these are persons who subconsciously believe they are the survivors of original pairs.

Spouses of twins, children of twins and parents of twins often join the merriment, as well. At least one evening is devoted to a banquet and dance. Twins entertain twins. Duos swap stories of the pleasures and problems their duplicated lives have brought them. This common experience makes strangers immediate friends, and even the competitions—for the oldest and the youngest pairs, for those who have come the furthest, those most alike, those most unalike and so forth—are friendly. When they walk into the grand ballroom, whether for the first time or the last in a long series of entrances, the twins experience the feeling of being "at home." They are enjoying the few days set aside for them when, instead of being in the minority, they are the overwhelming majority.

Along with the celebration and high spirits, there was also a sense of quiet congratulation. We all knew that we were survivors. The perils and predicaments, the risks and uncertainties of being born a twin were behind us now. Even the times of anxiety appeared amusing now that they were past. We only hoped that for twins of the future there would be fewer difficulties, that science could help more of us to be survivors, too.

When my sister and I were born, our identification tags were labeled "Adams No. 1" and "Adams No. 2." We weren't immediately named since only one baby had been expected and because we were two months premature. Our birth caused some initial consternation, of course, but eventually the fact that we were a surprise became nothing but a family joke since we were healthy and survived.

In August 1981, however, a Colorado couple was awarded $85,000 in a legal settlement against a doctor and hospital over the deaths of their infant twins. The mother was delighted to be pregnant. She hadn't been able to conceive and had been treated with a fertility drug. Then, during her twenty-fourth week, she felt a severe backache and strong cramps and reported them to her doctor. Recognizing the signs of labor, he hospitalized her. Shortly thereafter, she had a pair of fraternal twins—a boy and a girl. Her son was born alive but died immediately after delivery. The daughter, born partially blind and deaf, lived for fifteen months before she went into a coma and died. The couple sued, claiming that the physician should have given the mother drugs to delay labor until the babies were mature enough to survive.

In spite of comedians' jokes to the contrary, the lack of preparation for multiples is still no laughing matter. Behind the element of surprise lurks an enormous number of dilemmas, both for the parents of multiples and for the infants themselves. Extreme prematurity is certainly one life-threatening possibility. When my sister and I were born, medical resources weren't anywhere near what they are today. With the increased sophistication of those resources, parents' expectations, as in the case of the Colorado couple, naturally have changed.

As doctors focus on the interuterine progress of twins and larger groups of multiples, they are in a position to understand more fully the intricacies involved in all pregnancies. So important are these special twin studies that some physicians at the International Congresses for Twin Studies decided to meet more regularly to present their findings and discuss new obstetric procedures. The first such meeting was held in Aberdeen, Scotland in April 1979, with Dr. Ian MacGillivray, chairman of the Working Group on Multiple Pregnancy, at its helm. Specialized research will, in the future, undoubtedly offer couples new ways to cope with the life-threatening aspects of multiple gestation.

The Center for Study of Multiple Birth

The risk of spontaneous abortion or miscarriage in multiple gestation is at least three times as high as for a singleton pregnancy, according to experts such as Dr. Louis Keith. Not only that, but during the first two years of their lives, twins have a mortality rate five times greater than single babies do. Because he is both a concerned physician and a twin, Dr. Louis Keith has joined forces with his brother, Donald, to found the first major multibirth research facility in the United States. Called The Center for Study of Multiple Birth, it has been in operation since 1977, and is affiliated with the Department of Obstetrics and Gynecology of Northwestern University Medical School, and the Prentice Women's Hospital, where Dr. Keith practices obstetrics and gynecology.

The Center, operating thus far on private funds, naturally has a dual purpose. A major thrust of the Center's efforts to date has been the dissemination of the most up-to-date information relating to all aspects of the special problems facing parents caring for their twins, triplets or quadruplets. A second aim is to further research into ways of reducing birth risks for multiples and their mothers. Regarding the former purpose, in 1978 the Center published the book *The Care of Twin Children, A Commonsense Guide for Parents*. The authors, Rosemary T. Theroux and Josephine F. Tingley, are both registered nurses and themselves the mothers of twins. Since these women are rearing twins, they well know the problems—family adjustments, sibling rivalry, constant confusion and exhaustion, clothing, equipment, safety hazards and so forth—that face all parents of multiples. They have covered nearly every possible contingency in their helpful book.

The Center's research projects have included a series of studies on infant twin mortality. One significant danger that newborn multiples face is Respiratory Distress Syndrome (RDS), a condition responsible for approximately half the perinatal deaths associated with multiple gestation. In one five-year study involving thirteen hospitals called the Northwestern University Multihospital Twin Study, Dr. Louis Keith and his colleagues came up with startling statistics concerning the gestation and early lives of twins. In spite of recent advances in obstetric practice and new-born care, as well as the most modern facilities available, twins and higher multiples still are often faced with many of the dangers that threatened their brothers and sisters centuries ago. The study concluded: "Based on current standards of obstetrical and neonatal care, it is possible that at least six of the eight deaths in infants weighing more than 2000 grams might have been prevented. Similarly, it is possible that all five deaths related to Respiratory Distress Syndrome in infants weighing more than 1500 grams might have been avoided given optimal circumstances." Another primary finding was that more often than not, it is the second twin who dies in infancy. The death rate for this second child in any pair, especially if he or she weighs less than 1500 grams, is twice as high as that for the firstborn infant. During its early months, this secondborn twin continues to live in double jeopardy. Statistics also show that identical twins have a much higher rate of mortality during their first month of life than do fraternals.

Author Judith Krantz may or may not have been aware of these statistics when she wrote *Princess Daisy*, but the secondborn twin's dilemma is a prominent theme in her novel. Although Daisy's twin Danielle lives, she is mentally retarded and institutionalized for the major part of her life.

Since many twins are still born prematurely, low birth weight is very often the main problem for both members of a pair. As a mother myself (of three full-term single-tons), I now appreciate our parents' early concern when my sister and I weighed in at a fraction over three pounds each. Like so many multiple premies, we spent many weeks in incubators before we were large enough to be brought home. Many duos have shared our conditional start. Statistics show that twins more often than not are born at eight and a half months, or earlier. In the five-year

Northwestern study, over 11 percent of the twins were delivered prior to thirty-three weeks in the womb.

Another study conducted in Missouri over a five-year period in the mid-1970s showed that twin pregnancies accounted for over 10 percent of the perinatal deaths. Low birth weight as well as prematurity appeared to be the major causes. Even with more Caesarean sections being done, there seemed to be no change in this perinatal death rate. Statistics also show that twins born to mothers under twenty years of age are in the most life-threatening situation of all—both babies die in approximately 20 percent of those cases. In a twin pregnancy which is the mother's first pregnancy—the case with my sister and myself—the babies do not survive the birth process in 16 to 18 percent of all cases.

Surprise, however, is still perhaps the most common and life-threatening element in the arrival of multiples. The study by the Center for Study of Multiple Birth showed that most twin pregnancies were not diagnosed until sometime during the third trimester, and in nearly 25 percent of the cases, they weren't discovered until after labor had begun or, indeed, until after the first twin had already been delivered.

As Donald Keith, executive director of the Center, points out, "Nationally, approximately 50 percent of multiple births are not diagnosed until the last two weeks before delivery. There are just too many instances in which no one suspects there is more than one baby until the mother is on the delivery table. Early diagnosis is very important, although it is all too seldom accomplished. Mothers carrying twins need greater care throughout their pregnancy."

Unfortunately, according to Dr. Louis Keith, doctors and nurses sometimes forget the increased risks associated with twin pregnancies. He believes, therefore, that today they face a particular challenge. There is a crucial need for intensive prenatal and postnatal care, as well as special delivery techniques to improve the survival rate of a mother and her multiple children. Death or serious illness in the first month of life of the newborns needs to be considerably reduced. So, too, do the risks of complications for the mother, complications brought on by conceiving and delivering more than one child at a time. A few of these risks include aggravated hypertension, maternal anemia from acute blood loss, iron deficiency, foliate deficiency and hemorrhage, as well as extraordinary problems related to premature, prolonged and otherwise complicated labor.

A mother's psychological state is also a factor to be remembered. She can go to the hospital with a "full belly" and come home with "empty arms." Pregnancy wastage is devastating to encounter under any circumstances. To lose two infants at once naturally doubles the trauma. The risks awaiting a multiple pregnancy and birth are many: spontaneous abortion, the mysterious anomalies related to the "vanishing twin" and a potpourri of reasons for perinatal mortality, growth retardation and malformations, including fetal hemorrhage, "locked twins," placental "steal," amniotic fluid infections, cord prolapse and the twin transfusion syndrome in identical pairs. The earlier the diagnosis of a twin pregnancy can be made, the sooner steps can be taken to lessen these dangers.

Until now, there have been several ways doctors used to diagnose a twin, or larger multiple, pregnancy: (1) A mother might speak of a sensation of feeling larger than she did in previous pregnancies; (2) she might gain more weight than normally expected; (3) she might have unusually rapid uterine growth; (4) the doctor might have located fetal parts for more than one infant, heard two different heartbeats or discovered more than one infant by X ray. With the availability of ultrasound, multiple pregnancy can now be verified much earlier than was previously possible. Precise determination of gestational age, as well as verifying the number of fetuses, is now a reality. So, too, is the ability of doctors to spot the fearsome abnormalities that may be occurring. However, although ultrasound is available in many hospitals, if a doctor does not suspect that a woman is carrying more than one baby, such a test may not be ordered. Since lower costs for ultrasound scans are becoming more feasible, Dr. Keith foresees the time when every pregnant woman will have a routine scan to determine if she is carrying multiples, whether or not she or her physician suspects it.

Twins who are heavier in the womb are more often diagnosed early and weigh more when born, which gives them a better chance at normal lives. The smaller, late-diagnosed twins are more apt to be born prematurely, which is a distinct threat to their health and lives. When doctors fail to diagnose twins at all before labor begins, the second twin's danger stems from such factors as the drugs used to contract the mother's uterus after delivery, as well as natural conditions out of the physician's control.

Besides being aware early enough that twins or other multiples are on the way, what can doctors do to decrease the risk of multiple gestation and birth? Physicians don't know for certain all that is involved in the birth of any child. They are perhaps especially unsure of what actually sets off parturition, or the birth process, and are hence hard put to prescribe a course of action that consistently will prevent premature labor. There are drugs that will, in some cases, prohibit uterine contractions. Whether or not they should be used to attempt to delay delivery is a matter for the physician to decide. There are other drugs that may speed the growth of a fetus's lungs. This acceleration may save a premature baby from the complications of Respiratory Distress Syndrome. These drugs must, however, be administered at least twenty-four to forty-eight hours before birth to be effective. Also, how safe they are is still the subject of intense investigation; their long-term effects are as yet unknown. Another method that is sometimes tried in an attempt to forestall premature labor is bed rest, at home or in the hospital.

Bed rest is a therapy not adequately used by many physicians in the United States, according to Dr. Keith, usually because of the prohibitive costs of prolonged hospitalizations. "Realistically," he says, "it is practically impossible for a pregnant woman with other small children at home to stay in bed for the last two months of her pregnancy. The prescription of bed rest for such a mother is perhaps more psychologically beneficial to her physician than to the outcome of the pregnancy. One way to overcome such problems, though, might be the use of a nonhospital facility, such as a motel or hotel, located within a few minutes of the hospital and staffed by nurse midwives.

"In North America," Dr. Keith adds, "patients with uncomplicated pregnancy are examined monthly until well into the second trimester, biweekly until the thirty-sixth week and then weekly until delivery. Because of the risks associated with twin pregnancy, patients with twin gestation should be examined more frequently, particularly after the twentieth week of gestation." He believes that certain tests should be given more frequently than normal to check on such risks as iron deficiency, and that doctors should anticipate foliate deficiency anemia as well. More frequent blood tests, too, are apt to catch abnormalities early enough so that they might be corrected. As for the delivery of twins, Dr. Keith emphasizes that "only through careful preparation and the closest attention to detail can this high mortality rate be reduced.

"Actually, the majority of twins are going to be perfectly well and healthy once the initial problems have been hurdled," Dr. Keith says. "But there is a need for a well-baby clinic for multiples. Twins and their parents also need a sympathetic pediatrician and psychologist who will be able to advise on what is normal and what is not normal *for twins.*" As an example, he cites a call from a friend of his, a father of twins. The man was extremely distressed because his wife had taken the children to a clinic where she had received some frightening news. The children were just over two years old. A psychologist who had never examined them, but who had relied on written reports from the nurses, declared the children to be severely mentally retarded. Actually, there was nothing wrong with them. They were acting according to well-known *twin* behavior. A re-evaluation by physicians and psychologists experienced in twin care revealed that nothing was wrong. Then, too, the fact that they were in the phase all children go through known as the "terrible twos" should have been taken into account.

According to both Keiths, parents of twins are subjected to advice and old wives' tales from all sorts of well-meaning people. They are told that a mother can't breast-feed two or more babies at once, and yet many mothers manage it successfully. Whether the mother wants to breast-feed her twins or not—or has been persuaded not to—twins are less often given the benefit of this close, early tie with their mother. In a longitudinal study in coping conducted in Israel, the results showed that the mothers of twins spent more time on infant-centered activities than did singleton mothers, but less time on each individual twin than they would have on a singleton baby. More often than not, the twins were treated physically and psychologically as "a unit."

Parents of twins may also hear that because the twins are small when they are born, they will remain small and weak—not necessarily true. Many others are of the misguided belief that if twins don't speak as early as singletons, or if the pair have their own twin language, that they'll have speech defects for life. Again, although there are some sets with their own highly developed twin language, the majority of pairs learn how to speak properly when they go to school with other children, if they haven't before that time. The reaction to such misinformation, naturally, is dependent upon the situation and the parents' level of understanding: Some see it as nearly catastrophic; some merely another burden; others, a challenge.

The Center for Study of Multiple Birth, therefore, acts as a clearinghouse for the many questions people raise regarding twin pregnancy, twin births and the raising of twin children. Donald Keith, as executive director, deals with the bulk of the correspondence and coordinates the numerous aspects of the Center's efforts from an office in his home in Reston, Virginia. Seemingly indefatigable, he also travels extensively, speaking to interested groups, in an attempt to spread the word about help that is available. His message concentrates on the need for more research and more shared communication about the complicated, often precarious lives of twins and other multiples, as well as their overburdened parents.

"We receive more than one hundred letters a week," he says, " requesting all sorts of advice and information. These letters come from deserted mothers, bewildered teachers, desperate parents and proud grandparents. Sometimes the siblings of twins write. They are all trying to deal with the psychological or practical problems brought about by the appearance of twins in their midst. Sometimes we hear from mothers who think they're going crazy. They need reassurance that that is not happening. Most likely, it's only a matter of sheer exhaustion. They desperately need a support mechanism they can rely on, especially during those very early months when the babies first come home." The role of the father becomes extremely important at this time,

too, since any mother has only two hands. "If the parents
don't work together as a team, the marriage as well as the
twins may be in grave trouble," says Donald Keith. "It
takes each partner's concerted efforts and complete cooperation to get through those first hectic months."

When a call or letter arrives from frantic parents, the
Center is quick to refer them to their local Mothers of
Twins Club. There they can find other mothers, in their
same situation, who understand what they are going
through.

The Mothers of Twins Clubs

In 1960, the National Organization of Mothers of Twins
Clubs, Inc. (NOMOTC) was formed. Its aim is to act as a
clearinghouse for information on twins to benefit twins,
their parents and scientific research. Marion Meyer is executive secretary and the only paid staff worker at its
headquarters in Rockville, Maryland. The NOMOTC
works with the International Society for Twin Studies
(ISTS) to keep communications open among scientists,
twins and their families.

Mothers of Twins Clubs are located in many cities and
towns throughout the country, as well as abroad. These
local groups are the primary source of outside support for
parents of multiples. Normally, they meet monthly for
the exchange of ideas, sympathy, equipment and clothing,
as well as for talks from a wide variety of experts on the
problems of raising multiple children. Although all local
Mothers of Twins Clubs are not affiliated with the national organization, the national organization keeps a record
of all known clubs and draws upon their members regularly in research projects. Most members are mothers of
preschool twins, since this, without question, is the most

difficult time in the lives of multiples' parents. NOMOTC has begun an Adult Twin Registry, so that it will be in a position to contact those adult twins willing to participate in scientific research. It also recently instigated a cooperative effort with Parents of Multiple Birth Association, Canada (POMBA) in the first known international MOTC research project.

Special Problems, Special Aid

In June 1981, the world press eagerly spread the word: Amanda was in excellent condition. Stephen needed heart surgery immediately following his birth but was in satisfactory condition after the operation. Why was this pair so special? They were the world's first test-tube twins. Not surprisingly, the happy father was quoted as "shaking so much I can hardly stand." The infants, born in Melbourne, Australia, after doctors had implanted two fertilized eggs into thirty-one-year-old Radmila Mays' womb, were delivered by Caesarean section. They weighed around five pounds each. Stephen, however, was a "blue baby." His heartbeat was slow and he was barely breathing. Nevertheless, at birth he managed an ear-piercing yell. The doctor in charge, Dr. E. C. Wood, used new laboratory techniques, which included, with a mother's approval, implantation of two eggs at once to enhance chances of a successful pregnancy. Given this breakthrough with the delivery of the Mays twins, there well may be more test-tube twins joining the ranks of multiples in the not-too-distant future.

Stephen did not have surgery until immediately after his birth. Michael Skinner, however, had his operation (this time to clear a blocked urethra) before he was born. He became the second fetus in medical history on whom surgery was performed and the first to undergo anything more complicated than a transfusion. Doctors had been able to ascertain, through ultrasound scan, that he needed help to prevent serious—perhaps fatal—kidney damage. Part of the problem was that Michael was a twin. When his blocked urinary tract and distended bladder were first discovered, the doctors wanted to operate to correct them. But they realized that the stress from the operation might accidentally induce the twins' birth long before either baby was large enough to survive. On the other hand, to wait to operate until they were born at or near term jeopardized Michael's life and health. After considerable discussion with the physicians in charge, the twins' parents gave their consent for the surgery on the condition that the doctors wait until the infants were mature enough so that at least one might survive a possible premature birth. Two operations were in fact performed, since the first, which involved insertion of a catheter into Michael's bladder to drain the urine, worked only temporarily. The doctors tried again, using ultrasound to help them see what was happening inside his mother's womb. They also modified some of their instruments. This time the catheter remained in place until both Michael and Mary were born.

Such prenatal operations to correct abnormalities that would otherwise kill one or both fetuses are just beginning to offer new hope to parents of severely threatened fetuses. One of the physicians on the team operating on Michael was quoted as stating that similar techniques could be useful in the case of a fetus with an abnormality of the brain which, without surgery, would undoubtedly result in hydrocephalus (an excess of fluid on the brain), or one whose lungs were not developing properly and needed surgical repair.

What happens, however, when doctors conclude that a mother is carrying a fetus so deformed it cannot, if born, live a normal life? The moral questions are enormous and just beginning to come to light. One mother and doctor, however, faced the situation in New York the same year both Stephen and Michael's operations occurred. The forty-year-old woman had no children and had never been pregnant before. Seventeen weeks into her pregnancy, she learned, as a result of tests, that she was carrying twins and that one of them had Down's Syndrome, or mongolism. After receiving permission from the New York State Supreme Court, the doctors, again using ultrasound as their guiding hand, operated to halt the gestation of the severely deformed fetus. They pierced the heart of the abnormal twin with a needle, withdrawing blood and thus causing cardiac arrest and death. The other twin continued to develop normally, while the stricken fetus shrank in what was described as "almost a mirrorlike regression." This dead fetus was eventually delivered a short time after the birth of the normal baby, a boy.

The story of the Muellers, too, and their conjoined twins is one of tragic proportions. They had tried to have children for a number of years. When Pamela became pregnant, she was naturally elated, but after a very difficult labor in May 1981, while her husband Robert, a doctor, stood by, she delivered twin boys so deformed that they had only one body below the waist and three legs. They could hardly breathe; they barely cried. The parents were devastated. Eventually, a legal battle put their story on the pages of the world press. The twins—Jeff and Scott—weren't being fed. Essentially, they were being left to die without medical care. The Muellers were arraigned in court, along with their obstetrician. There was emotional testimony on both sides of the question of whether euthanasia might be justified under such extreme circumstances. The case was finally dismissed by a circuit-court judge. The Muellers once again had custody of the twins. They took them home, knowing, they said, that the boys had only months to live. "The Lord blessed us with two sons. He's seen to it that they won't be with us long, but while they are, we want to give care on a twenty-four-hour basis," their mother told the judge.

Until very recently, there was nothing to be done in many cases of twin gestations but to deliver severely retarded or crippled infants, or conjoined twins such as the famous Bunkers; the Hansens of Salt Lake City, who were born conjoined in 1977 and who have been successfully separated; and the Muellers. Scientific advancement has now made it possible, however, to predict severe problems such as mongolism from sampling the embryonic fluid. When such a test is positive, parents are confronted with the need to decide whether the afflicted fetus or fetuses should be aborted. Such moral dilemmas are multiplying in direct proportion to the rate of disappearance of the physical afflictions.

Coping

"They were such beautiful babies. For the first year and a half, we had no idea there was anything wrong at all." As Larry and Phyllis Roof of South Carolina, the parents of teenage autistic twins, reflect on their family situation, they say, "Maybe if there had been just one, it might have been different, but with two . . ." Doctors advised them that the boys should be institutionalized since there was no hope for them to live normal lives. The Roofs refused to accept the idea and have kept them at home. The story of the Roof twins, who are locked away in a world without speech, is frightening and discouraging. Yet perhaps because there are two children, the parents have found within themselves an extra dose of strength and love. Parents like the Roofs seem to gain enormous strength from what appears to others as adversity. They are fighting hard to achieve their dream—of providing help to their own children and to others with similar afflictions. Schoolteachers with little extra financial resources, the Roofs have started Sparkleberry School on 112 wooded acres of heavily mortgaged land. Their chances of paying debts and keeping the school going are extremely slim, but the Roofs feel that they have no choice. While all twins take a special kind of parenting, their boys need constant loving attention, and the Roofs are determined to give it to them. "Sparkleberry," Larry Roof recently told a reporter, "will not just care for the severely handicapped. We'll also explore new methods of teaching these puzzled minds."

Willa Jones found her extra strength when, in 1949, at thirty-eight years of age, she gave birth in Los Angeles to Yvonne and Yvette. The girls were joined at the tops of their heads. Doctors call them a rare form of conjoined, or craniopagus, twins. Black, divorced, with five other normal children at home, their mother was also in poor health after their births, but she refused to give up her babies to an institution. They did spend their first two years, however, in the hospital, where doctors tested and retested them to see if they could be safely separated. They had separate brains, normal bodies and quite different temperaments, but they shared a common bloodstream. Finally, the doctors concluded that the tragedy was irreversible. No separation was possible. Willa Jones took her babies home, saying, "God gave them to me, so I guess He'll show me the way to raise them." The women are now past thirty. They still live at home. They are almost always smiling and joking. They don't consider themselves handicapped—just different. Both they and their mother concentrate on positive thoughts about their predicament as the best way to survive.

Laura Frazier, a widow living in Iowa, mother of eight,

discovered what it is like to cope with recalcitrant twins.
She was given a jail sentence in 1981 because at fifteen, her
girls, Cheryl and Carol, refused to go to school. The judge
could have given her one hundred years and it wouldn't
have persuaded her daughters to go, she admitted to a local
reporter. Actually, her sentence was for thirty days for
breaking Iowa's compulsory-school-attendance law. Obviously, aberrant behavior in one teenager is tough enough
to deal with. When parents have two teamed up against
them, or, as in Laura Frazier's case, two against one, their
ability to cope with their offspring may diminish proportionately.

Even the autistic Roof twins team up on occasion. Larry
Roof disconcertedly described it this way: "What do you
do when one runs away? I had to decide whether to have
one in my hand or two running loose. The first time, I
decided one should run with me while I chased the other.
But then he decided not to run. He just dropped to the
ground like an anchor."

This problem of "one in the hand or two in the bush" is
faced by all new parents of multiples. And it is only one
of many that continually crop up to plague them. Ask almost anyone who has raised or lived closely around a pair
of twins, and they will tell you it is different from raising
any other two singleton children. In fact, experts who have
not tried it but who have become acquainted with its
problems all agree that the job of parenting twins may
be the most difficult job there is. "You're damned if you
do, damned if you don't," a father of teenage twins reports. "The hardest part, for us, is appearing to be fair to
each of the girls. When they are going through their
phases of demanding separate but very, very equal treatment—and I say phases advisedly, because ours seem to
have gone through several already—you've got your hands
full for sure."

I know our father and mother felt the same way about

dealing with my sister and me. Fairness was a crucial issue at times in our house. Once one of us won a prize, a bicycle, in a contest. I don't remember now which one of us won, because the other one also received a bicycle. I have often wondered whether, in order to keep the peace, Dad had to arrange matters so that it looked as if both of us had won.

Not only do parents of twins daily have to face the question of fairness at home, they often have to deal with apparent unequal attitudes by the outside world. They have to juggle the emotions of the twins' siblings, often a major problem since the world showers so much attention on the twins, ignoring the siblings. "The public takes twins as public domain, touches them, kisses them and is completely insensitive to the needs of the other sibs," says Marion Meyer, executive secretary of the National Organization of Mothers of Twins Clubs, Inc. When not coping with that, mothers and fathers of multiples report that discipline is the major problem they face. In Laura Frazier's case, this dilemma didn't disappear, as in most instances it does, once her twins were past the toddler stage. The simple fact is that twins draw moral support from each other, and that can get some pairs bent on mischief into a good deal of trouble.

This interaction between twins is one of the first things new parents recognize. One astonished father of young boys said, "In the hospital they constantly faced each other, even though they were in separate cribs. I remember wondering about that at the time. I didn't know if my twins were different or if it was usual behavior. No one could account for it. Now, at the age of three, their feelings for each other are even stronger and more positive."

As teenagers, another pair strives for independence and, according to their mother, Jeanne Erlich, is achieving it. "They go in different directions, but they look over their shoulders to make sure the other one isn't far behind."

Interestingly, Elyse and Denise Erlich have found a way to complement each other's achievements and weaknesses. When one is better at baking, say, than her sister, it is agreed that she will shine at that activity, while her twin stakes out a separate area in which to excel. Sibling rivalry, nevertheless, does crop up among some pairs and is so intense that the parents cite it as their most difficult problem. To parents worried that their twin pairs are too competitive with each other, envious or jealous, child psychiatrist Richard A. Gardner's words may help: "Constant sibling rivalry is natural and healthy," he asserts. He is backed up by many others who say that a great deal of learning occurs as a result of it. Many twins I've talked with agree with the psychiatrists. Although they admitted there was rivalry between them when they were young, they felt that inevitably it had helped them face a competitive world as adults and that it was probably the reason for their healthy closeness as the years progressed. "For one thing," a female pair in their late fifties said, "it taught us how to forgive each other and still be friends. We know the other one will always be there if there is a need. And we don't hold grudges. It's probably the best part of being a twin, something that singletons may never know."

If twins and twin studies are a hot ticket in scientific circles these days, the subject of how parents and teachers can ensure that twins and other multiples will achieve a strong sense of their individual identities is the liveliest subject wherever these concerned elders gather. The current drift of opinion that twins, left alone, will not manage to "find themselves" as singletons do is a revisionist notion that is given a good deal of reinforcement from education experts, psychologists and psychiatrists. Thus, many parents of multiples embrace the idea that twins should not be dressed alike, given similar names or kept together in school. The strength of this body of thought hit me rather forcefully when I spoke to an MOTC group about my sister's and my early years together. Since I look back now and am amused by those times, I was shocked to hear not a laugh but a gasp in the audience when I described our tandem earlier years. Out of worry and misunderstanding, some people attempt to de-emphasize the likenesses between twins too much. They worry excessively about the pair's psyches and make strong attempts to force them into a nonidentical, singleton mold. As I've talked with twins of all ages, I have found they feel that this is an unnecessary annoyance, since there was never a doubt in their minds about their own individuality, no matter how close they were to their twin partners.

Helen Kirk Lauve, supertwin statistician, described how one of the Key quadruplets—Roberta—addressed a Texas Mothers of Twins Club. She was extremely witty as she told how, when they were born in 1915, the first set of U.S. quads in which all reached maturity, the doctor seemed not to know what quads were, let alone how to take care of them. So both the doctor and their mother played it by ear. The mother breast-fed all four of them, plus their eighteen-month-old brother. She did everything wrong. Their names all sound alike; they were dressed alike; they went to school together; they did everything together. "Yet," said Roberta, "if I stand up straight and hold my tummy in, I don't think I'm so bad at all." Apparently, Baylor University in Waco, Texas, had to play it by ear, too, when the Key girls arrived at school together. One of the many interesting tidbits from Lauve's vast collection of information about twins and other multiples includes the detail that Baylor authorities set aside a special set of rooms for the Key girls as living quarters. Naturally, it was dubbed "The Quad-Wrangle."

Teachers debate the subject of whether or not twins successfully achieve individual identities. Many advise or even

attempt to force the separation of twins into different class-
rooms or schools. Mothers of twins are told by educators,
"Separation, especially for identicals, is important to help
each child to find his own identity early," and then again,
"It all depends upon the children and how much independence is fostered in the home environment." Some
teachers even insist that parents dress twins differently just
as a convenience for the teacher, not particularly as an
impetus toward differentiation for the twins themselves,
saying, "Dressing twins alike is primarily an attention-
getting device." "Twins treated as a unit have problems,"
says one educator. Yet another thinks that separating twins
who are intellectually equal is unfortunate since, "What
you are doing is holding one back simply because he is a
twin."

Peggy Scantland, a mother of twins in Ohio who was
trained as an elementary schoolteacher, told the editors
of *Double Talk*, a newsletter for parents of multiples, "My
feelings about separation . . . of multiples in school have
been developed as a mother of twins, not as a teacher. I
do *not* think twins should be routinely separated in school,
particularly in the early grades. The child leaving home
for the first time is making a tremendous change. To be
leaving Mom and a twin sibling at the same time would be
too much to ask. Mothers of singletons try to find play-
mates . . . who will share the same classroom with their
anxious kindergarteners. We don't try to split up friends
from being in the same classroom, so why should we split
up twins?"

A mother of fraternal twins, on the other hand, points
out that her pair probably should be separated when they
reach school age since they are fraternal and have such
different personalities.

Teachers report that there is very little discussion in education journals of whether multiples should be separated in

school or how to maintain individuality for them. They are therefore on their own in solving those quandaries, as well as multiples' competitiveness or dependency, their leader-follower roles, their maturity, attitudes toward discipline or the pressure they may exert on others by ganging up. Since twins face a double separation as they enter school—separation from home and separation from each other—the traumatic experience may so affect them that they present the teacher with disciplinary problems, whereas they have never before been anything but model children. Because of all of these possible problems, teaching teachers to teach twins is another area of research that both the Center for Study of Multiple Birth and the Mothers of Twins Clubs are interested in furthering.

There are obviously many chicken-and-egg questions regarding rearing and educating twins and other multiples, but future inquiries may focus on areas little examined until now. For instance, according to recent research in Greece, just the fact that twins are labeled "high risk" babies ultimately produces its psychological effect on all concerned, one that must be overcome by the multiples with or without help. Interestingly, early speech and language problems may turn out to have their genesis somewhere other than has been previously understood. Dr. Louis Keith pointed out in the Northwestern study how often multiples face respiratory distress at birth. Now, new insight into the effect a respirator has on premature infants, twin or not, is coming to light. In a study of forty-one premature infants in Rhode Island, it was found that 58 percent who had been on a respirator for more than twenty days had some hearing loss brought about by an excess of fluid in the ear. This fluid acts as a conductor of sound vibrations. It was an unusually high incidence of hearing problems in newborns, and such problems are believed to lead to poor speech development during the preschool years. Of the infants tested who had received oxygen for less than six days, the hearing loss appeared in 39 percent of the cases. For infants who do not have to be put on a respirator, such hearing loss is common only 10 percent of the time. According to Dr. Betty Vohr who conducted the study, if a child cannot hear properly, his or her ability to learn language is affected. There remains considerable debate about what causes this excess of fluid in the infants' middle ears.

Obviously, the concern for the well-being of twins and other multiples is real—for themselves and for the help their lives offer the rest of mankind. However numerous the group gathered at the International Twins Association appeared to onlookers, we were undeniably only a small fraction of the twins now alive in the world. While we are survivors and are pleased to be able to join together from time to time to celebrate our twin condition, we are increasingly aware, too, of how much more needs to be done to further the healthy and happy lives of all multiples.

Resources:

Twin Studies and Twin-Related Organizations

The Center for Study of Multiple Birth
  333 E. Superior Street, Suite 463–5
  Chicago, Illinois 60601
or
  1415 Green Run Lane
  Reston, Virginia 22090

Handprint/Footprint Research
  Joyce E. Maxey, International Coordinator
  910 26th Street
  Marion, Iowa 52302

International Society for Twin Studies
  2101 Constitution Avenue, NW
  Washington, D.C. 20418
or

  The Gregor Mendel Institute
  Piazza Galeno 5
  00161 Rome, Italy

International Twins Association
  114 N. Lafayette Drive
  Muncie, Indiana 47303

National Organization of Mother's of Twins Clubs, Inc.
  5402 Amberwood Lane
  Rockville, Maryland 20853

Helen Kirk Lauve
  Supertwin Statistician
  P. O. Box 254
  Galveston, Texas 77553

Dr. Thomas J. Bouchard, Jr.
  Twins-Reared-Apart Project
  University of Minnesota
  Minneapolis, Minnesota 55455

Bibliography

BOOKS:

Abbe, Kathryn McLaughlin, and Gill, Frances McLaughlin. *Twins on Twins*. New York: Clarkson N. Potter, Inc., 1980.

Ames, Delano, trans. *Egyptian Mythology*. London: Paul Hamlyn Ltd., 1965.

Andreski, Iris. *Old Wives Tales: Life Stories from Ibibioland*. New York: Schocken Books, 1970.

Bach, Dr. George R., and Goldberg, Dr. Herb. *Creative Aggression, The Art of Assertive Living*. Garden City, New York: Doubleday & Co., Inc., 1974.

Balandier, George, and Maquet, Jacques. *Dictionary of Black African Civilization*. New York: Leon Amiel, 1974.

Brinton, Daniel G. *The Myths of the New World, A Treatise on the Symbolism and Mythology of the Red Race of America.* Philadelphia: David McKay, 1896.

Bulfinch's Mythology. New York: Modern Library, Random House, Inc., 1855.

Bulmer, M. G. *The Biology of Twinning in Man.* Oxford: Clarendon Press, 1970.

Buringame, Dorothy. *Twins: A Study of Three Pairs of Identical Twins.* New York: International Universities Press, 1952.

Campbell, Joseph. *The Masks of God: Occidental Mythology.* New York: The Viking Press, 1964.

Collier, Herbert L. *The Psychology of Twins.* Phoenix, Arizona: O'Sullivan Woodside and Co., 1976.

Crail, Charles S. *My Twin Joe.* New York: Doubleday, 1932.

Dunkling, Leslie Alan. *First Names First.* New York: Universe Books, 1977.

Eisely, Loren. *The Immense Journey.* New York: Random House, 1946.

Farber, Susan L. *Identical Twins Reared Apart, A Reanalysis.* New York: Basic Books, Inc., 1981.

Fehrenbach, T. R. *Comanches: The Destruction of a People.* New York: Alfred A. Knopf, Inc., 1974.

Funk and Wagnall's Standard Dictionary of Folklore, Mythology and Legend. 1950, vol. 2.

Galton, Francis. *Inquiries into Human Faculty and Its Development.* New York: Macmillan, 1883.

Gedda, Luigi. *Twins in History and Science.* Springfield, Illinois: Charles C. Thomas, 1961.

Gedda, Luigi, and Brenci, Gianni. *Chronogenetique, L'heredité du Temps Biologique.* Hermann, 1975.

Genesis, 25:23.

Gray, George W. "The Organizer." *From Cell to Organism.* San Francisco: W. H. Freeman and Company, 1957.

Gregory, R. L. *The Intelligent Eye.* New York: McGraw-Hill, Inc., 1970.

Guinness Book of World Records.

Hagedorn, Judy W. and Kizziar, Janet W. *Gemini, The Psychology and Phenomena of Twins.* Anderson, S.C.: Droke House/Hallux, 1974.

Hand, Wayland D. ed. *Popular Beliefs and Superstitions from North Carolina,* vol. 6. Durham, N.C.: Duke University Press, 1961.

Harris, J. Rendel. *The Cult of the Heavenly Twins.* Cambridge: The University Press, 1906.

Harsanyi, Zsolt, and Hutton, Richard. *Genetic Prophecy: Beyond the Double Helix.* New York: Rawson, Wade, 1981.

Hart, Donn V. *Southeast Asian Birth Customs.* Human Relations Area Files Press, 1965.

Hastings, James, ed. *Encyclopedia of Religion and Ethics,* vol. 12, New York: Scribners, 1908–27.

Hatch, Olivia Stokes. *Olivia's African Diary, Cape Town to Cairo, 1932.* Washington, D.C.: 1980.

Hawthorne, Nathaniel. "The Birthmark." *Mosses from an Old Manse.* New York: Wyley and Putnam, 1846.

Herskovits, Melville J. *Dahomey, An Ancient West African Kingdom,* vol. II. New York: J. J. Augustin, 1938.

Hodge, F. W., ed. *Handbook of American Indians North of Mexico,* vol. II. New York: Rowman & Littlefield, 1971.

Hoffman, Ruth and Helen. *We Lead a Double Life.* Philadelphia and New York: J. B. Lippincott Company, 1947.

Hunter, Kay. *Duet for a Lifetime, The Story of the Original Siamese twins.* New York: Coward-McCann, Inc., 1964.

Huxley, Aldous. *Brave New World.* New York: Harper and Row, 1932.

James, Henry. "The Jolly Corner." *The Novels and Tales of Henry James.* New York: Charles Scribner & Sons, 1909.

Javert, Carl T. *Spontaneous and Habitual Abortion.* New York: McGraw-Hill, 1957.

Juel-Nielsen, Niels. *Individual and Environment, A Psychiatric-Psychological Investigation of Monozygotic Twins Reared Apart.* Copenhagen: Acta Psychiatrica Scandinavica, suppl. 183, 1956.

Koch, Helen L. *Twins and Twin Relations.* Chicago, Illinois: The University of Chicago Press, 1966.

Kohl, Marvin, ed. *Infanticide and the Value of Life*. Buffalo, New York: Prometheus Books, 1978.

Lepage, Frederic. *Les Jumeaux, Enquête*. Paris: Editions Robert Laffont, 1980.

Lindeman, Bard. *The Twins Who Found Each Other*. New York: William Morrow, 1969.

Mann, Thomas. *Stories of Three Decades*. New York: Alfred A. Knopf, 1936.

Mead, Margaret, and Bunzel, R., eds. *Golden Age of American Anthropology*. New York: Braziller, 1960.

Merriman, Curtis. "The Intellectual Resemblance of Twins." *Psychological Monographs*. 1924, vol. 33, no. 4.

Milunsky, Aubrey. *Know Your Genes*. Boston: Houghton Mifflin Co., 1977.

Morris, Desmond. *Manwatching, A Field Guide to Human Behavior*. New York: Harry N. Abrams, Inc., 1977.

Newman, Horatio Hackett. *Multiple Human Births, Twins, Triplets, Quadruplets and Quintuplets*. New York: Doubleday, Doran & Company, Inc., 1940.

Newman, Horatio Hackett; Freeman, F. N.; and Holzinger, K. J. *Twins: A Study of Heredity and Environment*. Chicago: University of Chicago Press, 1937.

Pfeiffer, John E. *The Emergence of Man*. New York: Harper and Row, 1969.

Pritchard, Jack A., and MacDonald, Paul, eds. *Williams Obstetrics*, Sixteenth edition. New York, Appleton-Century-Crofts, 1980.

Raffensperger, John G. *Swenson's Pediatric Surgery*, Fourth Edition. New York: Appleton-Century-Crofts, 1980.

Reinhardt, James Melvin. "Evidence from Studies of Twins." *Social Psychology*. Washington, D.C.: The American Sociological Association, 1938.

Rongy, A. J. *Childbirth: Yesterday and Today, The Story of Childbirth Through the Ages, to the Present*. New York: Emerson Books, Inc., 1937.

Rosen, Stephen. *Weathering: How the Atmosphere Conditions Your Body, Your Mind, Your Moods, Your Health*. New York: Evans & Co., 1979.

Rossner, Judith. *Attachments*. New York: Simon & Schuster, 1977.

Sanders, Roger C., and James, Jr., A. Everette, eds. *The Principles and Practice of Ultrasonography in Obstetrics and Gynecology*. Second Edition. New York: Appleton-Century-Crofts, 1980.

Scheinfeld, Amram. *Twins and Supertwins*. London: Chatto and Windus, 1968.

Schreiber, Flora Rheta. *Sybil*. Chicago: Regnery, 1973.

Schweitzer, Albert. *African Notebook*. Translated by C. E. B. Russell. Bloomington: Indiana University Press, 1958.

Shields, James. *Monozygotic Twins Brought up Apart and Brought up Together*. London: Oxford University Press, 1962.

Stevenson, Robert Louis. *The Strange Case of Dr. Jekyll and Mr. Hyde*. London: Longmans Green and Co., 1886.

Strong, S. J., and Corney, G. *The Placenta in Twin Pregnancy*. Oxford: Pergamon Press, 1967.

Thigpen, Corbett H. and Cleckley, Hervey M. *The Three Faces of Eve*. New York: McGraw-Hill, 1957.

Thomas, William I. *Primitive Behavior, An Introduction to the Social Sciences*. New York: McGraw-Hill Book Co., Inc., 1937.

Thompson, Robert Farris. *Black Gods and Kings*. Bloomington: Indiana University Press, 1976.

Tingley, Josephine F., and Theroux, Rosemary T. *The Care of Twin Children, A Common-Sense Guide for Parents*. Chicago: The Center for Study of Multiple Birth, 1978.

Wallace, Ernest, and Hoebel, E. Adamson. *The Comanches, Lords of the South Plains*. University of Oklahoma Press, 1952.

Wallace, Irving, and Wallace, Amy. *The Two*. New York: Simon and Schuster, 1978.

Watts, Alan W. *The Two Hands of God, The Mythos of Polarity*. New York: Macmillan Publishing Co., 1963.

Webster, Hutton. *Taboo, A Sociological Study*. Stanford, California: Stanford University Press, 1942.

Weltfish, Gene. *The Lost Universe*. New York: Basic Books, 1960.

Westermarck, Edward. *Ritual & Belief in Morocco*, vol. II. New Hyde Park, New York: University Books, 1968.

Weston, Lee. *Body Rhythm, The Circadian Rhythms Within You*. New York: Harcourt Brace Jovanovich, 1979.

White, Newman Ivey. *The Frank C. Brown Collection of North Carolina Folklore*. Durham, N.C.: Duke University Press, 7 vols., 1952–64.

Wilde, Oscar. *The Picture of Dorian Gray*. London: Ward Lock and Co., 1891.

Williams, Gurney III. *Twins*. New York/London: Franklin Watts, 1979.

Willis, R. A. *The Borderland of Embryology and Pathology*. Second Edition. London: Butterworth & Co., 1962.

JOURNALS:

Abrahams, R. G. "Spirit, twins and ashes in Labwor, Northern Uganda." *The Interpretation of Ritual* (1972) pp. 115–134.

Acta Geneticae Medicae et Gemellologiae, The Mendel Institute, Rome, 29: 1,2,3,4; 23; 28: 4; and *Book of Abstracts*, Second International Congress of Twin Studies, Alan R. Liss, Inc., New York.

Andrada, M. G., et al. "Developmental Assessment of 'At Risk' Baby For Early Detection of Handicap." International Workshop on the "At Risk" Infant. *Book of Abstracts*, Tel Aviv, 24–31 July 1979.

Annett, M. A. "A single gene explanation of right- and left-handedness and brainedness." *Lanchester Polytechnic* 1978.

Azriely, Sara. "Prematurity as linked to physical and mental stress of women during pregnancy." International Workshop on the "At Risk" Infant. *Book of Abstracts*, Tel Aviv, 24–31 July 1979.

Beit-Hallahmi, Benjamin, and Paluszny, Maria. "Twinship in Mythology and Science." *Comprehensive Psychiatry*, vol. 15, no. 4. July/August 1974. 345–353.

Campbell, Stuart, and Dewhurst, C. J. "Quintuplet Pregnancy

Diagnosed and Assessed by Ultrasonic Compound Scanning." *Lancet* 17 January 1970, p. 101.

Cadoret, Remi J. "Psychopathology in Adopted-Away Offspring of Biologic Parents with Antisocial Behavior." *Arch. Gen. Psychiatry* 35: (1978) 176–184; "Evidence for Genetic Inheritance of Primary Affective Disorder in Adoptees." *Amer. Psych.* 135:4: (1978) 463–466.

Cadoret, Remi J., and Gath, Ann. "Inheritance of Alcoholism in Adoptees." *Brit. J. Psychiat.* 132: (1978) 252–8.

Carter-Saltzman, Louise, et al. "Left-handedness in twins: incidence and patterns of performance in an adolescent sample." *Behavioral Genetics* 6 (1976).

Cederlof, R., et al. "Cancer in MZ and DZ Twins." *Acta. Genet. Med. Gemellol.* 19: (1970) 69–74; "The Swedish Twin Registry, Past and Future Use." *Ibid.*, 351–354.

Cederlof, Rune. "The Twin Method in Epidemiological Studies on Chronic Disease." Institute of Hygiene of the Karolinska Institute, Stockholm, 1966.

Crowe, Raymond R. "An Adoption Study of Antisocial Personality." *Arch. Gen. Psychiatry* 31: 785–791, December 1974; "Adoption Studies in Psychiatry." *Biological Psychiatry* 10, 3: (1975) 353–371.

de Heusch, Luc. "Le sorcier, le Pere Temples et les jumeaux." *La Nation de Personne en Afrique Noire* (1973) 231–242.

Dornan, S. S. "Beliefs and ceremonies connected with the birth and death of twins among South African natives." *South African Journal of Science* 29: (1932) 690–750.

Engel, George L. "The Death of a Twin: Mourning and Anniversary Reactions. Fragments of 10 years of self-analysis." *International Journal of Pyscho-Analysis* (1975) 56.

Evans, Pritchard, E. E. "Customs and beliefs relating to twins among the Nilotic Nuer." *Uganda Journal* 3: (1936) 230–238.

"The Evolution of Cooperation." *The Research News*. University of Michigan, March/April 1980.

Friberg, Lars, et al. "Mortality in Twins in Relation to Smoking Habits and Alcohol Problems." *Arch. Environ. Health* 27: (November 1973) 294–304.

Floderus, Birgitta. "Psycho-social Factors in Relation to Coronary Heart Disease and Associated Risk Factors." *Nordisk
Hygienisk Tidskrift* Suppl. 6 (1974) Stockholm.

Friedman, S. L., et al. "A Comparison of Temperament in
Pre-Term and Full-Term Infants." International Workshop
on the "At Risk" Infant. *Book of Abstracts*, Tel Aviv, 24–31
July 1979; "Visual Responsiveness at 40 Weeks Conceptional
Age: Comparisons of Pre-Term and Full-Term Infants."
Ibid.

Glenn, Jules. "Anthony and Peter Shaffer's Plays: The Influence of Twinship on Creativity." *American Image* 31: (Fall
1974) 270–92.

Gosher-Gottstein, Esther R. "Families of Twins: Longitudinal
Study in Coping." *Twins, Newsletter of the International
Society for Twin Studies*, March–July 1979.

Granzberg, Gary. "Twin infanticide—A cross-cultural test of
a materialistic explanation." *Ethos.*

Harlap, Susan and Joseph Eldor. "Births Following Oral Contraceptive Failures." *Obstetrics & Gynecology* 55: (April
1980) 447–451.

Hellman, Louis M., et al. "Ultrasonic diagnosis of embryonic
malformations." *American Journal of Obstetrics and Gynecology*, 1973, p. 115.

Journal of Personality and Social Psychology v. 35: (1977)
no. 2.

Keith, L., et al. "Differential Mortality Rates Between First
and Second Twins." International Workshop on the "At
Risk" Infant. *Book of Abstracts*, Tel Aviv, 24–31 July 1979;
"The Northwestern University multihospital twin study."
American Journal of Obstetrics and Gynecology, 1 Decem-
ber 1980.

Keith, Louis, and Keith, Gail E. "Zygosity Determination
Among Twins." *J. C. E. Ob/Gyn.* July 1975.

Keith, Louis and Hughey, Michael John. "Twin Gestation."
Clinical Obstetrics 2: (1979) Ch. 2. Hagerstown, Maryland:
Harper & Row.

Levi, Salvator. "Ultrasonic assessment of the high rate of human multiple pregnancy in the first trimester." *Journal of Clinical Ultrasound*, 1976, p. 4.

Livingston, J. E., and Poland, B. J. "Study of Spontaneously Aborted Twins." *Teratology* 21 (1980) New York: Alan R. Liss, Inc.

Lipsitt, Lewis P. "Developmental Consequences of Prenatal and Neonatal Risk Factors: Crib Death and Failure-to-thrive." International Workshop on the "At Risk" Infant. *Book of Abstracts*, Tel Aviv, 24–31 July 1979.

Loesch, Danuta, and Swiatkowska, Zofia. "Topologically Significant Dermatoglyphic Patterns in Twins." *Acta. Genet. Med. Gemellol.* 26: 246–258.

Maratos, Olga. "Implications of Risk Factors in Infant Development and Communication Between Mother and Infant." International Workshop on the "At Risk" Infant. *Book of Abstracts*, Tel Aviv, 24–31 July 1979.

Mason, Sue H. "Two Papers on Twins: I. A Survey of Facts and Theories About Twins; II. A Comparative Study of Four Pairs of Twins Examined in Kindergarten and in Junior High School, with Special Reference to Personality." *Smith College Studies in Social Work*, vol. 4: (March 1934) no. 3.

McManus, I. C. "Handedness in Twins: A Critical Review." *Neuropsychologia*, vol. 18. no. 3. (1980) 347–55.

Medearis, Arnold L., et al. "Perinatal deaths in twin pregnancy: A five-year analysis of statewide statistics in Missouri." *Am. J. Ob/Gyn.* 134: (June 15, 1979) 413–419.

Naeye, Richard L., et al. "Twins: Causes of perinatal death in 12 United States cities and one African city." *Am. J. Ob/Gyn.* 131: (June 1, 1978) 267–272.

Nance, W. E. "A Model for the Analysis of Mate Selection in the Marriages of Twins." *Acta Genet. Med. Gemellol.* vol. 29: (1980) no. 2.

Rehan, N., and Tafida, D. S. "Multiple Births in Hansa Women." *British Journal of Obstetrics & Gynecology*, November 1980.

Ritzman, E. G. "The Multinipple Trait in Sheep and Its Inheritance." *Technical Bulletin 53*. University of New Hampshire Experiment Station.

Robinson, H. P., and Caines, Judy S. "Sonar Evidence of Early Pregnancy Failure in Patients with Twin Conceptions." *British Journal of Obstetrics and Gynecology* 84: (1977) 22.

Schapera I. "Customs relating to twins in South Africa." *Journal of the African Society*. 26 (1927) London.

Southall, A. "Twinship and Symbolic Structure." *The Interpretation of Ritual* (1972) 73–114.

Turpin, R. and Lindsten, J. "Identical Twins of Opposite Sex." *Lancet*, 9 March 1963.

Varma, Thankam R. "Ultrasound evidence of early pregnancy failure in patients with multiple conceptions." *British Journal of Obstretrics and Gynecology* 86: (1979).

Wieder, Serena. "Clinical Intervention with High Risk Mothers and Infants: A Model for Infant Mental Health." International Workshop on the "At Risk" Infant. *Book of Abstracts*, Tel Aviv, 24–31 July 1979.

Wright, Logan. "A Study of Special Abilities in Identical Twins." *Journal of Genetic Psychology*, 1961.

OTHER SOURCES:

Allsbrandt, Barbara. "The joys and problems of being a twin." *Fort Collins Coloradoan*, 9 May 1976.

Ames, Walter. "Twin Tells of Quarrel, Firing Fatal Rifle Shot." *Los Angeles Times*, 22 May 1965.

Baker, Louise and Williams, Greer. "What Would You Do with Triplets?" *Saturday Evening Post*, 29 December 1951.

Battelle, Phyllis. "The Triplets Who Found Each Other." *Good Housekeeping*, February 1981, p. 74.

Baugh, Gene. "For 37 Years, Woman is 'Supertwinologist.' " *MOTC's Notebook*. vol. XVI: (Spring 1976) no. 3.

Bean, Ed. "Couple counting their blessings in triplets." *Des Moines Tribune*, 17 September 1981.

Begley, Sharon with Carey, John. "The Wisdom of Babies." *Newsweek*, 12 January 1981.

Begley, Sharon with Kasindort, Martin. "Twins, Nazi and Jew." *Newsweek*, 3 December 1979.

"Birth Rarity in Cleveland, Twins Aren't, Doctors Declare." *Cincinnati Enquirer*, 9 August 1961.

Born, David O. "Twins Study: Mirror, Mirror." *The Saturday Evening Post* vol. 253: (April 1981) no. 3, p. 32.

Brozan, Nadine. "Twins or Triplets: How Families Cope." *New York Times*, 14 September 1981.

Cassini, Igor. "Tale of the Two Glass Slippers." *Saturday Home Magazine* (King Features Syndicate 1950).

Chambers, Andrea. "Trouble." *People*, 5 May 1980.

Chen, Edwin. "Twins Reared Apart: A Living Lab." *New York Times Magazine*, 9 December 1979.

Clark, Matt. "Double Take." *Newsweek*, 12 March 1979.

Cocco, Marie and Demoretcky, Tom. "Identical Twins . . . Are Triplets." *Newsday*, 24 September 1980; Cocco, M. "A Three-Star Show of Fraternity," *Ibid.*, 27 September 1980.

Cohen, Jim. "Badger Basketball Grows with Hughes Twins." *Sporting News*, 9 February 1974.

Colby, Lester B. Interview with Richard Neison Wishbone Harris: "Toni Twins on Tour Personalize Main Street 'Perm' Promotions." *Sales Management*, June 1949.

Coppola, Jo. "Their Troubles Come Triply." *New York Sunday News*, 28 December 1952.

Crowley, Kieran. "Amazing twins are now seeing triple as a third brother surfaces." *New York Post*, 23 September 1980.

Davis, Flora and Orange, Julia. "The Strange Case of the Children Who Invented Their Own Language." *Redbook*, March 1978.

Dietz, Jean. "50 Twins Volunteer for Heart Study." *Boston Sunday Globe*, 26 March 1961.

Distelheim, Rochelle. "The Mysteries of Identical Twins." *McCall's*, January 1981.

Emery, C. Eugene, Jr. "Preemie hearing loss linked to respirator." *Providence Bulletin*, 22 June 1981.

Farber, Susan. "Telltale Behavior of Twins." *Psychology Today*, January 1980, pp. 58–60.

Farnsworth, Marjorie. "Super-Ma Thinks It Over, Says Her 16th Is the Last." *New York Journal American*, 25 February 1950.

Fields, Sidney. "Children of Her Love." *New York Daily News*, 5 January 1970.

Fine, Benjamin. " 'Scientific' Twins Come of Age Today." *New York Times*, 18 April 1953.

Foltz-Gray, Dorothy. "House of Mirrors." Unpublished paper.

Forist, Thalia. "Chips off the Old Block." Unpublished paper.

Frey, Richard L. "We're solving the mystery of twins." *Good Housekeeping*, February 1953.

Gaines, Bob. "The Memory Twins Who Baffle Science." *Family Weekly*, 6 March 1966.

Gedda, Luigi. "Les Jumeaux." *La Recherche*, September 1975, pp. 731–739.

Gerston, Jill. "Twins: Are they double trouble or are they double the fun?" *Des Moines Sunday Register*, 5 April 1981.

Gorney, Cynthia. "The Twins, Identical Brothers Who Grew Up Apart, One Raised As a Nazi, One As a Jew." *The Washington Post*, 10 December 1979.

Harvey, Paul. "Surprise Endings." *Good Housekeeping*, June 1980.

Holden, Constance. "Identical Twins Reared Apart." *Science*, vol. 207, March 1980; "Twins Reunited." *Science 80*, vol. 1, no. 7, November 1980, pp. 54–59.

Hoover, Willis David. "Girls won't go to school; Mom jailed." *Des Moines Register*, 29 March 1981.

Hunt, Morton. "Doctor Kallmann's 7000 Twins." *Saturday Evening Post*, 6 November 1954.

Hurlburt, Mary. "Teachers Explore Separation/Togetherness." *Double Talk*, Summer 1981.

"Inherited Personality Traits Not Found in Twins Study." *Family Practice News*, vol. 10, no. 21, 1 November 1980.

Iowa, University of. *Health News Service*, 14 December 1979.

"It's Twins Again." *Ebony*, July 1974.

Jackson, Donald Dale. "My Brother, My Self." *Smithsonian*, December 1980.

Jahr, Cliff. " 'Dear Abby' Speaks out on Marriage, Success and 'Ann Landers.' " *Ladies' Home Journal*, September 1981.

Jeffrey, Barbara, "Your Health Is in Your Hands." *Family Circle*, 14 June 1978.

Jenkins, Patricia L. "Twinsburg, Out of the Wilderness, Into the Future." *Danko Graphics,* 1980.

Johnston, Joseph. "Science's Too-Plump Twins Who Prove You *Can Too* Reduce." *Chicago Sun Mirror Magazine,* 7 June 1953.

Kavanaugh, Mary Lou. "Doubling gets dizzying . . . and confusing." *Cranston Herald,* 10 October 1979.

Kennedy, Ray. "Sextuplet birth story called false." *Des Moines Tribune,* 21 February 81.

Kessler, Robert E. and Finger, Alan. "The Face Looked Familiar." *Newsday,* 17 September 1980.

Kristof, Nicholas D. "A life is saved as doctors operate on unborn twin." *Providence Bulletin,* 27 July 1981.

Leo, John and White, Arthur. "A Sad, Baffling Dependency." *Time,* 6 April 1981.

Mallett, Grant. "Leading a Double Life." *Kansas City Star,* 16 November 1980.

Maxey, Joyce E. *Research Letters,* April 1976, Spring 1980, June 1981.

McCarthy, Joe. "All About Twins." *McCall's,* August 1953.

McClure, Mabel. "She's Mad About Multiples." *Galveston News,* 17 May 1964.

Meier, Peg. " 'U' Studies environmental effects of identical twins." *Minneapolis Tribune,* 30 November 1979.

Modersohn, Robert J. "A Twin City in Iowa? You'd Better Believe It." *Des Moines Sunday Register,* 3 September 1978.

"Moral Dilemma of Siamese Twins." *Newsweek,* 22 June 1981.

Munro, Keith. "The Strange Case of the Dionne Quints." *Collier's,* 23 April 1949.

"Murder on the Doorstep." *Newsweek,* 8 December 1975.

"New Blood test is aiding courts in determining paternity suits." *Providence Journal,* 1 June 1981.

O'Brien, Diane. "The Twins Who Made Their Own Language." *Family Health,* September 1978.

"Offers pour in for twins abandoned in dumpster." *Providence Bulletin,* 25 March 1981.

"Of this and that." *Cincinnati Post,* 9 August 1961.

Osborne, Kathy. "The Twins, Scientists probe genetic mysteries." *States-Item* (New Orleans), 25 February 1980; "The Twins, Researchers finding intriguing similarities." *Ibid.*, 27 February 1980; "The Twins, They were probed, pinched —and it's worth it, pair insist." *Ibid.*, 28 February 1980; "The Twins, Learning about each other more important than tests." *Ibid.*, 29 February 1980.

O'Shea, Margaret N. "The Invisible Wall." *The State Magazine* (New Orleans), 20 April 1980.

"Our Family Goes for Doubles." *Parents Magazine*, May 1966.

Parrott, Jennings. "These Twins Are Doubly Interesting." *Los Angeles Times*, 23 February 1979.

Peterson, West F. "Deuces Wild." *Mechanix Illustrated*, September 1952.

"Police Detective Solve the Baffling Case of the Equal Cheeks." *Providence Bulletin*, 21 October 1978.

Rabinovitz, Margot E. "Some Thoughts on the Inter-Twin Relationship and Its Effect on the Personality Development of Twins as Individuals." *Gemini Review*, May 1980.

Rawson, Rosemary. "Two Ohio Strangers Find They're Twins at 39—and a Dream to Psychologists." *People*, 7 May 1979.

Robbins, Jhan and June. "Can Twins Read Each Other's Minds?" *This Week Magazine*, 28 January 1962.

Rodgers, Joann. "Me, Myself and Us: Twins." *Science Digest*, November/December 1980.

Rovner, Sandy. "Healthtalk: 'Sparkleberry.'" *Washington Post*, 14 March 1980.

Satin, Joseph H. "It Pays to Multiply." *This Week*, 4 December 1948.

Schecter, Bruce. "Seeing Double—New Research About Heredity's Impact on Twins." *Family Weekly*, 26 April 1981.

Segal, Julius and Yahraes, Herbert. "The 'Problem' Child." *Family Health*, Spring 1981.

"SIDS Kills Twins Simultaneously." *Providence Bulletin*, 10 March 1981.

Slocum, Bill. "Twin Actresses Turn Into Singles at Last." *New York Mirror*, 10 March 1959.

Spatz, Frances. "Exactly Like My First Husband." *The American Weekly*, 7 October 1971.

Stahl, Jerry. "Two-fers." *Los Angeles Magazine*, June 1980.

Stearn, Jess. "There Are 2 Aspects to This Story." *New York Sunday News*, 23 April 1950.

Stocker, Carol. "Twins." *Providence Sunday Bulletin*, 25 July 1976.

Stumbo, Bella. "Yvonne and Yvette: Siamese twins." *Des Moines Tribune*, 28 August 1981.

Symons, Bill. "Twin Battles Back Against Rare Disease." *Denver Post*, 7 September 1981.

"Teaching Teachers to Teach Twins." The Center for Study of Multiple Birth (pamphlet).

Thistle, Mary B. "What Everybody Wants to Know About Twins." *Parents*, August 1953.

Thone, Dr. Frank. "Twins May Become Unlike." *Science Newsletter*, 4 September 1937, pp. 154–55.

Turner, Bunty. "How three families are coping with triplets." *The Australian Women's Weekly*, 9 January 1980.

"Twins' Two Fathers Asked to Divide Custody of Babies They Both Claim." *United Press International* (Tom Mahoney archives).

Urban, Glenn. "You won't have to work at having fun this weekend." *Colorado Springs Gazette Telegraph*, 4 September 1981.

Varro, Barbara. "Twins take special kind of parenting." *Des Moines Sunday Register*, 4 November 1979.

Wax, Judith. "Dear Ann Landers: Is Incest Hereditary?" *New York Sunday Times Magazine*, 13 October 1974.

Welshimer, Helen. "Nature Hurls the Direct Lie at Science." *Minneapolis Sunday Tribune* (King Features Syndicate 1938).

West, Michael. "One Mind in Two Bodies, British Twins Identical in a Bizarre Twin Life." *Associated Press*, 1 April 1981.

Wolfe, Linda. "The Strange Death of the Twin Gynecologists." *New York Magazine*, 8 September 1975.

Ziegler, Edward. "The Mysterious Bonds of Twins." *Reader's Digest*, January 1980.

Zumbo, Paul. "School Is Knee Deep in Twins—and Irish, Too." *New York Sunday News*, 20 November 1949.

Other than those publications listed above, I also consulted: *Advertising Age; American Medical News; Boston Herald; Cincinnati Post; Detroit Free Press; Life; London Sunday Times; Look; Houston Post; New York Herald Tribune; Parade; Rocky Mountain News; Today's Health; Twins, Newsletter of the International Society of Twin Studies;* and the personal files and archives of Dr. Thomas Bouchard, The Center for Study of Multiple Birth, Ruth Eason, Dr. Luigi Gedda, Marilyn Holmes, Helen Kirk Lauve and Tom Mahoney.

Appendix

A Further Note on Attitudes Toward Twins

Africans have long held widely divergent attitudes toward multiple births. Along the Niger Delta, historically, the mother of twins generally was put to death along with her twin children. If she was allowed to live, hers was not a happy existence. She was cast out and moved about in the wilderness searching for food, traveling at night so others would not see her. In the Congo, a thousand miles away, however, a mother of twins is even to this day given a special amulet to wear declaring she is the mother of twins. Her name is changed to honor her condition. Others greet her by bowing to her twice.

Among the Turkana tribesmen who live in northeast Africa, twins are called *emu* and are feared as a bad omen of an impending death of someone in their family or in their tribe. Mothers have been known to strangle their twin children so their singleton children will remain well. Fathers of twins must slaughter additional animals when human multiples are born as retribution for having produced them. The Bagandans of east central Africa, however, consider that the arrival of twins heralds the intervention of the god Mukasa, but many taboos are invoked so that the tribe may continue in the god's favor. If the twins fall ill, the parents are considered at fault and the god's anger will be extended to the entire clan.

A neighboring tribe—the Bakitaras—are also happy when twins arrive. Nevertheless, if both infants are boys, the Bakitaras believe the god has favored the father and was unhappy with the mother and her people. If both are girls, it is the father and his clan that has been disgraced.

The Herero tribe in southwestern Africa are among those who consider twins a bad omen. When twins arrive, the entire tribe is called together, despite the fact that some may live far away or, because of their advanced age, may need to be carried. All the tribe's animals, too, must be gathered together. Anyone who fails to observe this ritual surrounding the *epaha* (twins) will fall under a spell and die. Additional rituals, which may last an entire year, are performed by the twins' parents. Since offerings of animals are also given to them, the parents may become quite rich, in the process.

The southeastern African tribes of Thonga require that the mother of twins be purified, since the arrival of twins indicates that in place of a birth a sort of death has occurred. If this purification is not carried out, the mother will contaminate other women of child-bearing age. In earlier days the Thonga killed twins; now the twins are allowed to live but are not treated well. Cinders are thrown at them and people shy away from them. If a singleton child is naughty he is told "You are acting like a twin!" "Twins are troublesome" is another common chant among these people.

Twins are only one person to the people of the Neuer tribes. Twins of the sex opposite the parent are the most feared: the spirit of the girls will kill their father, the spirit of twin boys will kill their mother. But a fraternal pair of opposite sexes is a better omen since they will undoubtedly quarrel and neutralize the danger to the parents. Twins in these tribes are not allowed to have any contact with singletons of the opposite sex. Thus, a young female twin cannot be courted. If a singleton male unwittingly approaches a female twin, she shuns him saying, "I am a twin" and he will immediately turn away. There is, however, a sham or counterfeit marriage for twins—between the pair and one singleton of the opposite sex. The twins are dressed in men's clothing if they are female and women's if they are male. Their singleton spouse is likewise dressed for the ceremony in clothing of his or her opposite sex.

Taboos surround the subject of marriage and twins in many areas of the primitive world. Some natives feel that a boy-girl pair have violated the incest taboo by being together in the womb. Others—the Balinese in the Dutch East Indies, for example—call these couples "betrothed twins." In the Philippines and also in Japan in primitive times, opposite sex fraternal twins were forced to marry their twin.

The birth order of twins is open to differing interpretation as well. The Yuman tribes in America believed the firstborn twin was the younger and came to this conclusion because one always allows a younger person through a doorway first. In the Ashanti tribes in Africa the firstborn was also considered the youngest because he was preparing the way for his twin.

In certain places one of a pair was put to death, tribal customs dictating whether it would be the first- or secondborn. In the Solomon islands it was the firstborn; this twin was killed by its grandmother and buried immediately, with care taken that no men should see the burial procedure. The Kayan tribe of Borneo usually killed the girl if the pair was an unlike-sexed fraternal set. A tribe of northern Luzon believes that one of a twin pair is a spirit of a dead person. The quieter one—or the larger one if both are quiet—is put in a jar and buried alive. Among the Zulus, twins are considered such a disgrace that they are seldom talked about and it is thought very likely that twins are still killed at birth either by their mother or the midwife. They are supposed to be placed together in one pot and put in a damp grave to ward off future drought.

In British Columbia, the Thompson Indians referred to twins as the "grizzly-bear" children or "hairy feet" because the woman who bore them dreamed repeatedly of this animal before their birth. And although the Quinaults of northwestern America showed no horror of twins, the father and mother of the pair could not fish for twenty days after their birth or the fish would stop running. Nor could the father hunt for two years, since if he did it was suspected he would scare away the game animals for the whole tribe.

Index

Kay Cassill has written about twins and twin studies for Science Digest, Cosmopolitan *and* Marathon World, *and has contributed to the* Smithsonian, People *magazine (for which she is a special correspondent)*, McCall's, *and many other publications. She is a Fellow of the International Society for Twin Studies and a Director of The Center for Study of Multiple Birth. At one time she was, with her twin sister, Marilyn, a model and a top-ranked synchronized swimmer; she has since pursued a career not only as a writer (she is the recipient of a Penney-Missouri Journalism Award) but also as an artist, with a self-portrait in the permanent collection of the Metropolitan Museum of Art.*

Kay Cassill lives with her husband, novelist R. V. Cassill, in Providence, Rhode Island, separated by two time zones from her identical twin.